PRAISE FOR

Living Your Divine Life:
Experience God's Glory, Absolute
Happiness, and Great Prosperity

Living Your Divine Life is the best book I have ever read. It unifies over 100 authoritative teachers, saints, and leaders of different religions, philosophy, physics, mathematics and biblical history into a matchless message. The message that Bedrij articulates and the Bible and science corroborate is that we are an aspect of God, the All in all, in which we live and move and have our being. The work demonstrates how by living a divine life we can experience God's glory, absolute happiness, and great prosperity. This is what we need to heal ourselves.

—Stan Kardatzke, MD
President, Indiana Urgent Care

Like a tree, that lives effortlessly, day and night, receiving only what is provided, giving freely to all who come, asking nothing in return . . . . This work is pure love, and love is of the Spirit. In *Living Your Divine Life,* Bedrij shows us how to let the Spirit guide us, so we too might live effortlessly, be productive, find peace, joy, prosperity and happiness, and be a blessing to all."

—Clancy D. McKenzie, MD
Author, "Babies Need Mothers"

"How powerful it is to read page after page of wisdom and truth testifying to our oneness with each other and with God! Orest Bedrij brings a clear, unwavering and timely message to a world beset by confusion and conflict. He calls each of us to embrace the reality of our own divinity, and he urges each of us not to delay in taking personal responsibility for acknowledging and manifesting that divinity for the sake of all mankind and ourselves.

Albert Einstein insisted, 'The world we have made as a result of the level of thinking we have done thus far creates problems that we cannot solve at the same level of thinking as they were created.' Bedrij's *Living Your Divine Life* leads the way to that new level of thinking, one that is sorely needed in today's world."

—**Barbara Benjamin**
Director, Intuitive Discovery, Inc.

Praise for Orest Bedrij's Previous Books

Celebrate Your Divinity:
The Nature of God and the Theory of Everything

"In the midst of guns and glamour and the ascendant loss of life in the name of serving them, here is a manual for raising the human dimension and struggle to its cosmic significance. Its encyclopedic scope and depth are the product of a lifetime of dedicated study. Orest Bedrij brings fresh light to the Divine disguised in time, the pecking order of Graces, the evolutionary adventure, and located in the Heart of God. He picks his grapes in bunches, harvests clusters—not solitary fruits—and always has hold of the stems.

"The book turns out to be a brilliant translation of the insight of contemporary mathematical physics into the coinage of everyday parlance. This is no bedside novel to nurture sleep, but a wake-up call on the rim of disaster. It is not addressed to the faint of heart or to those with tired minds, but a summons to *know* what it is to *be* fully human and *do* now what is invited, yes, required of us. Thank Bedrij for blowing a clear, clean, warning signal. It is born of his deepest optimism about the human venture, rooted in his contagious religious and scientific outlook. *Sersum Corda!* (*Lift up your hearts!*)"

—**Dr. Glenn A. Olds**, Former President of Kent State University, US Ambassador to the UN Economic and Social Counsel

"All who thirst for genuine meaning behind life and explanation of greater reality will find what they are looking for in Orest Bedrij's book *Celebrate Your Divinity*. Many contemporary 'theories of everything' conclude with an all-encompassing particle or astronomic singularity. This book covers the unfinished terrain, showing a mathematical unity behind the physics and how such discoveries relate to our deepest sensibilities about God, the All-in-All, and the world. The book weaves also together many vistas of history and recent sociopolitical events with this arcane matter. It shows the reader where humanity must go, and provides material suggestions on simple approaches they can use to improve life's quality at any immediate moment . . . His guidance is a wonderful stepping-stone toward a fulfilled life."

—**Professor Stephen Modell**, MD, MS, Director Research, Genetic Policy, University of Michigan

"This is a visionary work of monumental proportions, a masterpiece of man's highest thoughts and insights. Orest Bedrij has trodden where most dare not. He has had the courage to visit and deliberate in the great disciplines and then to reap the harvest of the world's greatest minds—minds from those at the dawn of the understanding of man's consciousness to those at the forefront of today's level of understanding. Just as so many of the great minds before us in their flashes of inspiration, Bedrij has seen the thread of new unity among the fruits of the disciplines of science, philosophy, religion, mathematics, bringing them under one brilliant universal umbrella to share with us all. This work will bring to us a new vision of the world. It will bring inspiration to those seeking new and deeper insights into reality. It will encourage these pioneers of human thought to move ever boldly forward."

—**Professor Peter Kotzer**, President, Washington Natural Philosophy Institute

One

"I have not seen any recent book which encompasses a greater range of factual information nor does so under a more poetic guise than *One* . . . Quotes from the great religious writings of our own and other civilizations link it to the best thinking of all times and all ages."

—Professor John Archibald Wheeler,
Princeton University

You

"This book is an important stepping-stone to a quantum jump in evolution, a world of Oneness which is in the making under our very eyes. May this book inspire leaders to catch up with the sages of our times who are revealing to us the fundamental Oneness of humanity and of all creation."

—Dr. Robert Muller,
Chancellor of the United Nations University for Peace,
Former Assistant Secretary General of the United Nations

"This very original book is both a work of science and mysticism . . . It will nourish both the mind and the spirit . . . a genuine contemporary spiritual anthology . . . with meditations that succeed each other like beads on a rosary."

—Professor Antoine Faivre,
Chair of Esoteric and Mystical Studies,
University of Paris (Sorbonne)

LIVING YOUR DIVINE LIFE:

Experience God's Glory, Absolute Happiness, and Great Prosperity

LIVING YOUR DIVINE LIFE:

Experience God's Glory, Absolute
Happiness, and Great Prosperity

Orest Bedrij

Xlibris

Library of Congress Control Number: 2009906592
ISBN: Hardcover   978-1-4415-5187-0
                   Softcover   978-1-4415-5186-3

Library of Congress Cataloging-in-Publication Data

Bedrij, Orest, 1933— p. Living Your Divine Life: Experience God's Glory,
Absolute Happiness, and Great Prosperity / Orest Bedrij. — 1st ed. cm.

Includes bibliographical references and index.
1. Divine Life—Nature. 2. Absolute—The, nature. 3. God—The, science, religion.
4. Zero—'1' in physics and Spiritual Calculus. 5. Life—Philosophy. 6. Science—
The Unchanging. 7. Pure Awareness—Ultimate reality. 8. Enlightenment—
Cosmic consciousness. 9. Second Nature. 10. Evolution—Unchanging aspects.

I. Title

Published in the United States by Xlibris, a strategic partner of Random House
Ventures, LLC, a subsidiary of Random House, Inc.

Printed and bound in the United States of America.
October 2009
First Edition
10 9 8 7 6 5 4 3 2 1

To order additional copies of this book, contact:
Xlibris Corporation
1-888-795-4274
www.Xlibris.com
Orders@Xlibris.com
60045

For You
Absolute Love—the Light of the world.
    You
Gazing forth from every face.
    You
In Your infinite splendor and glory.

CONTENTS

O Absolute Splendor! This Work Is about You and Your Infinite Life • Our Universe Is a Disney World Theme Park: Experience God's Glory in Yourself and in Others • Personal Happiness Is Our Responsibility: We Need a Deeper Understanding of the Christ and His Work • Growth Expands Our Concept of God: It Reminds Us of Our Magnanimous and Compassionate Hearts • O God, My God, Oh Infinite Splendor and Light, All Things Are Yours: The Heavens, the Earth, and the Nations Are Yours! Why Not Make Your Divine Life More Accessible to You?

I

Omnipresence, Omniscience, Omnipotence Is Our Natural State: Wake Up, My Love, to Your True Nature; Let Your Eyes See Eternity • A New Science of Life: The Unchangeable Miracle Way, The Light of Human Existence • From Strength to Strength: Immense Success • The Secret of Secrets: Your True Identity: The Life of Humanity Is the Life of God • Toward Our Home in God, Toward the Father's Heart: Seek First the Infinite Splendor within You, Experience the Presence of God in Absolute Happiness • In the Journey to God, Each Day Is Enlightenment: Organize Your Life So that the World

Does Not Consume You • Spiritual Calculus: One Heart and One Mind: We Must Put Our Trust in the "Unchangeable" Laws of Physics • You Live in Your Personal Universe: '1' Is Unchanging Rest and Perpetual Stillness • All People Are Members of Your Immediate Family: Become a Driving Force of the Eternal Love and Grace

Honor Be to God in Man! Blessed Are the Pure in Heart for They Shall See God • Awakening to the Consciousness of Effortless Living: Awake, O Sleeper, Arise from the Dead, and Christ Will Give You Light • God Knows Himself: He Who Knows Himself Knows God • It Is the Spirit, '1', That Gives Life: HE WHO IS Is the Projection of the Unchangeable Godhead at Rest • Insights into the Nature of Your Being: All Tell the Same Story • The Absolute Dwelling in All Life Forms • Oh, How Could it Have Been Otherwise! How Could We All Have Been So Blind So Long • Truth Seeks the Wise and the Righteous: Truth Alone Triumphs • I Am: The Absolute Principle • I Am Who I Am: God in the World

Thy Kingdom Come, Thy Will Be Done: Complete Transformation of the Self into God Enhances Your Vitality, Enriches Your Life • God Does Not Need Advisors: Let God Work through You without Consulting You • Goodness Knows: We Can't Improve On Love, We Are Meant to Reveal Love in Us • The Heart of the Gospels: "There Is No Division in the Body" • All Scriptures Are Full of Gems of Knowledge; Core of All Scriptures: The Oneness of All • The Self as a "Triumphing Power": Nothing in Themselves, All in God: The Life in which Our Will Is United with God •

Make the Best Use of Your Life: "Walk the Talk" with Love and Compassion for All Existence • Living at the Source: You Can't Improve on God • In the Miracle Zone: That Which Is God Is the Best That Can Be

IV
Perfections for Living Your Divine Life:

We Are Children Until We Become Perfect

V

We Are the Light of the World: It's Time We Came out of the Cave of Pain and Grief to Enjoy Our Sacredness • What People Know, They Do! Violence Is Never a Solution: A Crime against Humanity • Our Challenges Now: I Feel Your Pain, I Feel Your Grief • Training in Holiness: We Need a Sustainable World-View, We Must Rise Above Animals and Act Like Gods • See the Glory of God Displayed: Rejoice! This Brother of Yours Was Dead, and Has Come Back to Life • May God's Face Consciously Shine in You • Abolition of the World Slavery: A New Birth of Freedom, Happiness, and Prosperity

VI

What Are We Searching For? Please Share Your Joys with Me • Grace Be with You: Find Your Inner Light

INTRODUCTION

Like the bee gathering honey from different flowers, the
wise man accepts the essence of different
Scriptures [and Sciences] and sees only the good in all
religions [and knowledge].

—Srimad Bhagavatam

Concerns for men himself and his fate must always be the
chief interest of all technical endeavors . . . in order that the
creations of our mind shall be a blessing and not a curse to
all mankind.

—Albert Einstein

O Absolute Splendor!
This Work Is about You and Your Infinite Life

My dearest reader, this book can be a defining event in your life. It is
designed to shine new light on you, your Infinite Splendor and your
absolute life of endless possibilities. You can partake of the divine glory
and the vastness of God's transcendence in this life.

It is a very happy event for all of us to make ourselves more
knowledgeable about our true identity, the development of the highest

form of human consciousness, and our unlimited life in God the Father Almighty and the "miracle zone" of effortless living.

Here, it is also our grandest happiness that every child, woman, and man, through direct experience of God's glory in themselves and in others can break the chains of their slavery and share a new birth of freedom, or, as Saint Paul wrote in his letter to the Romans:

> Indeed, the whole created world eagerly awaits the revelation of the sons of God . . . because the world itself will be freed from its slavery . . . and share in the glorious freedom of the children of God (Rom. 8:19, 21).

Here, where compassion and genius embrace and kiss one another, you experience the "absolute perfection and light": marriage of love and peace, unlimited bliss and knowledge, immeasurable wisdom and superabundant vitality, prosperity, and union with the Absolute Life.

Our Universe Is a Disney World Theme Park: Experience God's Glory in Yourself and in Others

To refine and enhance communication and our take-home message on our Absolute Heritage, using concrete knowledge and wisdom that you already have and which is more easily grasped, I use the "Disney World"-metaphor examples and analogies, within The Great I Am/cosmos description. Metaphors and analogies have been employed by the prophets and Christ Jesus (parables), computer sciences (interface metaphors), psychotherapy (therapeutic metaphors), and so forth. Consequently, my dearest reader and Absolute Splendor of Light, just as Disney World is a huge theme park in the world for children, so our universe is a gigantic theme park for us.

Please note, however, that although parables and analogies are useful tools in communication, they are not the real thing. To know what an orange tastes like it must be tasted; "to share the divine nature" (2 Peter 1:4) and experience God's glory in yourself and in others, absolute happiness and great prosperity, we must personally experience it.

Also, as an aid to comprehension, please make a note that all emphases in this book's excerpts from the Bible (the collection of Jewish and Christian texts), Bhagavad Gita, Koran, the Vedas, and the Upanishads are mine. These sacred scriptures comprise a universe of "unchangeable" wisdom and a practical guide to the purpose driven life that have the ability to inspire any woman or man to absolute enlightenment, freedom, and accomplishment.

Personal Happiness Is Our Responsibility: We Need a Deeper Understanding of the Christ and His Work

Where do we come from? Who is God? Why is God's still-small voice (the voice of the silence, soundless sound, or the Silent Speaker: '**1**') so challenging to hear? Who are we, my dearest reader and Infinite Splendor? What have we come to do in this world? How can we realize this ideal in daily life and help the divine within us to advance?

When I posed these *summum bonum* (the highest good) challenges of our communication and relationship with God to a number of prominent scientists, educators, clerics, philosophers, sages, and saints, with diverse intellectual temperament as well as spiritual literacy and foremost authorities on God, from all corners of the earth, they had very similar answers mightily in tune to the true and the holy. Although many have different starting points and approaches to discovering the ageless wisdom, all answers are connected to the Absolute Light; the divine Ground, Knower and Source of all existence, which, like a seed of a giant sequoia, is "latent" in all of us.

Their insights and treasures of wisdom were published more than thirty-five years ago in *Yes It's Love: Your Life Can Be a Miracle*, which is provided here in an appendix. Those unacquainted with that work might find it valuable to take a quick look at the appendix before proceeding to the body of this work. It presents a general primer of spiritual wisdom, technology, and development that the majority of world religions (in the traditional faith of the Church, "servants of Christ and administrators of the mysteries of God" [1 Cor. 4:1]) cherish, advance, and promote.

Specifically, "infants" in the Life of God (newborn in the kindergarten of the spiritual school) are nursed with infant "milk"—lollipops of baby talk and spun immortal fables, parables, and primer (Pre-K-12) spirituality on the most sublime wisdom about the Spirit of God and the "Absolute Infinity in us." On the other hand, "meat," or the "solid food" is not given to individuals who are not advanced in the spiritual life (babies "without any experience in the matter of right and wrong" [Heb. 5:13]). To quote from one of the most enlightening sacred documents, the First Epistle of Paul to the Corinthians, written in the 50s CE, approximately twenty years after the resurrection of Jesus (Matt. 28:1-20; Mark 16:1-20; Luke 24:1-49; John 1-21:25):

> Brothers, the trouble was that I could not talk to you as spiritual men but only as men of flesh, as infants in Christ. I fed you with milk, and did not give you solid food because you were not ready for it. You are not ready for it even now, being still very much in a natural condition. For as long as there are jealousy and quarrels among you, are you not of the flesh? (1 Cor. 3:1–4).

Professor Manlio Simonetti teaches at the University of Rome. With a fearless simplicity, in his penetrating *Biblical Interpretation in the Early Church*, he cuts to the heart of the human challenge, "the need for a deeper understanding of the significance of the Christ and his ministry." By uncommon directness and an insightful grasp, Simonetti acknowledges:

> Indeed, neither the prophets nor Our Lord himself expressed the divine mysteries in a simple way which would be accessible to all, but they spoke in parables (i.e., allegories) as the apostles themselves declared (Matt. 13:34). There were various reasons for this: To encourage the more zealous to sustained and skillful research, and because those who are not sufficiently prepared would receive more injury than help from knowledge of Scripture. The sacred mysteries are reserved for the elect; those predestined for this "gnosis" [knowledge into the absolute infinity and unchanging in all and above all in us]. This explains the characteristic use of the parable-style in Scripture (*Strom.* VI 15:124).

Growth Expands Our Concept of God: It Reminds Us of Our Magnanimous and Compassionate Hearts

The "meat" of the secret of secrets (1 Cor. 3:2) and of "who have trained and used their tastes to know the difference between good and evil" (Heb. 5:14), along with the beyond–the–primer "milk" of college, graduate, and postgraduate spiritual wisdom are generally not offered by the majority of world religions or intellectual and learning centers. The tragedy lies in interdenominational wars and subversive thinking: "Our religion is the only true religion—we are in sole possession of truth," and a basic lack of understanding of the total nature of God's absoluteness in the universe and grasp of the exact nature of things.

Specifically: the "meat" (Eph. 6:19), the solid food for grown-ups of the divine mysteries in the gospels (Christ in me; me in Christ [2 Cor. 11:10, Gal. 2:20]), is the awareness of the union of every individual with all other individuals, of every object with all other objects, and of all individuals and objects with the Absolute Infinity, '**1**'. We do not think deeply and live out in our daily lives all the considerations respectfully, on the essential unity of all values that there is:

> One God and Father of all ['**1**'], *who is over all*, and *works through all*, and *is in all* (Eph 4.6).

Additionally, the barbaric history of birthright (a right to which a person is entitled by birth) identity theft and mass murder perpetrated in the great cause of God's defense by different religions (Islamic jihads, the 9/11 mass murder, India's Thuggee pactices, the Albigensian Crusades against the Cathar heresy, the Northern Crusades, the Papal and Spanish Inquisitions, burning people *alive* at the stake, and so on) has been a menace to permanent world peace, great prosperity, freedom, and humanity living a divine life of true purity, love, and compassion.

Paul the Apostle called himself the "Apostle to the Gentiles." He was with Saint Peter and James the Just, the most prominent of initial Christian missionaries. In the same Epistle to the Corinthians, Paul shares a direct encounter with absolute truth and our splendors of transcendent beauty:

> Are you not aware that "you are" the temple of God, and that the Spirit of God dwells in you? . . . For the temple of God [the Temple of Absolute Infinity] is holy, and *you are that temple*" (1 Cor. 3:16–17).

Swami Vivekananda (1863–1902) has inspired millions of people worldwide with his spiritual teachings, free of dogma and sectarianism. His fundamental message is: "I call upon men to make themselves conscious of their divinity within"—*living each moment with a sense of God's presence in them*. In the vein of Saint Paul, Vivekananda states:

> The moment I have realized God sitting in the temple of every human body, the moment I stand in reverence before every human being and see God in him—in that moment I am free from bondage, everything that binds vanishes, and I am free.

O God, My God, Oh Infinite Splendor and Light, All Things Are Yours: The Heavens, the Earth, and the Nations Are Yours!
Why Not Make Your Living a Divine Life More Accessible to You?

My Infinite Splendor of Love, by a life of perfection (see "Perfections for Living Your Divine Life," Chapter IV), we can stop "worshiping god of gold" (Ex 32) or "turning our Father's house into a marketplace" (John 2.16). "God is Spirit ['1'], and those who worship him must worship in spirit and in truth" (John 4.24).

To unlock wisdom and promote love, compassion and understanding, we not only quote the minds and hearts of the Bible—we look at what is good for us, what profits us—*we live it* every moment. We realize that there is "no separation between God and us." We, the transmuted humanity, whose life is *one* in nature and essence with the infinite Absolute, become conscious, as Paul of Tarsus did in his Epistle to the Corinthians, that:

> All things are yours, whether it be [me] . . . or the world, or life, or death, or the present, or the future: all these are yours, and you are Christ's, and Christ is God's (1 Cor. 3:21–23).

Dominican preacher, theologian, and mystic of precision and compassion, Meister Johann Eckhart (1260–1328) put it this way: "In the kingdom of heaven [which is the empty space, and which is within you and outside of you] all is in all, as is one, and all is ours."

Saint John of the Cross (John Yepes, 1542–1591)—was one of the greatest Christian mystics and cofounder of the contemplative order of Discalced Carmelites. He experienced God's infinite light in himself. Like Paul the Apostle to the Corinthians and Meister Eckhart, John of the Cross-reiterates the timeless reality, which we will present in this work again and again through different people of different viewpoints and of different awarenesses:

> The heavens are mine, the earth is mine, and the nations are mine! Mine are the just, and the sinners are mine; mine are the angels and the Mother of God; all things are mine, God himself is mine and for me, because Christ is mine and all for me. What do you ask for, what do you seek for, O my soul? All is yours—all is for you."

Yes, O Absolute Splendor and Light, yes my dearest reader, beauty and heart: the totality of all that exists, ever existed, or will ever exist "are yours," as the Apostle Paul, Meister Eckhart, and Saint John of the Cross so magnificently affirm. Yes! The heavens are yours, the earth is yours, and the nations are yours! "All is yours—all is for you."

This is what we'll try to develop in this book; this is how we'll attempt to make your infinite living significantly more accessible to you. This is where, my dearest Light, Compassion, and Wisdom, your life can become miracle after miracle from moment to moment.

Love All and Serve All

Only once have I been mute.
It was when a man asked me: "Who are you?"

—Khalil Gibran

Without a meaningful, believable story that explains the
world we actually live in, people have no idea how to think
about the big picture.
And without a big picture, we are very small people.

—Joel R. Primack and Nancy E. Abrams

So long as we have no knowledge of our real nature, we are
beggars, jostled about by every force in nature and made
slaves of by everything in nature.

—Swami Vivekananda

Ultimately, we come into being from the Spirit of God from
the empty space.
The universes come and go but we'll always be around, to
love all and to serve all.

—Orest Bedrij

Disease is not cured by pronouncing the name of medicine, but by taking medicine. Deliverance is not achieved by repeating the word "Brahman" [the unchanging, infinite, immanent, and transcendent Reality], but by directly experiencing Brahman.

—Shankara

God is everywhere, he fills his creation. Among the movable and the immovable objects there is not an atom but has his presence in it.
He is like the heavens pervading all. He is like the air inhabiting my heart . . . .
Brahma and his creation cannot be separated even for a moment, but we, of the earth earthy, have no inkling of that vital principle; an owl may live for a hundred years and still will not know what the day is like.

—Mahatma Gandhi

Life is a song—sing it.
Life is a game—play it.
Life is a challenge—meet it.
Life is a sacrifice—offer it.
Life is love—enjoy it!

—Sai Baba

Emptiness is unborn
Emptiness does not pass away.
When you know emptiness
You are not different from it.

—Wu-men Hui-k'ai

I

In the Miracle Zone: Effortless Living

The first sign that you are living a Divine Life is that
you are becoming full of inner peace, compassion,
and great happiness.

—Orest Bedrij

Omnipresence, Omniscience, and Omnipotence Is Our Natural State:
Wake Up, My Love, to Your True Nature; Let Your Eyes See Eternity

What is the "miracle zone" of effortless living? To answer this question, we have to take into account the relative or human frame of reference with limitations and the Absolute Infinity frame of reference without limitations.

If we consider the first person "I" as a "surface-mind" imprisoned in the body, similar to a hatchling chick in his shell with limited possibilities (Saint Paul's "infants in Christ"), we will experience one type of life. When we consciously realize that "the Spirit of God dwells in us" (1 Cor. 3:16), that "You are the light of the world" (Matt. 5:14), that "You are gods" (John 10.34), and thus hold ourselves in the highest regard as the Absolute Infinity (with unlimited possibilities and not the baby-bird in the shell), we will experience another type of life in our eternal journey of self-discovery and recreation. (Note: the "Spirit of God" is the *empty space* in which we, all the atoms, stars, and galaxies of our universe live, move and have our being.)

The surface-mind is the lower mind (*kama-manas* in Sanskrit), also known as the everyday mind, or the logical mind (*manas*), which includes the emotions (*kama*) and feelings. In the self-limiting, the less demanding ("infant") form of living, we walk, talk, write, sing, ride a bike, push the accelerator in a car, or feed ourselves with a spoon, in most cases without consciously concentrating on that activity. Professionals who play tennis, golf, or a violin do the same. Here pros do not think about how to hold the tennis racket, golf club, or violin bow when they play. Their behavior is *spontaneous*, natural, and effortless, or "second nature." They perform, like all inner systems in our being (i.e., neuron communication in our brain, DNA and RNA development in our body, etc.), automatically, *beyond the conscious influence of the human will.* Here our autopilot habits are deeply ingrained as to appear natural.

Second nature is a habit or characteristic practiced for so long that it seems to be part of a person's nature and appears as if it is innate. "If you want a quality," states Norman Vincent Peale (1898-1993), a progenitor of the theory of "positive thinking":

> act as *if* you already have it. If you want to be courageous, act
> as *if* you were—and as you act and persevere in acting, so you
> tend to become.

Before we learned to walk, talk, write, sing, keep our balance on a bike, or feed ourselves with a spoon, we had to acquire these second-nature (autopilot: automatic life-guidance system) *habits* through "repeated practice" and self-education. Like building interstate highways, we had to "connect and enlarge our neuron pathways," the "antennae in our brain," *to* the mathematical patterns within us. These mathematical patterns, which physicists call the laws of physics, is the hidden order to the universe or the unchanging software of God's inner structure. That unchanging software, or the "source code" of God the Father Almighty, the laws of physics represent with a symbol '**1**'.

David Bohm (1917-1992) was an American-born theoretical physicist who made important contributions in the domain of quantum physics, philosophy, and in the atom bomb development in the Manhattan Project. Bohm, in his Lecture at Berkeley in 1977, describes the process of the ultimate perception, or knowing the truth, '**1**', not originating in the brain:

> The ultimate perception does not originate in the brain or any material structure, although a material structure is necessary to manifest it. The subtle mechanism of knowing the truth does not originate in the brain.

The neuron antennae enable us to "receive high-speed communication streams of messages and experiences" on the conditions of the universe we are exploring within the '**1**'. They respond prior to the influence of the human will, but within the determination of the Absolute itself. Here the totality of all conditions of the universe are mathematical, unalterable (i.e., like the cycle of the seasons), have perfect solution, and are prior to the control of the individual willpower.

In the everyday mind, or the logical mind, similar to a baby bird in his shell, we, as the Absolute Infinity, live "partially" under the constancy of governing universal principles. Like slaves, we are incarcerated in the "prison" of optical delusion of our consciousness and therefore cannot express ourselves "fully" across the spectrum of actions, as the Infinite Splendor and "the light of the world" (Matt. 5:14).

Albert Einstein (1879–1955), the German-born theoretical physicist published over 300 scientific and over 150 non-scientific works and received the 1921 Nobel Prize in Physics for his work in theoretical physics, and particularly for his unearthing of the law of the photoelectric effect. With a courageous straightforwardness, Einstein, who did not follow the beaten track of other physicists and thinkers, in *The New York Post* November 18, 1972, stated:

A human being is a part of the whole, called by us the "Universe," a part limited in time and space. He experiences himself, his thoughts and feelings as something separated from the rest—a kind of optical delusion of his consciousness. This delusion is a kind of prison for us, restricting us to our personal desires and to affection for a few persons nearest to us. Our task must be to free ourselves from this prison by widening our circle of compassion to embrace all living creatures and the whole of nature in its beauty. Nobody is able to achieve this completely, but the striving for such achievement is in itself a part of the liberation and foundation for inner security.

A New Science of Life:
The Unchangeable Miracle Way,
The Light of Human Existence

In the Absolute Infinity (without limitations) frame of reference and the illuminated mind (*buddhi-manas* in Sanskit) of living a divine life, one realizes that "the temple of God is holy, and *you are that temple*" (1 Cor. 3:16)—"that the Father is in me and I in him" (John 10:38). This breakthrough awareness about yourself—and training of the intellect so that it can function in automatic pilot, like the "laws of physics," under "*total* say of the mathematical pattern of *unchanging* source code," expands one's capability, power, and effectiveness. At this juncture, the universe always works in your favor.

To be "unchanging," '**1**', is to be "consistent" (dependable, trustworthy) and "absolute." So living a divine life—like learning to walk, talk, write, sing, or feed yourself with a spoon— resides in the refining of personality with a life and habits of the inherent freedom, purity and perfection of '**1**' (see "Perfections for Living Your Divine Life;" "keep yourself in training for godly life" [1 *Tim* 4:7]; "keep yourself pure" [1 *Tim* 5:22]) and the transformation of the self more fully into God.

Here, unshackled from the shell of limitations ("free[d] ourselves from this prison," using Albert Einstein's words, or "when the dead shall hear the *voice* ['**1**'] of the Son of God (John 5:25), using Jesus' language), God lives totally through you and for you. Now you are able to advance on autopilot in the seamless robe of light, '**1**', from miracle to miracle in "All is yours—all is for you" Infinite Splendor. What's more, affirms Peale, "Miracles are of all sizes. And if you start believing in little miracles, you work up to the bigger ones."

Theoretical physicist and writer on the subject of quantum physics, Fred Alan Wolf (1934—) in *Taking the Quantum Leap* wrote:

> We are beginning a new age of awareness, the age of quantum consciousness, the age of conscious atom. By looking within ourselves, we may be able to solve the problems facing us on the final frontier—the frontier of human spirit.

Yes, states the Christ:

> No need for you to be surprised at this, for an hour is coming in which all those in their tombs [not enlightened to what they see and do] shall hear his ['**1**'] voice and come forth. Those who have done right share rise to live; the evildoers shall rise to be dammed (John 5:28).

Similar to generating electricity, there is a universal law, or a law of nature ('**1**') that rules our cosmos and is the way by which our universe continues to exist, thrive and expand. We can't rub two sticks and hope to produce electric power. We have to know how to create electromagnetic induction, which underlies the operation of generators, induction motors, transformers, and most other electrical machines.

The '**1**', or the Absolute Infinity, can be observed in the "effortless action" of electrons, protons, neutrons, planets, stars, galaxies, super clusters, and ultimately the universe. We can also see the unchanging (life-guidance system) in the functioning of the electron configuration of the periodic table, the laws of physics, the workings of electricity, gravity, and so forth.

The celestial mandate of living a divine life by means of the unchanging source code of the universe, '**1**', was what Confucius (551–479 BC) symbolized as *ming*. Ming, according to Confucius, is the will of Heaven, what Heaven confers, or going with the grain.

Lao-tzu, over 2500 years ago, in the classic Chinese text *Tao Te Ching*, illustrates this alignment with the unchanging power, or perfect equilibrium, '1', with *wu-wei*. Wu-wei points to the unchanging motionless "rest" of Heaven or "effortless doing." In contemporary expression it means, "*going with the flow*" or "nondoing" yourself, but allowing the autopilot, the '1' (like in walking and talking), to take over in the world of change.

Aikido is a living illustration of the Taoist nondoing concept. The practitioner is moving along with his opponent instead of resisting his attacks.

Lao-tzu's "nondoing" or "without action" attainment, in the language of the Hebrew Bible (Tanakh), is the "holy" seventh day of Genesis, where God "rested" from all His toil of creating that He has done:

> And God blessed the seventh day and made it holy, because on it he rested from all the work of creating that he has done (Gen. 2:3).

In the Old Testament, on the seventh day of Genesis, at some point God recognized that there is no need to create any more. Everything that had to be created already exists in God, '1'. And so, God can get things done through Confucius' what Heaven confers, or Lao-tsu's "without action" effortless rest. Like in Disney World, our attractions already exist in '1'; we have only to determine "what" attractions we want to journey.

In the New Testament (Greek Scriptures, or the New Covenant) Jesus, in the Lord's Prayer, refers to living a divine life by the absolute software of '1', as "*Thy* [unchanging] *will be done*, on earth as it in heaven" (Matt. 6:10). Similar to discovering new laws of physics, we must know how to bring Jesus' heaven (i.e., the unmanifest quantum potentiality, '1') to earth (i.e., new laws of physics). Learning to communicate with this gentle, silent, and absolute software, in the universe of change, rests deep in the weave of great emptiness. The act of surrendering to that reality brings whole-body enlightenment and effortless or spontaneous living.

Agnes Gonxha Bojaxhiu (1910–1997), well known as Mother Teresa of Calcutta, a symbol of humanity, love, and compassion, put it this way: "Let God use you without consulting you." God used Mother Teresa as the provision of help to "the hungry, the naked, the homeless, the crippled, the blind, the lepers, all those people who feel unwanted, unloved, uncared for throughout society, people that have become a burden to the society and are shunned by everyone."

Elena Petrovna Gan (1831-1891), better recognized as Helena Blavatsky, co-founder of the Theosophical Society, wrote:

> When we let the soul speak we put color into life.
> When we let the soul speak we change direction—to the soul's direction.
> When we let the soul speak we live with purpose—the soul's purpose.
> When we let the soul speak, we start to really live.
> The soul already knows that which the mind is desperately seeking to understand.
> The soul already knows that which we have not remembered in this lifetime.
> The soul already knows, and can, if allowed, remind us.
> Let the soul speak.

From Strength to Strength: Immense Success

President Ronald Reagan made an interesting observation: "If we ever forget that we're one nation under God ['1'], then we will be a nation gone under." Hence, like in the laws of physics under the unalterable design and power that is beyond the influence of the human will, living a divine life is an end result of not living for oneself. Here, like the elementary particles, the Milky Way with one hundred billion stars in its galaxy, among billions of galaxies in our cosmos, *moves effortlessly* under the direction and power of the unmovable and invariable Absolute Infinity, '1', or the laws of nature. In living a divine life, one lives in and for the Absolute in oneself and the Absolute in all existence. And so the Holy Love states:

> My doctrine is not my own, it comes from him ['1'] who sent me (John 7.16). [Furthermore,] I do nothing myself. I say only what the Father ['1'] has taught me (John 8:28). [Also,] You pass judgment according to appearance but I pass judgment on no man. Even if I do judge, that judgment of

> mine is valid because I am not alone. I have at my side the One ['**1**', the unchangeable] who sent me. It is laid down in your law that evidence given by two persons is valid. I am one of those testifying in my behalf, the Father ['**1**'] who sent me is the other (John 8:15-18).

And,

> I cannot do anything of myself. I judge as I hear, and my judgment is honest—because *I am not seeking my own will* but the will of him ['**1**'] who sent me. If I witness on my own behalf, you cannot verify my testimony [because it is not constant, '**1**'], but there is another ['**1**'] who is testifying on my behalf, and the testimony he renders me I know can be *verified* [because it is unchangeable] (John 5:30-32).

In an address to the New Jersey State Senate on February 21, 1861, six feet four inch Abraham Lincoln (1809–1865), with his great qualities of head and heart, similar to Moses who acted at God's behest leads the Hebrews out of slavery, spoke of himself as a "humble instrument in the hand of the Almighty." On another occasion Honest Abe, who was kind to everybody and everything and who saved the Union, freed the slaves, brought a new birth of freedom, and then died a martyr for his mighty deeds, stated, "I am satisfied that when the Almighty wants me to do or not to do a particular thing, he finds a way of letting me know it." Furthermore, the Great Emancipator acknowledged:

> If it were not for my firm belief in an overriding Providence, it would be difficult for me, in the midst of such complications of affairs, to keep my reason in its seat. But I am confident that the Almighty has his plans and will work them out; and . . . they will be the wisest and the best for us.

And the Apostle Paul in his Epistle to the Galatians writes:

> It is no longer I who live but Christ [the Absolute Infinity, the
> Author of all things] who lives in me [and creates astonishing
> miracles through me] (Gal. 2:20).

Everything in life has its price. Therefore, if we want to generate electricity, receive TV reception, fly jumbo jets, build skyscrapers, or safely come back from the moon, we must live by the absolute software of the universe, '**1**'. The same applies to going beyond the level of ordinary logical thought, to whole-body enlightenment where "your whole body will be full of light" (Matt. 6: 22), absolute happiness and great prosperity.

The Secret of Secrets: Your True Identity: The Life of Humanity Is the Life of God

Who is God? Where is God? Who are we, my Precious and Infinite Splendor of Love? Although these questions are perennial, God and you (who are the object of our quest) may be characterized as "*That Which Is*," as the same absolute nature and essence, '**1**'. What applies to you of course applies to your parents, your family, and your friends.

We can think of "That Which Is" as Disney World at night in a deep sleep, or Disney World during the day when it is wide awake, with Mr. Toad's Wild Ride on the go. That which we see as manifest reality during the day *preexists* at night at Disney; it is known as "quantum potentiality" in physics. The Epistle to the Hebrews characterizes it like this: "what is visible came into being through the invisible" (Heb. 11:3).

Richard Feynman (1918–1988), recipient of the 1965 Nobel Prize in Physics for his part in the development of quantum electrodynamics, expressed:

> If the same circumstances [identical rides at night and during
> the day] don't always produce the same results, predictions are
> impossible and science will collapse.

Thus, the universe is the visible image of God. The way in which we go from the invisible to the visible state of "That Which Is" is this: we decide "what" Disney World attractions we want to ride. Here God's being does not manifest itself in its totality (absolute) but only partially (relative) through our choice of the rides we experience.

In Einstein's (1905) formula of special relativity, $E = mc^2$, energy (E) and mass (m) are one and the same ("="), indistinguishable in essence. Like ice, water, fog, mist, or steam, all are identical in essence, only different in form. So Einstein's mass and energy can be regarded as mass of nuclear weapons, known mercilessly as the "Little Boy" and the "Fat Man," or they can be considered as energy of the mushroom clouds in Hiroshima and Nagasaki, heartless atom-bomb detonations against civilian city dwellers.

Mathematically, in physical relationships, "That Which Is" absolute (total) is characterized with the symbol '1' (i.e., $1 = E/mc^2$), while "That Which Is" relative (comparative) is characterized with the symbols E/mc^2. Therefore, all that is relative comes from '1', or That Which Is absolute. Furthermore, as mass and energy are identical in essence, so God (unmanifest) and you (manifest) are one and the same essence only in different form, like rides that are the same at night or during the day in Disney World. Thus we hear from Jesus (Yeshu or Yeshua, "God saves"):

> Whoever has seen me [i.e., E/mc^2] has seen the Father ['1']
> (John 14.9). The words I speak are not spoken of myself, it
> is the Father who lives in me accomplishing his works (John
> 14:10). [When your mind clears up, when you understand our
> unity] On that day you will know that I am in my Father, and
> you in me, and I in you (John 14:20).

In simple language: life, or nature, is the image of God (i.e., a reflection of God's attributes, $E/mc^2 = 1$)—our true (birthright) identity. That is to say, reflection of the absolute source code of the universe or mirror mage of quantum potentiality made visible to our personal observation and questioning.

As the distance between steps on earth determines the amount of a measure, so the distance between points in '1', determines the character of life, or nature, in '1'. And so the '1', or you, is the "Father of all, who is over all and *works through all*, and *is in all*" (Eph. 4:5–6) stated Saint Paul, elated with love, kindness, and compassion of Christ, in his Epistle to the Ephesians.

Toward Our Home in God, Toward the Father's Heart: Seek First the Infinite Splendor within You, Experience the Presence of God in Absolute Happiness

Jesus the Christ, the Holy and Compassionate One, who has come in his Father's, '**1**', name (John 5.43), is the most loved and the most revered of the human beings who have ever trekked this earth. He washed and dried his disciples' feet, resurrected the dead, walked on the water, and healed the sick without the aid of drugs, surgery, or supplements. He demonstrated the life of Infinite Splendor and of living a divine life through his wisdom, integrity, fearlessness, forgiveness, kindness, and unconditional love.

Jesus "was speaking of God ['**1**'] as his own Father, thereby making himself God's equal" (John 5:18). The concept of the *coming* (manifesting in our lives) kingdom of our Father (the "kingdom of heaven") is of central importance in Jesus' teaching. In total, the Gospels present over 120 accounts (Matthew has 54; Mark has 20; Luke has 43; John has 4) of the Beloved, the Son of the Blessed, regarding "the kingdom of God."

He stated that the kingdom of God is within and outside our own being, making the kingdom of the Absolute and sharing the heavens, which are ours; the earth, which is ours; and the nations, which are ours (Col. 1:12) not as a hoped-for future phenomenon but as a *present reality* and his primary "mission statement."

Our physicists and mathematicians do the same when they bring Jesus' "heaven" (i.e., absolute nothingness, quantum potentiality) to "earth" (i.e., discover new laws of physics)—when they seek physical relationships that are invariant—equations which are unchanging. In spiritual language, physicists seek equations that are "perfect" (Matt. 5.48).

The Infinite One, with dedicated persistence, advised searching for the kingdom of God, the Absolute Itself within us, and its magnanimity and truth, as the principal purpose in our life:

> Seek first his kingdom ["That Which Is" unchangeable under a transformation in physics] and his righteousness [trustworthiness, goodness], and all these things will be given to you as well (Matt. 6:33).

We know that Siddhartha Gautama (563–483 BC), the venerable sage of the Shakya clan, like Christ Jesus, had an air of wisdom, humility, loving kindness, sincerity, and compassion for all. He addressed the nature of life, the nature of self, the nature of the environment, and the nature of liberation. Similar to the Nazarene, Shakyamuni Buddha's priority was bringing to fruition the highest state of spiritual realization—to penetrate the veils of *maya* (illusion, the emptiness of the world, every man's consciousness) and perceive that one is the infinite Absolute or a Buddha.

The enlightened person perceives the Infinite Splendor of Divinity in all beings and the Christ's kingdom "near you," "among you," and "within you." This is a state of being where every thought and act in life is a spiritual exercise, and *our reality is the thought of God manifest in human form.* Namely, the Buddha set his monumental work and the highest goal for all beings on attaining complete liberation through the knowledge that one is not the body but rather absolute consciousness, or a Buddha. He pointed out:

> In the search for truth there are certain questions that are not important. Of what material is the universe constructed? Is the universe eternal? Are there limits or not to the universe? . . . If a man was to postpone his search and practice for enlightenment until such questions were solved, he would die before he found the path."

In the vein of Jesus the Christ and his parables, allegories, and examples, Siddhartha Gautama amplified his priority with a story of a hunter who has been wounded by a venomous arrow. The doctor wants to remove the lethal arrow, but the patient declares,

> The arrow shall not be pulled out until I know who the man is who shot me with it; to what family he belongs, if he is big, small, or of medium size; if his skin is black, brown, or yellow.

Just as the hunter wounded by the poisonous arrow would have expired before he obtained his answers, so perhaps it would be more beneficial to us to postpone many of our questions and hasten to attain liberation and live a divine life. Namely, we have to achieve complete peace of mind, absolute happiness, and the "great death" of ego to first experience and then remain in the zone of effortless living.

The enlightened ones made this case: don't just believe in God; experience God's infinite light in yourself and in others. Seek first the infinite splendor of love within yourself and in others "and all these things" which are yours in the first place, as the Apostle Paul and Saint John of the Cross put it, "will be given to you as well."

Similar to learning to walk, talk, eat, or write, when one devotes oneself to living a divine life as our "only" occupation it becomes effortless and pure space. That pure space is called in Sanskrit *nirvana, moksha*, and *liberation*. Jesus calls it "God the Father" and de Chardin names it "the omega point." The laws of physics, as mentioned earlier, represent it with a symbol '1'.

Here, our will is united with the will of God, or '1'. The heart is detached from all that is not God and the senses are fused into a single and ineffable act of awareness. Here one finds complete focus upon the business at hand and the *ruthless abandonment* of distractions, which are in the way of perfection and *experiencing the presence of God within us and in others and at every moment*. Now *your life is managed* not according to the helter-skelter world of men, but, like the unchanging laws of physics or the unchanging laws of nature, *according to the unchanging source code within you!*

In the Journey to God, Each Day Is Enlightenment: Organize Your Life So that the World Does Not Consume You

In a mosque at Fatehpur Sikri, India, we find this inscription: "Jesus said, 'This world is a bridge. Pass over it, but do not build your dwelling there.'"

Swami Rama (1925–1996), whose work seeks to unite science and spirituality; East and West; the contemporary world and the traditional wisdom; characterizes it this way in *A Call to Humanity*:

A human being should learn to organize his worldly life so that the external world does not consume too much of his time and energy. By taking care of one's duties lovingly and skillfully, a human being establishes harmony in his personal, family, and social life. A peaceful environment allows him to explore the higher Reality, which is more important than the reality of the manifest world . . . Making the best use of all of life's situations, events, and circumstances is the art of successful living.

As you read on, you will discover that a person having come to awareness beyond the infant "milk" (see "The Great I Am: Beyond the Infant Milk," Chapter II), ends the round of existence (see "Living at the Source: I Live, Yet Not I But God in Me," Chapter III), and returns, like the Prodigal Son, to nourish those horizons of Absolute Love from which they came (see "Each One Teach One, Living a Divine Life," Chapter V).

Having become conscious that *God is in us* and *we are in God*, united together as one that eternally cannot be divided, I have embarked on a search for a body of evidence on the nature of the essence and principle of all existence and living a divine life. All through life, I have been examining the masterpieces of literature for other "faithful servants" and the devout lovers of the Absolute Infinity who have purged themselves of their focus of self so that the divine Light is able to use them as a channel of love, compassion and grace. I am speaking of fully enlightened Ones. The Ones who have united with the Real "above all reason, beyond all thought" and have disclosed the unsuspected splendor of unbounded blessedness, goodness, and serenity in their lives.

Enlightened Ones from whom Absolute Light (spiritual and intellectual insight) pours into their humanity—those like the humble servants of science, who speak the same language and who come from the same unity of Light and Peace. I speak of fully enlightened Ones who have reached the absolute summit of compassion and happiness and become its ambassadors—sons and daughters of the Absolute Wisdom. Some of my findings, as they relate to this area, can be found in my book *Celebrate Your Divinity*.

Spiritual Calculus: One Heart and One Mind: We Must Put Our Trust in the "Unchangeable" Laws of Physics

In parallel to the above work, I have, with systematic rigor, experimental research, prediction and verification, been working to decode the foundation of nature—the order of infinities and the Spiritual Calculus. The Spiritual Calculus involves expressions about the transcendent and immanent Ground of Being and of the world conceived as its manifestation. At this juncture I employed the exactness of physics and mathematics: the validity of the mathematical definitions and demonstrations and the high-precision measurements of physics.

To express the special elegance and simplicity of the Absolute Infinity, '**1**'—(the concrete unmanifest or potential state of endless possibilities—the richly living yet *unchangeable* and indestructible principle that presides over all natural causes) and the relative infinity ("God in the World," manifest reality)—I have utilized verified physical relationships, the fundamental physical constants and mathematics. It was possible to integrate the work of some of the most profound thinkers of modern science into the natural spectrum of physics and the Spiritual Calculus via a logarithmic slide rule of physical relationships. The physics part of this work is described in *'1': The Foundation and Mathematization of Physics.*

Overflowing with happiness, awareness of marvelous serendipity, and joy of the very heart of Light, I discovered that the *empty-space* (the interstellar space through which light is propagated and where "we live and move and have our being" [Acts 17.28]) is the Absolute Infinity, and where "we are in fact God's offspring" (Acts 17:29). Here, in the unalterable empty space in which innumerable electrons, protons, neutrons, stars, galaxies, and super clusters are whirling and dancing about one other, and that which separates the particles of matter from each other, is the laws of physics' *unchanging frame of reference*, '**1**'. In '**1**' we find the mathematical unity behind the physics and the reality that the present, the past, and the future are already here and now. Similar to Disney World attractions, we just have to choose what rides we want to take—what life experiences we want to live.

You Live in Your Personal Universe:
'1' Is Unchanging Rest and Perpetual Stillness:

In the light of what we know, '**1**' is the everlasting unmovable principle and the source code of the universe that exists independently of our actions or knowledge, governing the universe, all things, and the succession of our ideas. Also, '**1**' is the "pure awareness," which at first, before manifestation, is like a clean paper on which nothing is written.

The pure awareness is of luminous clarity, immaterial, and is identical with the empty-space. It exists before time and is the ground of all being. *Time is the smallest increment* (reciprocal relation) *of motion* in '1'. '1' was never created and will never end. The pure awareness is also the *observer* of consciousness and thought. I consider pure awareness the absolute frame of reference and the *a priori* principle, or the first science, and the highest final cause, to which nothing else can be prior.

In addition, full of inestimable love, joy, and gladness of heart, I have observed and verified that our thoughts and our actions create and continually *recreate our personal universe*. Furthermore, our human mind can have an effect on time, space, energy, and matter not only inside the body (our health, beauty, happiness, and healing), but also at great distance outside the body. To quote from the "Union Without Ceasing" chapter, in *Yes It's Love*:

> If you could see your thoughts and their effect on your surrounding, you would literally be petrified to dwell on anything negative. You would realize that *the whole of your life's experience is but the outer expression of inner thoughts you have chosen to hold*. You would understand that what you think in your mind you will invariably produce in your experience. Think love, and love energy emanating from your mind will not only surround and modify you but all those about whom you think. Think thoughts of hate, and hate energy will be acting on you and on those about who you think.

We live in a universe that is, in common expression, the Thought of its Absolute Thinker, or Creator. "The Sanskrit word for creation is *srishti*, projection," writes Vivekananda:

What is meant by "God created things out of nothing [the empty space, '**1**']"? The universe [Disney World rides on the go] is projected out of God [Disney rides turned off]. He becomes the universe and it all returns to Him, and again it proceeds forth, and again returns. Through all eternity it will go on in that way.

What is more, our thoughts go from one place to another within '**1**' without traversing the intervening space and without the lapse of time. This can be compared to the action of electrons, which jump from outer to inner orbits of the atom in '**1**' "without taking time or passing through inter-orbital space."

All People Are Members of Your Immediate Family: Become a Driving Force of the Eternal Love and Grace

In the First Epistle of Paul to the Corinthians we read:

> When I was a child, I spoke as a child; I understood as a child, I thought as a child: but when I became a man, I put away childish things. For now we see in a mirror dimly, but then face to face. Now I know in part; then I shall understand fully, even as I have been fully understood (1 Cor. 11–12).

Niels Bohr (1885–1962) was one of the leading theoretical physicists of the 20th century. In 1921 he founded the Niels Bohr Institute. Bohr guided, mentored, and collaborated with many of the foremost physicists of the century at his institute in Copenhagen and the Manhattan Project. He won the 1922 Nobel Prize in Physics and made fundamental contributions to understanding atomic structure and quantum mechanics. Bohr, who had a very deep insight into the human spirit and physics, characterized our bond in this way:

> When searching for harmony in life one must never forget in the drama of existence we are ourselves both actors and spectators.

Saint Paul illustrated our unity along these lines:

> He who loves his wife loves himself (Eph. 5.28).

In the Gospel of Eve, which is not part of the canonical Bible, our unity is presented in this fashion:

> And he spoke to me and said, "I am you and you are I, and wherever you are, I am there, and in all things am I sown. And from wherever you wish, you gather me, and when you gather me, you gather yourself."

John Archibald Wheeler (1911–2008) was one of the preeminent theoretical physicists of the 20th century. He made many very significant contributions to our body of knowledge on particle, nuclei, and nuclear weapons. Yet, Wheeler's most noteworthy gift was not the quantity or quality of physics but rather the radiance of his enthusiasm, encouragement, and understanding that he skillfully brought to his students and to the community of physicists inside and outside Princeton University. Like Einstein and Bohr, his two inspirations, he never stopped thinking about physics and the universe. He once stated:

> The time left for me on earth is limited, and the creation question is so formidable that I can hardly hope to answer in the time left for me.

Wheeler stimulated me with helpful suggestions to look for the prediction and mathematization of physics. He wrote to me: "I was not bright enough to find a prediction in your paper, so I will have to wait for some new development. In the meantime, you may get some comfort from my motto, 'If you would learn, teach.'" Wheeler employed the one-on-one and each one teach one method in sharing his love and knowledge of physics. In 1976 he stated:

> We all know that the real reason universities have students is in order to educate the professors.

In the vein of Albert Einstein, David Bohm, Erwin Schrödinger, and many others, Wheeler understood our bond. He characterized the universe as "a self-excited circuit." Similar to Niels Bohr, Wheeler described our unity like this:

> We are participators in bringing into being not only the near and here but the far away and long ago. We are in this sense, participators in bringing about something of the universe in the distant past, and if we have one explanation for what's happening in the distant past why should we need more?

Martin Redfern notes:

> Many don't agree with John Wheeler, [as many did not agree with Moses, Siddhartha Gautama, Jesus, Shankara, Muhammad, and countless others] but if he is right then we and presumably other conscious observers throughout the universe are creators—or at least the minds that make the universe manifest.

The significance of above findings is extremely important for all of us. On one hand, as you will see in this work, many women and men through direct experience, principles of physical cosmology and physics, have already verified our unity ("The Father and I are one" John 10:30) and our divinity ("You are gods, all of you sons of the Most High," Ps. 82.6). Furthermore, the ground of all or the changeless "Absolute above all reasons, beyond all thought" is really "You." On the other hand, by applying physics and mathematics, we see corroboration of their findings with hard science.

We are members of the immediate and perfect family of God—of the Absolute Light, Absolute Life, and the Absolute Joy. Thus, the Absolute Infinity, or the All in all, '1', is everywhere. One of the most famous verses in the Torah (Exod. 3:14) characterizes this as: "I am that I am," or "I-shall-be that I-shall-be".

Furthermore, *the awareness of being one with God and with all mankind generates the strength and power of the Absolute Infinity within us* to move heaven and earth and to overcome challenges. *The greater that awareness,* the more we are Christ-like or Buddha-like, *the greater the strength and power of the Absolute Infinity within us,* the more we break the chains of our deep-seated slavery and experience a new life of freedom. And so, with the Compassionate One, we glorify our Father in us:

> If you live in me and my words stay part of you, you may ask what you will—it will be done for you. My Father has been glorified in your bearing much fruit and becoming my disciples (John 15:7-8).

Also, live on in love. Experience joy like never before:

> As the Father has loved me, so I have loved you. Live on in my love. You will live in my love if you keep my commandments, even as I have kept my Father's commandments, and live in his love. All this I tell you that my joy may be yours and your joy may be complete. This is my commandment: love one another as I have loved you. There is no greater love than this: to lay down one's life for one's friends
>
> You are my friends if you do what I command you. I no longer speak of you as slaves, for a slave does not know what his master is about. Instead, I call you friends, since I have made known to you all that I heard from my Father (John 15:9-15).

Advance. It's never been easier.

II

The Great I Am:
Beyond the Infant Milk

Knowledge of ourselves teaches us whence we come, where we are and whither we are going. We come from God and we are in exile; and it is because our potency of affection tends toward God that we are aware of this state of exile.

—Jan van Ruysbroeck

When I was looking for God
I have been looking for myself.

—Jalal al-Din Rumi

Honor Be to God in Man!
Blessed Are the Pure in Heart for They Shall See God

Our human awareness can observe itself and its universe. Awareness can thus know truth about itself, its kindheartedness, and its nature.

Who knows better than you when you are hungry, when you are thirsty, or when you are cold? Who knows better than you when you observe a sunrise, sunset, birth, or death? You yourself are the best judge for yourself.

Steady practice of self-purification and refinement of our awareness can teach "everyman's consciousness" how to turn inward and realize God's glory in themselves and in others: a new life of peace, the power and clarity of mind, pure awareness, absolute happiness, and living a divine life via the absolute source code of the universe. This higher level of existence, which has been confirmed and reconfirmed many times, is superior to our usual way of life. The experience can be compared to going cross-country with horses and wagons, without roads or a map four hundred years ago, versus today in cars on interstate highways with a map and a GPS.

Mother Teresa of Calcutta for over forty-five years ministered to the sick, poor, orphaned, and dying. She founded the Missionaries of Charity in 1950, now operating 610 missions in 123 countries with more than 4,000 Sisters/Brothers and over 100,000 volunteers. Mother Teresa, who was not a woman to indulge in mere lip service, declared:

> A clean heart can see God, can speak to God, and can see the love of God in others.

As Jesus stated in the Gospel of Matthew:

> Blessed are the pure in heart for they shall see God (Matt. 5:8).

The miracle worker of Puttaparthi, India, Sathya Sai Baba (1926–present), whose saintly life and motto is to "love all and serve all," expressed it like this:

> You need not search for God. You yourself are divine. How can you go in search of yourself? This is the mistake you commit. When everything is permeated by the Divine, who is the searcher of the Divine? It is because the world has lacked men who could proclaim this Vedantic truth with

authentic experience that it has sunk to such degrading levels.

Sai Baba is correct. "How can you go in search of yourself?" *How can an ocean wave search for water?* Swami Vivekananda put it in this fashion:

> When you look at that unchanging Existence from the outside, you call it God; and when you look at it from the inside, you call it yourself. It is but one. There is no God separate from you, no God higher than you, the real "you." All the gods are little beings to you, all the ideas of God and Father in heaven are but your own reflections. God Himself is your image.

Some of the acts of self-purification, egolessness and refinement of awareness include: self-restraint and spiritual discipline, worry and anger management, nonviolence, avoidance of injury to any life form, not stealing, truthfulness, trustworthiness, inner silence (stilling the body and mind), kindness, love and compassion, fasting, "your will be done," and transformation of our mind to the mind of God [Jesus' (Matt. 5:1–12; Luke 6:20–42)].

Awakening to the Consciousness of Effortless Living: Awake, O Sleeper, Arise from the Dead, and Christ Will Give You Light

Like cleaning a window, when a high level of self-purification and refinement in perception has been attained, one sheds the limited personality, the egoistic character; and advances to the state of total peace beyond all conditions and qualities, or "pure awareness" and direct perception of God's glory ("*That Which Is*" unchangeable) in all.

Direct perception means we are face to face with the "wonder of wonders" and are "seeing God face to face" (1 Cor. 13.12, Matt. 5:8, Ps.

17:15). "God," says Eckhart, "is nearer to me than I am to myself; He is just as near to wood and stone but they do not know it."

In the process of self-purification and refinement of awareness one "synchronizes" one's consciousness to the "empty-space" instead of the movement of particles (observed, i.e., in a protective eggshell), as we do in our regular daily life. In the zone with God, one harmonizes oneself to a splendor of perfections (see "Perfections for Living Your Divine Life").

Some of these perfections include inner peace, unassuming nature, and stillness of the mind, magnanimity, the almighty silence, and non-attachment to anything in life. Here, in the development of the highest form of human consciousness, our awareness becomes free from any overlay (unshackled from the shell of limitations). Now, as the pure awareness, one can see oneself in attributes such as unity, infinity, eternity, and the Absolute Godhead.

As in Disney World with the lights on and off, consistent with the understanding of Buddhism, a person cannot become a Buddha (the Absolute Infinity), because one been a Buddha for eternity. However, a person trapped in a "surface mind"—the everyman's consciousness or "protective eggshell"—is not aware of this fact, and thus it seems to him as though he "becomes" a Buddha when he realizes his Buddha-nature for the first time.

Merwan Sheriar Irani (1894–1969), known to many as Meher Baba, who brought new understanding of spiritual value and truth to humanity, knew that he is the Infinite Splendor and "the light of the world." Traveling incognito throughout India, similarly to Buddhists, in what he called "The New Life," stated:

> After the attainment of God-realization, the soul discovers that it has always been the Infinite Reality, and that its looking upon itself as finite during the period of evolution and spiritual advancement was an illusion. The soul also finds that the infinite knowledge and bliss that it enjoys have been latent in the Infinite Reality from the beginning of time and that they became manifest at the moment of realization.

Jesus also tried to make us aware of our Infinite Splendor with acts of kindness, love and compassion, resurrecting the dead, feeding multitudes, and reminding us that:

> You are the light of the world" (Matt. 5:14); "you are gods" (John 10:34); and "Truly, truly, I say to you, he who believes in me, the works that I do he do also; and greater works than these shall he do" (John 14:12).

Furthermore,

> As often as you did [give a cup of water] for one of my least brothers, you did for me [Absolute Infinity] (Matt. 25:40).

And so Saint Paul in his Epistle to the Ephesians wrote:

> Awake, O sleeper, arise from the dead, and Christ will give you light (Eph. 5:14).

William Blake (1757–1927), to remove barriers to spiritual vitality, had a similar proclamation:

> Awake! Awake O sleeper of the land of shadows, wake! Expand! I am in you and you in me, mutual in love . . . Lo! We are one.

In Christian theology of various denominations, including the Lutheran Church, Catholic Church, and the Methodist Church, the direct perception of God or "pure awareness" is termed as the "beatific vision" of the Absolute. In "Union Without Ceasing" of *Yes It's Love*, "beatific vision" was characterized by Dr. R. M. Bucke as "cosmic consciousness." As stated previously, the Sanskrit term Buddhists use to describe that state is "nirvana." For Hindus it is the supreme universal consciousness or "moksha," and for Zen in Japanese it is "jakumetsu."

In physics this omnipresent, omnipotent, and omniscient state is an attempt to limit the Limitless (Latin definere). It can be measured, verified, and corroborated with high precision instruments as "That Which Is" unchangeable. All laws of physics are unchangeable. All laws of physics describe the unchangeable character of '**1**'.

God Knows Himself:
He Who Knows Himself Knows God

During five thousand years of humanity's history, a number of individuals through varied acts of self-purification and refinement of their awareness realized and validated the unchangeable order of Reality. Their minds cut deeply to first principles. With effort and concentrated attention they characterized that order of Reality via the attributes of God as the unchangeable essence, omnipotence, omnipresence, omniscience, Spirit of God, or the Creator of all. They awakened to the awareness of the Absolute Infinity within themselves, others and the universe.

Take, for example, Abraham Isaac Kook (1865–1935) an extraordinary thinker and a leading Jewish spiritual leader of the twentieth century. He served as the first chief rabbi of Palestine Jewry, under the League of Nations mandate to Great Britain to administer Palestine. Kook wrote,

> Special individuals, the sages of great understanding [Lao-tzu, Zoroaster, Isaiah, Patanjali, Ramakrishna, and a universe of others], always knew the secret of spiritual unity. They knew that the human spirit is a universal spirit, that although many divergences, spiritual and material, tend to separate person from person and society from society, greater than all the differences is the essential unity among them.

Lao-tzu (also known as Laozi, Lao-tse) had a significant influence on Chinese culture, spirituality, and literature. According to Chinese tradition, Lao-tzu lived in the sixth century BC. His writings teach the philosophy of "the Tao," which means "the Way," and they deal with the "virtue" or "integrity" and "the Way" of the unchangeable, and the zone of effortless life, which existed before the universe came into being.

The Tao, which is described in Lao-tzu's *Tao Te Ching*, can be verified by experiencing the essential unity, or the oneness of all. The *Tao Te Ching* is a "Teacher of teachers" and a diamond mine of wisdom and insight on the nature of '1'. It is one of the most sacred texts of Taoism. Following are nine lines quoting Lao-tzu's characterization of the '1':

> There is a thing inherent and natural
> Which existed before heaven and earth.
> It is motionless and fathomless.
> It stands alone and never changes [is invariant];
> It pervades everywhere and never becomes exhausted.
> It may be regarded as the Mother of the Universe [the foundation of nature].
> I do not know its name [it's "nameless"];
> If I am forced to give it a name,
> I will call it Tao [the Absolute Infinity], and I name it as supreme.

It Is the Spirit, '1', That Gives Life: HE WHO IS Is the Projection of the Unchangeable Godhead at Rest

Through the laws of physics, science has also confirmed our unity and that the observer and the observed are fundamentally one. Today, we find among the ranks of those awakened to their absolute identity scientists like: Einstein, Bohr, Bohm, Wheeler, Schrödinger, Bernard d'Espagnat, Freeman Dyson, Arthur Eddington, David Finkelstein, Wilhelm Fushchych, and others.

Albert Einstein, whom we have mentioned earlier, wrote:

A human being is a part of the whole . . . He experiences himself . . . as something separated from the rest—a kind of

optical delusion . . . This delusion is a kind of prison for us . . .
Our task must be to free ourselves from this prison by widening
our circle of compassion to embrace all living creatures and
the whole of nature in its beauty.

David Bohm in *Wholeness and the Implicate Order* describes our unity
through the empty-space in contemporary physical terms,

It is being suggested here, then, that what we perceive through
the senses as empty space is actually the plenum, which is the
ground for the existence of everything, including ourselves.
The things that appear to our senses are derivative forms
[primordial images], and their true meaning can be seen only
when we consider the plenum, in which they are generated
and sustained, and into which they must ultimately vanish.
This plenum is, however, no longer to be conceived through
the idea of a simple material medium, such as ether, which
would be regarded as existing and moving only in a three-
dimensional space.

Rather, one is to begin with the holomovement, in which
there is the immense "sea" of energy described earlier. This sea is
to be understood in terms of a multidimensional implicate order
[the Absolute Itself, '1'], while the entire universe of matter
as we generally observe it is to be treated as a comparatively
small pattern of excitation. This excitation pattern is relatively
autonomous and gives rise to approximately recurrent stable
and separable projections into a three-dimensional explicate
order of manifestation, which is more or less equivalent to that
of space as we commonly experience it.

Insights into the Nature of Your Being:
All Tell the Same Story

Austrian theoretical physicist Erwin Schrödinger (1887–1961), a towering
genius with a broad education, was a contributor to the wave theory of
matter that helped elucidate the fundamentals of quantum mechanics. He

received the 1933 Nobel Prize in Physics with British physicist Paul A.M. Dirac (1902–1984) for developing the elegant wave equation, a widely used mathematical tool that became the heart of modern quantum mechanics. Schrödinger is highly prized for his lucidity of thinking and clarity of expression. He served as director of the School for Theoretical Physics at the Institute for Advanced Studies in Dublin and wrote the well-known little book "What is Life?" 1944. Schrödinger states:

> In Christian terminology to say, "Hence I am God Almighty," sounds both blasphemous and lunatic. But please disregard these connotations for the moment and consider whether the above inference is not the closest a biologist can get to proving God and immortality at one stroke.
>
> In itself, the insight is not new. The earliest records, to my knowledge, date back some 2,500 years or more. From the early great Upanishads the recognition ATMAN = BRAHMAN (the personal self equals the omnipresent, all-comprehending eternal self) was in Indian thought considered, far from being blasphemous, to represent the quintessence of deepest insight into the happenings of the world. The striving of all the scholars of Vedanta was, after having learned to pronounce with their lips, really to assimilate in their minds this grandest of all thoughts . . .
>
> To Western ideology, the thought has remained a stranger, in spite of Schopenhauer and others who stood for it and in spite of those true lovers who, as they look into each other's eyes, become aware that their thought and their joy are numerically one, not merely similar or identical—but they, as a rule, are emotionally too busy to indulge in clear thinking, in which respect they very much resemble the mystic.

Unless one tunes in to the exact frequency channel on a TV one cannot see the program; unless one synchronizes one's awareness to the unchangeable of the empty-space one cannot experience the Absolute Infinity. Swami Rama states:

Unless one corrects and purifies one's heart and mind, one cannot know Reality. If there be the slightest longing for anything on the material plane one cannot grasp the Divine and will be tied down. He who is full of desires should gratify them first and be rid of them through experience. We have come to this world to learn through experience.

The Absolute Dwelling in All Life Forms

From the earliest spiritual revelations in the history of mankind we know that some of these enlightened individuals understood that "the Word became flesh" (John 1:14)—that the Absolute Infinity, like a pilot of a vessel, can employ different means of transportation or forms for self-expression and reality exploration.

These vessels of our life, similar to physical quantities, elements, minerals, plants, animals, and humans, ascend hierarchically from a lesser awareness to a greater or purer awareness, perfection and flawlessness, enabling the pilot (the Absolute Infinity) to change the mode of self-expression and self-exploration.

And so, when Moses (c. the 1300s BC or c. the late 1100s BC), the most important figure in Judaism, "who was in conversation with the angel on Mount Sinai" (Acts 7:38), "the one whom *God* ['**1**'], *through the angel* appearing to him in the thornbush" (Acts 7:35), asks, "If they should say to me, 'What is His name?' what shall I say to them?" The Lord said unto Moses, "I AM THAT I AM," and adds, "Say to the children of Israel: HE WHO IS hath sent me to you" (Exod. 3:13–14). This is a most profound name of *unmanifest* (He Who Is) and *manifest* (I Am That I Am) God, because it signifies that the manifest form, organism, or vessel of the Absolute Infinity is his very unmanifest essence and existence.

Saint Bernard of Clairvaux (1090–1153) was one of the greatest spiritual masters of all time and one of the most imposing church leaders in the first half of the twelfth century. He was the founding abbot of Clairvaux Abbey in Burgundy and a most gifted spiritual writer with extraordinary personal magnetism. Saint Bernard put pen to paper:

Who is God? I can think of no better answer than He who is.
Nothing is more appropriate to the eternity which God is. If
you call God good, or great, or blessed, or wise, or anything
else of this sort, it is included in these words, namely, He is.

"Your real life is Christ [the foundation of life, '1']" (Col. 3:4), said Saint
Paul in his Epistle to the Colossians.

Mahatma Gandhi declared, "I am a man of God disguised as a
politician." And so are you, my dearest reader, love, and Absolute Infinity
disguised in your living being!

The *Bhagavad Gita* ("Song of God"), also called the Upanishad of
the Upanishads and a scripture of liberation, is one of the most important
religious classics of the world and is revered as a sacred scripture of
Hinduism. It states:

> As a person casts off worn-out clothes and puts on those that
> are new, so the embodied Self casts off worn-out bodies and
> enters into others that are new.

Sathya Sai Baba describes the evolutionary process this way:

> Man has evolved from the stone through plant and tree, worm
> and insect, bird and mammal; but some are still groveling
> in the early stages though they have achieved the human
> form . . . So you should cast off all the impediments, all the
> encumbrances that drag you down and make you a boulder
> instead of a Devotee of God and a realized person, or even a
> Paramatma [Absolute Consciousness, '1'].

The Linnaean Society of London was founded in 1788. It seeks to advance
the study of all facets of the biological sciences. At a get-together of the
Linnaean Society in 1858, Alfred Russell Wallace (1823–1913) and Charles
Robert Darwin (1809–1882) presented their theories of evolution by
"natural selection," now one of the cornerstones of modern biology.

Six centuries prior to the Linnaean Society meeting, Jalaluddin Rumi (1207–1273), Persian poet, Sunni Islamic jurist, theologian and mystic, offered a more advanced perspective of the evolutionary progression. In his more than 25,000-verse poem *Mathnawi*, Rumi observed in deep stillness the chronology of hierarchical sequence and transformation in nature. The *Mathnawi*, which is deemed by some to rank in importance with the Koran, is a loosely structured and at times metrically rough and colloquial in style one of the best known influential works of Muslim mysticism. Here is Rumi's awe-inspiring vision of his divine universal forms:

> I died as mineral and became a plant,
> I died as plant and rose to animal.
> I died as animal and I was Man.
> Why should I fear? When was I less by dying?
> Yet once more I shall die as Man,
> To soar with angels blest;
> But even from angelhood I must pass on:
> All except God ['**1**'] perishes.
> When I have sacrificed my angel soul,
> I shall become what no mind e'er conceived.
> O let me non-exist,
> For Nonexistence [the empty-space, absence of manifested objects] proclaims in organ tones,
> "To Him ['**1**', nonexistence of form, the Absolute Infinity] we shall return."

Oh, How Could it Have Been Otherwise!
How Could We All Have Been So Blind So Long

Who is transforming through different forms and organisms in fantastically large numbers to obtain what we call existence? Who has disguised her/himself in masquerade costumes of physical quantities and whirling particles in the universe? Who pretends to be a bottomless ocean, gigantic sequoia, a captivating woman, or a charismatic man? Who has, in temporary amnesia, forgotten who one is? "This is the God to Whom the Christian refers when he says 'in Him we live, and move, and have our being'" (Acts 17:28), says Alice Bailey in *The Consciousness of the Atom*:

> This is the force, or energy, which the scientist recognizes; and this is the universal mind, or the Oversoul of the philosopher. This, again, is the intelligent Will which controls, formulates, binds, constructs, develops, and brings all to an ultimate perfection. This is that Perfection which is inherent in matter itself, and the tendency which is latent [as empty space] in the atom, in man, and in all that is. This interpretation of the evolutionary process does not look upon it as the result of an outside Deity pouring His energy and wisdom upon a waiting world, but rather as something which is latent within that world itself that lies hidden at the heart of the atom of chemistry, within the heart of man himself, within the planet, and within the solar system. It is that something [pure awareness, empty space] which drives all on toward the goal, and is the force [the Existence, the Logos, the enfolding consciousness whom we call God] which is gradually bringing order out of chaos [empty, formless reality]; ultimate perfection out of temporary imperfection; good out of seeming evil; and out of darkness and disaster that which we shall some day recognize as beautiful, right, and true. It is all that we have visioned and conceived of in our highest and best moments.

Truth Seeks the Wise and the Righteous: Truth Alone Triumphs

Below you will find a treasury of insights, sayings, teachings, and quotations by different individuals with citations expressing the awakening and growth to a state of consciousness of the Absolute that is present within each one of us. The list is intended to show an integrated meaning of our birthright "identity" (*who we are*) and where we are heading.

The treasury of quotations is divided into two subdivisions: 1. I Am: The Absolute Principle and 2. I Am Who I Am: God in the World. In the "I Am" section we can consider the Absolute Principle as unmanifest (Disney World attractions: Magic Kingdom, Animal Kingdom, and Epcot, with the lights turned off). And the "I Am Who I Am" section we can regard the Absolute Principle as manifest (Disney World with the lights turned on). In real life, we the observer, with our thoughts and our actions energize different parts of Reality (Christ's "mansions") and experience what we choose to experience.

This treasury can be a very valuable tool in your growth to consciousness of Absolute Infinity, by researching each personage in more detail. Most of the individuals in this treasury of insights have been discussed in *Celebrate Your Divinity*. You may also want to consider that exploration. To help you navigate the volume, we are providing orientation codes to references and chapters as: part 1 or 2, chapter (ch.) yy, reference xx in *Celebrate Your Divinity*. For instance, if a quotation by Meher Baba is from part 1, chapter 19, reference 25 in this book, the orientation code is "1 ch. 19:25."

I Am: The Absolute Principle

Anselm, Saint
No one who understands what God is can conceive that God does not exist.

Baba, Meher
Out of the depths of unbroken Infinity arouse the Question, Who am I? And to that Question there is only one Answer—I am God! 1 ch. 19:25.

If you look within and experience your own soul in its true nature, you will realize that you are infinite and beyond all creation. 1 ch. 19:26.

Bedrij, Orest
The Godhead, or the Absolute Infinity, is the empty-space and unchanging: '**1**'.

'**1**' is the pure awareness.

He Who Is (God in the World) is Godhead in action.

Just as '**1**' so every part of '**1**' contains within itself the history of all things.

Bhagavad Gita
Everything is situated within Him ['**1**']. 1 ch. 7:6.

All created beings are unmanifest in their beginning [lights turned "off" on Disney World rides], manifest in their interim state [lights turned "on" on Disney World rides], and unmanifest [lights turned "off" on Disney World rides]. (2.28: Chapter 2, line 28).

There never was a time when I did not exist [as an archetype or a potential in Disney World], nor you, nor any of these kings. Nor is there any future in which we shall cease to be. Just as the dweller in this body passes through childhood, youth and old age, so at death he merely passes into another kind of body. (2.12–13). 1 ch. 10:10.

There is no Truth superior to Me. Everything rests upon Me ['**1**'], as pearls are strung on a thread. I am the taste of water, the light of the sun and the moon, the syllable *om* in the Vedic mantras; I am the sound in ether [the empty-space] and the ability in man. I am the original fragrance of the earth, and I am the heat in fire. I am the life of all that lives, and I am the penance of all ascetics. I am the original seed of all existence, the intelligence of the intelligent, and the prowess of all powerful men. All states of being—be they of goodness, passion or ignorance—are manifested by My energy. I am, in one sense, everything—but I am independent. I am not under the modes of this material nature (7.7–12). 1 ch. 19:11.

Bible, the
The Spirit [the empty space, '**1**'] of the Lord fills the whole universe and holds all things together (Wisd. of Sol. 1:7). 1 ch. 11.

Lord, You have been our dwelling place (Ps. 90:1). 1 ch. 7.

Bohm, David
What we perceive through the senses as empty space is actually the plenum, which is the ground for the existence of everything, including ourselves [Disney World rides with lights turned "off"]. The things that appear to our senses are derivative forms [Disney World rides turned "on"], and their true meaning can be seen only when we consider the plenum, in which they are generated and sustained, and into which they must ultimately vanish [Disney World rides turned "off"]. 1 ch. 10:12.

Eckhart, Meister Johann
The Godhead gave all things up to God. The Godhead is poor, naked and empty as though it were not; it has not, wills not, wants not, works not, gets not. It is God who has the treasure and the bride in him, the Godhead is as void [empty space] as though it were not. 1 ch. 10:22.

I am that which I was and shall remain, now and forevermore. 1 ch. 11:14.

Einstein, Albert
[Reality] is precisely not to be influenced, since it is changeless and unmovable, either by configuration of matter or by anything else. 1 ch. 14:2.

Gandhi, Mahatma
There is an inmost center in us all, where truth abides in fullness.

Truth is within us.

Gautama, Siddhartha (the Buddha)
Verily, there is an unborn, unoriginated, uncreated, unformed. If there were not this unborn, unoriginated, uncreated, unformed, then an escape from the world of the born, the originated, the created, and the formed would not be possible. 1 ch. 14

Muslim Sufis
What marvel! That a Being colorless displays a hundred thousand hues, tints, shades! What wonder! That being void of form enrobes in forms beyond all numbering!—May we behold Him in all hues and forms! Yet lifts to every name an answering head, the name of Him who is the changeless One amidst the changing many, and within whose oneness all this many is confined, may we begin our loving work of peace. 1 ch. 6:20.

Muhammad, Holy Prophet
I, verily the I All-One, am God, there is no other God than I [the '1': the universal all-pervading self], and I alone should be adored by all. 1 ch. 20:15.

Peebles, Phillip Edwin
One might well ask what the universe is expanding into, or where the space opening up between the particles came from.

Plato
To find out the Maker and Father of this universe is difficult; and, when found, it is impossible to declare Him to all. 1 ch. 5:15.

Shankara

The Atman is that by which the universe is pervaded, but which nothing pervades; which causes all things to shine, but which all things cannot make to shine . . .

Brahman has neither name nor form, transcends merit and demerit, is beyond time, space and the objects of sense-experience. Such is Brahman and "thou art That." Meditate upon this truth within your consciousness.

The nature of the one Reality ['1'] must be known by one's own clear spiritual perception; it cannot be known through a pandit (learned man). Similarly the form of the moon can only be known through one's own eyes. How can it be known through others?

Suso

All creatures have existed eternally in the divine essence, as in their exemplar [lights turned "off" on Disney World rides]. So far as they conform to the divine idea, all beings were, before their creation, one thing with the essence of God. (God creates into time what was and is in eternity.) Eternally, all creatures are God in God . . . So far as they are in God, they are the same life, the same essence, the same power, the same One, and nothing less.

Vivekananda, Swami

There is but one Infinite Being in the universe, and that Being appears as you and as I; but this appearance of division is after all delusion. He has not been divided, but only appears to be divided. This apparent division is caused by looking at Him through the network of time, space, and causation. When I look at God through the network of time, space, and causation, I see Him as the material world. When I look at Him from a little higher plane, yet through the same network, I see Him as an animal, a little higher as a man, a little higher as a god, but yet He is One Infinite Being of the universe, and that Being we are. I am That, and you are That. Not parts of It, but whole of It.

I Am Who I Am: God in the World

Athanasius, Saint

The Divine Word became human in order that every human being may become God. 1 ch. 9:5.

Augustine, Saint

Lord, I have sought you in all the temples of the world and lo, I found you within myself. If a man does not find the Lord within himself, he will surely not find Him in the world. 1 ch. 25:29.

We are all members of one Body, whether we are here or anywhere else on earth, now or at any other time from Abel the Just to the end of the world. 1 ch. 11:3.

Bedrij, Orest

The empty space connects atoms, stars and galaxies; the empty space connects everything in the universe.

He who knows himself is God.

Just as light attracts light and life attracts life, so happiness attracts happiness and success attracts success.

Benjamin, Barbara

I am, the cross I carry; I am, the light you see; I am, the choices that I make; I am, my destiny.

Bible, the

The God who made the world and everything in it is the Lord of heaven and earth and does not live in temples build by hands (Acts 17:24). 1 ch. 7.

You are the light of the world (Matt. 5:14). 1 ch. 11.

Is it not written in your own Law that God said, "You are gods"? (John 10:34) 1 ch. 11.

Whoever has seen me has seen the Father (John 14:9). 1 ch. 7.

I am in my Father, and you in me, and I in you (John 14:20). 1 chs. 5, 7.

In him we live and move and have our being (Acts 17:28). 1 chs. 1, 8, 11.

We, many though we are, are one body (1 Cor. 10:17). 1 ch. 11.

Each one of you is a son of God (Gal. 3:26). 1 ch. 19.

All are one (Gal. 3:28). 1 ch. 20.

One body and one Spirit (Eph. 4:4). 1 ch. 20.

Whoever looks on me is seeing him who sent me (John 12:45). 1 ch. 7.

All that the Father has belongs to me (John 16:15). 1 ch. 7.

You are in me and I am in you (John 14:20). 1 ch. 11.

The body is one and has many members, but all the members, many though they are, are one body (1 Cor. 12:12). 1 ch. 20.

Blake, William
I am in you and you in me. 1 ch. 8:8.

Bohm, David
The entire universe has to be understood as a single undivided whole, in which analysis into separately and independently existent parts has no fundamental status. 1 ch. 19:19.

Carey, Ken
I am always with you . . . You and I are one in your consciousness. As we have ever been one in Reality. I beat with every throb of your heart, feel with every touch of your hand, cry your every tear, breathe your every breath. I am never far away. 1 ch. 19:21.

Cidade Caleixnese
The kingdom of heaven is within you, and whosoever shall know himself
shall find it. 1 ch. 20:23.

Descartes, Rene
I clearly see that existence can no more be separated from the essence
of God than can its having its three angles equal to two right angles be
separated from the essence of a rectilinear triangle, or the idea of a mountain
from the idea of a valley; and so there is not any less repugnance to our
conceiving of God (that is, a Being supremely perfect) to whom existence
is lacking, than to conceive of a mountain which has no valley.

Eckhart, Meister Johann
When is a man in mere understanding? I answer, "When a man sees
one thing separated from another." And when is a man above mere
understanding? That I can tell you: "When a man sees All in all, then a
man stands beyond mere understanding."

If it is true that God became man, it is also true that man became God.
1 ch. 9:8.

In thus breaking through, I perceive what God and I are in common.
There I am what I was. There I neither increase or decrease. For there
I am the immovable which moves all things. Here man has won again
what he is eternally and ever shall be. Here God is received into the soul.
1 ch. 11:9.

Emerson, Ralph Waldo
Every man is a divinity in disguise, a god playing the fool. 1 ch. 11

Farid, Ibn al-
I knew for sure that we are really One, and the sobriety of union restored
the notion of separation, and my whole being was tongue to speak, an eye
to see, an ear to hear, and a hand to seize. 1 ch. 4:21.

Everything you see is the action of the One ['1']. 1 ch. 4:20.

Gandhi, Mahatma
I am that immaculate Brahma.

He who knows himself is Brahman.

Gospel of Eve
And he spoke to me and said, "I am you and you are I, and wherever you are, I am there, and in all things am I sown. And from wherever you wish, you gather me, and when you gather me, you gather yourself."

Gospel of Thomas, The
Jesus said, "I am the light that is over all things. I am all: from me all has come forth, and to me all has returned. Split a piece of wood; I am there. Lift up the stone, and you will find me there." (verse 77). 1 ch. 10.

Jesus said, If they say to you: "From where have you originated?" say to them: "*We have come from the Light, where the Light has originated through itself. It (stood) and It revealed itself in their image.*" If they say to you: "(Who) are you?" say: "We are His sons and we are the elect of the Living Father." If they ask you: "What is the sign of your Father *in you*?" say to them: "It is a movement and a rest [stillness, empty-space]" (50). 1 ch. 9:3.

[God's kingdom] is inside you [and outside you], [whoever] knows [oneself] will find this. And when you know yourselves, [you will understand that] you are [children] of the [living] father. [But if] you do [not] know yourselves, [you are] in [poverty], and you are the [poverty]." (3).

Huang Po
The Mind is no other than the Buddha, and Buddha is no other than sentient being. When Mind assumes the form of a sentient being, it has suffered no decrease; when it has become a Buddha, it has added nothing to itself.

Huxley, Aldous
It is because we don't know Who we are, because we are unaware that the Kingdom of Heaven is within us that we behave in the generally silly, the

often insane, the sometimes criminal ways that are so characteristically human. We are saved, we are liberated and enlightened, by perceiving the hitherto unperceived good that is already within us, by returning to our eternal Ground and remaining where, without knowing it, we have always been. 1 ch. 20:1.

Kabir
Behold but One in all things; it is the second that leads you astray.

Krishna, Gopi
This unimaginable Cosmic Intelligence is present at every spot in the universe, and our whole personality, ego, mind, intellect and all—is but an infinitely small bubble blown on this boundless ocean. 1 ch. 17:14.

Muller, Robert
The soul of the universe, incarnated in a human being, lost much of its qualities and became imperfect. 1 ch. 11:6.

Jami, Maulana "Abdurrahman"
Neighbor and associate and companion—everything is He. In the beggar's coarse frock and in the king's silk—everything is He. In the crowd of separation and in the loneliness of collectedness by God! Everything is He and by God! Everything is He. 1 ch. 20:9

Mechthild of Magdeburg:
I am in you and you are in me. We cannot be closer. We are two united, poured into a single form by an eternal fusion. 1 ch. 25:24.

Merton, Thomas
Our very life loses its separate voice and resounds with the majesty and the mercy of the Hidden and Living One. 1 ch. 20:8.

Muslim Sufis
There's naught within your robe but God Himself, the knower and the known are but the same. He who knows God is God; God knows Himself. 1 ch. 25:25.

I saw you not before—I see you now, Belov'd! You peep forth from every face! I saw you not before—behind the clouds, Beloved! You did not hide. I see you now! 1 ch. 26:10.

Patanjali
The causes of suffering are not seeing things as they are.

Paul VI, Pope
Stand in admiration, rejoice; we have become Christ. 1 ch. 26:8.

Planck, Karl Ernst "Max"
In the last analysis, we ourselves are part of nature, and, therefore, part of the mystery that we are trying to solve. 1 ch. 7:15.

Plotinus
God is sovereignty present through all. We cannot think of something of God here and something else there, nor of all of God gathered at some one spot: there is an instantaneous presence every where, nothing containing and nothing left void, everything therefore fully held by the divine.

Each being contains in itself the whole intelligible world. Therefore All is everywhere. Each is there All, and All is each. Man as he now is has ceased to be the All. But when he ceases to be an individual, he raises himself again and penetrates the whole world.

Rama, Swami
He who wants to know God, should know himself.

God is not away from us, but dwells within us.

The Vedic scriptures declare that the Brahman [the Eternal] became "Many" [individual selves] to realize its own glory and greatness. This manyness or plurality is but a transformation assumed by the Absolute, which in its totality remains the One without a second. 1 ch. 9:13.

Rumi, Jalaluddin al-
The Beloved is all in all; the lover merely veils Him; The Beloved is all that lives, the lover a dead thing. 1 ch. 20:7.

I am you and you are me. 1 ch. 25:21.

Van Ruysbroeck, Jan
The image of God is found essentially and personally in all mankind. Each possesses it whole, entire and undivided, and all together not more than one alone. In this way we are all one, intimately united in our eternal image, which is the image of God and the source in us of all our life. Our created essence and our life are attached to it without mediation as to their eternal cause.

Schimmel, Annemarie
God is visible in every trace of His creation, and although the common folk, the blind and dumb, animal-like, do not recognize Him, the mystic drinks not a single drop of water without discovering His vision in the cup. 1 ch. 5:9.

Schrödinger, Erwin
I am God Almighty. 1 ch. 7:5.

I am in the east and in the west, I am below and above, I am this whole world. 1 ch. 15:10.

Spinoza, Benedict de
The human mind is part of the infinite intellect of God.

There cannot be any substance excepting God, and consequently none other can be conceived. [From this it follows that] whatever is, is in God, and nothing can be or be conceived without God.

Reality and perfection are synonymous. 1 ch. 11.

Symeon of Mesopotamia

As the master says, "God's kingdom is spread out upon the earth, and people do not see it."

Tagore, Rabindranath

Oh my heart, arise! Arise in this land of purity, on the shores of the sea of great humanity. 1 ch. 8:10.

Tasawwuf

The wise see in their heart the face of God, and not in images of stone and clod! Who in themselves, alas! can see Him not, they seek to find Him in some other spot. 1 ch. 19:33.

Ta-shih, Yung-chia

One Nature, perfect and pervading, circulates in all natures, One Reality, all-comprehensive, contains within itself all realities.

Thales of Miletus

All things are full of gods. 1 ch. 7.

Theologia Germanica

Goodness needeth not to enter into the soul, for it is there already, only it is unperceived.

Traherne, Thomas

Pigs eat acorns, but neither consider the sun that gave them life, nor the influence of the heavens by which they were nourished, nor the very root of the tree from whence they came.

Upanishads, the

Cows are of many different colors, but the milk of all is one color, white; so the announcers who proclaim the Truth use many varying forms to put it in, but yet the Truth enclosed in all is One. 1 ch. 19:36.

Verily, this whole world is Brahman. Tranquil [still and calm], let one worship It, as that from which he came forth, as that into which he will be dissolved, as that in which he breathes. 1 ch. 19:12.

As the bees, my dear, prepare honey by collecting the essences of different trees and reducing the essence to a unity, as they are not able to discriminate "I am the essence of this tree," "I am the essence of that tree"—even so, indeed, my dear, all creatures here, though they reach Being, know not "We have reached Being" . . . . These rivers, my dear, flow, the eastern toward the east, the western toward the west. They become the ocean itself. As there they know not "I am this one," "I am that one"—even so, indeed, my dear, all creatures here, though they have come forth from Being, know not "We have come forth from Being." 1 ch. 19:14.

Atman alone is the whole world. 1 ch. 19:13.

The One God hidden in all living beings, the Living Witness biding in all hearts—the Wise who seek and find Him in them-Self, to them, the None Else, is Eternal Joy. The all-pervading Inner Self of all, who from His Formlessness creates all Forms—the Wise who see that One within them-Self, to them alone belongs Eternal Joy . . . The Colorless, who from His secret store exhaustless, countless colors draws, to paint, efface, repaint the worlds upon the face of empty-space with Mystic Potency—may He endow us with the lucid mind! 1 ch. 6.19.

You are woman. You are man. You are the youth and the maiden too. You as an old man totterest with a staff being born, you becomest facing in every direction. You are the dark blue bird and the green (parrot) with red eyes. You hast the lightning as thy child. You are the seasons and the seas. Having no beginning. You do abide with all-pervadingness. Where from all beings are born. 1 ch. 19:20.

I Myself am He! 1 ch. 19:15.

The world is His ['**1**']; indeed, He is the world itself. 1 ch. 19:16.

Verily, this Soul is the overlord of all things, the king of all things. As all the spokes are held together in the hub and felly of a wheel, just so in this Soul all things, all gods, all worlds, all breathing things, all these selves are held together. 1 ch. 19:17.

I am the Infinite; what you are, that same am I; you are all This; I am all This. 1 ch. 19:20

Vedas, the
Truly, you are Godhead yourself . . . He is you. 1 ch. 19:37.

The countless heads, eyes, ears, and hands and feet of living beings are all parts of One Man. 1 ch. 20:10; 2 ch. 1:18.

The progeny of Adam, all are parts and limbs of one and the same organism, risen from the same essence, everyone; and can it be, while one limb is in pain, that other limbs should feel at restful ease? 1 ch. 20:14.

Vivekananda, Swami
There is no help for you outside of yourself; you are the creator of the universe. Like the silkworm you have built a cocoon around yourself. Who will save you? Burst your own cocoon and come out as the beautiful butterfly, as the free soul. Then alone you will see Truth.

What we are, we see outside, for the world is our mirror.

Every being is divine, is God. Every soul is a sun covered over with clouds of ignorance; the difference between soul and soul is owing to the difference in density of these layers of clouds.

Look upon every man, woman, and everyone as God. You cannot help anyone, you can only serve: serve the children of the Lord, serve the Lord

Himself if you have the privilege . . . it is the greatest privilege in our life that we are allowed to serve the Lord in all these shapes.

Wilber, Ken
All things, including subatomic particles, are ultimately made of God. 1 ch. 19:18.

Wingate
Call Me Omega or God, or Jehovah, or Brahman, or Allah, or anything else you would like to call Me. I AM all of these. Yet I AM also none of them. I AM the Cosmos, the Universe. Everything That Is . . . I AM the First Cause. I AM the Last Effect. I AM Every Cause and Every Effect. I AM Spirit. I AM Soul. I AM Matter. As Spirit, I AM the inexpressible, indefinable Source of All Being, infinite and eternal. As Soul, as Spirit manifest for an evolution, I AM Mind. I Am Consciousness. I AM Beingness. And as Matter, as Soul manifest for a lifetime, I AM Everyone and Everything. I AM Perfect; and Every Cause and Every Effect and Everyone and Everything are Part of My Perfection. I AM THE ONE. I AM ALSO THE MANY. AND WHATEVER IT IS THAT SAYS I AM, I AM THAT I AM. 1 ch. 17:9.

III

Living at the Source: It Is Not I But God Who Lives in Me

The wise say that this threefold way is like an iron chain,
binding the feet of him who aspires to escape from the
prison-house of this world.
He who frees himself from the chain achieves Deliverance.

—Shankara

Thy Kingdom Come, Thy Will Be Done: Complete Transformation of the Self into God Enhances Your Vitality, Enriches Your Life

Now we will address humanity's ultimate triumph: the unqualified achievement of the spirit in which the source code of the universe, God's kingdom, is our own operational guidebook and our own personal mode of living. To be precise, we let God's *choice* ('**1**') and God's *will* ('**1**') be done, in our lives by letting our own individual choice and our own will go. This is the holy seventh day of Genesis, where "God had finished the work he had been doing; so on the seventh day he rested from all his work" (Gen. 2:2).

As we have pointed out earlier, in the foundations of physics, scientists characterize God's "unchanging" kingdom and God's "unchanging" will as the "unchanging" *laws of physics*. And therefore, if we want to produce electric power for our homes or observe magnificent images of the universe through the robotic 11-ton Hubble Space Telescope (orbiting the Earth at 593 kilometers (km) above see level) we must utilize the absolute source code of the universe, '**1**'. We can not orbit the Hubble at 5 km nor can we orbit it at 10 km above see level. Like generating electricity, we must follow exactly the laws of physics, '**1**'.

Jesus, in the Lord's Prayer, refers to the source code of the universe as *Thy kingdom come, Thy will be done*. The Lord's Prayer, also known as Our Father or Pater noster, is the most important of all the Christian documents and is the most time-honored prayer in Christianity, and Christians all over the world unite around it. The Great Prayer was carefully constructed by Jesus as a condensed principle for the growth of humanity.

Dr. Emmet Fox (1886–1951), who was one of the outstanding spiritual teachers of our times, describes the Great Prayer in more detail in the appendix. The context of the prayer is recorded in the Gospel of Matthew (6:9–13) and in the Gospel of Luke (11:2–4). And so in the Lord's Prayer, which is a distillation of all Christian sanctity, we read:

> May your [unchanging] Kingdom come, May your [unchanging] will be done on earth as it is in heaven (Matt 6:10).

In creating electromagnetic induction from quantum potentiality (Jesus' heaven) to manifest reality (Jesus' earth), one goes beyond personal way of thinking, preference, or choice, as in all laws of physics, one goes to the '1'. Here, in creating electromagnetic induction, "Christ is risen from the dead (quantum potentiality), trampling down death by death, and upon those in the tombs bestowing life!" And when electricity is flowing, "Indeed, He is risen!" Now our life takes its meaning: a new life given a new humanity characterized by resurrection principles. Now, one does not live for oneself; now one lives *in* and *for* the unchangeable Absolute in oneself and in all beings. Now, through the development of the highest splendor of human consciousness, one lives a divine life of harmony, absolute happiness and abundance.

Saint Basil the Great, archbishop of Caesarea in Cappadocia of Asia Minor, was a spiritual giant with a towering generosity of heart and a penetrating mind. He understood that the human being is a divine being, and that life is about character development and human growth in the broadest sense. He motivated populace to manifest the divinity within oneself—to live in the zone of effortless Spirit (considered through immense masterpieces of thousands of pages of Saint Basil's works) and to rise above the countless challenges. The following insights describe the stages of awakening and transformation into God:

> Through His aid, hearts are lifted up, the weak are led by the hand, and they who are advancing are brought to perfection. By His illumination of those who are purified from all defilement, He makes them spiritual by fellowship with Him. Just as bright and transparent bodies, in contact with a ray of light, themselves become translucent, and emit a fresh radiance from themselves, so souls wherein the Divine Spirit dwells, being illuminated thereby, themselves become spiritual and give forth their grace to others.
>
> Hence comes their foreknowledge of the future, the understanding of mysteries, the comprehension of what is hidden, the distribution of good gifts, the heavenly citizenship, a place in the choir of angels. Hence comes to them unending joy, abiding in God, being made like unto God, and which is the highest of all, being made God.

Saint Catherine of Genoa's (1447–1510) dissertation parallels those of Saint Basil the Great. She was one of the most penetrating gazers into the secrets of the Absolute Infinity, living a divine life, and into the total transformation of the self into God, stating: "My Being is God, not by simple participation, but by a true transformation of my being;" akin to Saul becoming Paul or a grain of wheat transforming into many grains of wheat. In rest and in work, with mind undisturbed, with heart full of tranquility and compassion, Saint Catherine put pen to paper:

> When the loving kindness of God calls a soul from the world [of fear, worry, failure, and pain], He finds it full of vices and sins; and first He gives it an instinct for virtue, and then urges it to perfection, and then by infused grace leads to true self-naughting, and at last to true transformation. And this noteworthy order serves God to lead the soul along the Way; but when the soul is naughted and transformed, then of herself she neither works nor speaks nor wills, nor feels nor hears nor understands, neither has she of herself the feeling of outward or inward, where she may move. And in all things it is God ['**1**': the unchangeable source code] who rules and guides her without the mediation of any creature. [We consciously live in a state of eternal blessedness, or the Buddhist "it thinking."] And the state of this soul is then a feeling of such utter peace and tranquility that it seems to her that her heart, and her bodily being, and all both within and without is immersed in an ocean of utmost peace; from whence she shall never come forth for anything that can befall her in this life. And she stays immovable, imperturbable, [and] impassible. So much so that it seems to her in her human and spiritual nature, both within and without, she can feel no other thing than sweetest peace. And she is so full of peace that though she presses her flesh, her nerves, her bones, no other thing comes from them than peace.

Sri Ramana Maharshi (1879–1950) was one of the most profound sages and liberated beings of current India. He was treasured and respected equally by Buddhists, Christians, Hindus, and Taoists for his spiritual wisdom and teachings. Ramana arrived at "nirvana" (the uncompromising

Absolute Infinity, liberation, pure awareness) at the age of 16 and stated that the purest mode of his practice was the omnipotent silence, which radiated from his being and hushed the minds of those attuned to it. Maharshi declared:

> The whole of wisdom is contained in two biblical statements: "I am that I am" and "Be still and know that I am God." The sense of I pertains to the person, the body and the brain. When a man knows his true Self for the first time, *something else* ['**1**'] *arises from the depths of his being and takes possession of him.* That something is behind the mind; it is infinite, divine, eternal ['**1**']. Some people call it the kingdom of heaven, others call it the soul, and others again Nirvana, and Hindus call it Liberation; you may give it what name you wish. When this happens, a man has not really lost himself; rather he has found himself. Unless and until a man embarks on this quest of the true Self, doubt and uncertainty will follow his footsteps through life. The greatest kings and statesmen try to rule others when in their heart of hearts they know that they cannot rule themselves. Yet the greatest power is at the command of the man who has penetrated to his inmost depth . . . What is the use of knowing about everything else when you do not know yet who you are? Men avoid this inquiry into the true Self, but what else is there so worthy to be undertaken?

God Does Not Need Advisors: Let God Work through You without Consulting You

Before a rebirth into a new life, every seed must die. At some point during one's self-purification, the surface-mind (every man's consciousness), imprisoned in the body similar to an oyster or a baby bird in his shell, emerges from the cave of fantasy and unawareness.

Similarly to a minuscule amoeba, the surface mind of separate individuality (a force of discord, pride, greed, infatuation, cruelty, and ignorance) becomes more conscious and enters into lucid self-knowledge and realization of the Absolute Infinity within itself. One recognizes that the Absolute or Universal Mind that created and maintains our universe is more knowledgeable and more commanding than the infinitesimal awareness that one possesses. That God's "map" and God's "way" of the laws of nature are better than our personal map and our personal way. That God's advice is superior to our own counsel and that if I want to live I must die in my approach and my direction, and choose the "unchangeable" Absolute Infinity as my way and my God in me.

Visualize a helter-skelter interstate expressway and railroad systems where road and rail networks don't connect. Picture a disorganized company or a government where every individual and every department has its own agenda, where individuals and departments don't work together toward the same objective. Imagine a stomach where what goes into the stomach stays in the stomach, where "the business of the stomach is growth of the stomach" and not performing its function of sharing nutrients with regards to the whole body.

Willis W. Harman (1918–1997), president of the Institute of Noetic Sciences and professor emeritus of engineering-economic systems at Stanford University, was a seminal thinker in the area of consciousness and human transformation within the international business community. In his search for knowledge and for a higher-synergy society at Stanford, he did not limit himself to one school of thought or one partisan explanation but instead journeyed far and wide throughout the entire spectrum of scholarship, science, and reason. Willis expressed the business of the stomach story to me this way:

> When reality is wholeness, there is no greater error than separateness thinking. Imagine if the stomach were to get the idea that it could pursue its self-interest independent of the well being of the whole body/mind/spirit. Justifying its appetites with the maxims "What's good for the stomach is good for the whole," and "The business of the stomach is growth of the stomach," it seeks to maximize its absorption of nutrients and minimize the fraction going to other parts of the body. It worries about such indicators as getting its "market share" of food value, and "gross abdominal product."

It sounds absurd, of course, because the stomach doesn't do anything of the sort. It concentrates on performing its function with regard to the whole system, and trusts that if it does that, the system will see to it that its nutrient, protection, and other needs are met.

In the pursuit of identity with, or conscious awareness of God within oneself, one breaks through into the "infinite, divine, eternal" effortless life of perfection, where our will is united with the unchangeable Absolute of the Inner Light; where one acts not out of a superficial emotion of friendship and kindness but out of inner awareness of the "Absolute in oneself, in others, and in all that is."

In Eckhart's language: "God expects but one thing of you, and that is that you should come out of yourself in so far as you are a created being and let [the unchangeable] God be God in you."

Instead of divide, destroy and die, this is unite, build and live in the inexhaustible richness of the divine nature. Instead of "I thinking," it is insight into "Thy [unchanging] will be done" of effortless and miracle thinking. Thus, by becoming selfless in every circumstance of life (activity according to its nature, tranquility according to its essence), one opens up new paths for the inflow of that triumphing "power of life," super-bountiful energy and knowledge, and partakes directly in the absolute World of Pure Being.

The human being, like the Prodigal Son, having finally come to full awareness of cosmic unity and the joy of the infinite River of Life, completes the circle of life and returns to fertilize those levels of reality from which it originated. "In the body," states Sri Aurobindo (1872–1950), the great modern sage of India:

> it reveals itself as an ecstasy pouring into it from the heights of the spirit and the peace and bliss of a pure and spiritualized physical existence. A universal beauty and glory of being begins to manifest; all objects reveal hidden lines, vibrations, powers, harmonic significance concealed from the normal mind and the physical sense. In the universal phenomenon is revealed the eternal Ananda [Bliss, Joy, Absolute].

Goodness Knows: We Can't Improve On Love, We Are Meant to Reveal Love in Us

Throughout the centuries, individuals who have tried to reach a higher level of righteousness, sanctity, and godliness were characterized by different names in different traditions: yogis; rabbis; mystics; Sufis; theologians; saints; Bodhisattvas; Buddhas; and avatars, or incarnations of God. Because we live in the West, I will touch briefly on the Early Christian Fathers, Doctors (or Teachers) of the Church and saints who demonstrated holiness of life and gave Christianity commitment to various modes of living, preaching, discipleship, theological language, and liturgy.

The leading causes of the rapid growth of Christianity in the face of great persecutions and challenges are to be found in the immaculate life of its founder, the truth and self-evidencing primacy of his message, and its renewing and purifying effect on the knowledge and the brotherly love of humanity. The early Christianity gave birth to many prominent writers, theologians, and saints. They include Irenaeus of Lyons (2nd century AD–c. 202), Clement of Alexandria (150–215), Tertullian (160–220), Origen (185–254), Athanasius of Alexandria (293–373), Basil of Caesarea (328–379), Gregory of Nyssa (335–394), Ambrose of Milan (339–397), John Chrysostom (347–407), Jerome (347–420), Augustine of Hippo (354-430), Gregory the Great (540–604), Isidore of Seville (560–636), and John of Damascus (676–749).

"Christianity is the imitation of Christ," declared Saint Basil. "Christ appeared," stated Saint Augustine of Hippo, modern Souk-Ahras in Algier, "to the men of the decrepit, decaying world, that while all around them was withering away, they might through Him receive new, youthful life." Saint Ambrose wrote of the Seven Gifts of the Holy Spirit: 1. Spirit of Wisdom; 2. Spirit of Understanding; 3. Spirit of Counsel; 4. Spirit of Strength; 5. Spirit of Knowledge; 6. Spirit of Godliness; 7. Spirit of Holy Fear. Some gifts of the Spirit, also called *charismata*, are listed in 1 Corinthians 12.

The unknown author of the "Epistola ad Diognetum," in the early part of the second century, recorded:

> The Christians . . . dwell in the Grecian or barbarian cities, as the case may be; they follow the usage of the country in dress, food, and the other affairs of life. Yet they present a wonderful

and confessedly paradoxical conduct . . . They marry, like others; they have children, but they do not cast away their offspring. They have the table in common, but not wives. They are in the flesh, but do not lust after the flesh. They live upon the earth, but are *citizens of heaven*. They obey the existing laws, and *excel the laws by their lives*. They *love all*, and are persecuted by all.

Christians were reminded "You must be perfect—just as your Father in heaven is perfect" (Matt. 5:48). Also:

I may be able to speak the language of men and even of angels, but if I have not love, my speech is no more than a noisy gong or a clanging bell. I may have the gift of inspired preaching; I may have all knowledge and understand all secrets; I may have all the faith needed to move mountains—but if I have not love, I am nothing. I may give away everything I have, and even give up my body to be burned—but if I have not love, it does me no good. Love is patient, love is kind. It does not envy, it does not boast, it is not proud. It is not rude, it is not self-seeking, it is not easily angered, it keeps no record of wrongs. Love does not delight in evil but rejoices with the truth. It always protects, always trusts, always hopes, always perseveres.

Love never fails. There are inspired messages, but they are temporary; there are gifts of speaking, but they will cease; there is knowledge, but it will pass. For our gifts of knowledge and our inspired messages are only partial; but when what is perfect comes [the realization that we are one body—that "I have been looking for myself"] then what is partial will disappear (1 Cor. 13:1–10).

The Heart of the Gospels: "There Is No Division in the Body"

The central idea in spreading Christianity from Jesus to Constantine (AD 30–312) was the "unity of the Spirit" ("I am in my Father, and you are in me, and I am in you" [John 14:20]) and the "unity of divine service" (the deeper meaning of Jesus washing the disciples feet in John 13:14).

Jesus said, "The greatest one among you must be your servant" (Matt. 23:11). Christ's profound wisdom became the Christian "mystery of Christ in us" (Col. 4:3, Eph. 3:4–6), teachings for the assemblies of the primitive faithful, the world of pagan antiquity, and those less educated in spiritual matters.

The implementation of the Christian message was by means of the imitation of Christ, the "experience of living by Christ's principles." Christianity ("Christianismos") stood for "essence" of the Absolute Splendor, a sign of *God's glory in humanity*. To be called Christian (Acts 11:26; 26:28) meant that a person who lived by Christ's principles was aware that the Spirit of Unity and Spirit of God rested in them (1 Pet. 4:14–16).

The Spirit of Unity related to "the interdependence of the human race," the shift from the part to the Oneness of the whole, as "one body with many parts," and the celebration of the Christ mystery in *us*! For example, to survive we need air, water, and food; they are our lifelines to sustaining life. To think differently is childish. To not know that we are "one body with many parts" means to not reveal Christ in us.

This includes everyone, not merely those who call themselves Christians. It was understandable that the kingdom of God ['1'] is within us (Luke 17:21), along with a growing appreciation of our Oneness and therefore *one had to accept one's responsibility to each other and responsibility for each other's welfare.* The sooner we learn the lesson," states Pradeep Talwalker in *The Theosophist*:

> the sooner we will be ready for the next lesson, the next class. The more the number of classes that we clear in any life, the sooner we will finish our curriculum and be graduated. With each lesson, our lives will be filled more and more with happiness, durable joy . . . The more mistakes we commit; the more miseries will come our way. Miseries, therefore, are friends in a way that show us the red lantern of danger and keep us on the right track.

All Scriptures Are Full of Gems of Knowledge; Core of All Scriptures: The Oneness of All

Our interdependency, working together as One, and responsibility to care for one another and creation in love, respect, forgiveness, and gratitude, was presented by way of numerous teachings and the development of cultural, economic, and social skills. Here is an example from Saint Paul's First Letter to the Corinthians:

> For Christ ['1'] is like a single body, which has many parts; it is still one body, even though it is made up of different parts [similar to an airplane with many parts] . . .
>
> For the [human] body [like a mechanical body] itself is not made up of only one part, but of many parts. If the foot [Indian] were to say, "Because I am not a hand [Arab], I don't belong to the body," that would not make it stop being a part of the body. And if the ear [American] were to say, "Because I am not an eye [Chinese], I don't belong to the body," that would not make it stop being a part of the body. If the whole body were just an eye [Chinese], how could it hear? And if it were only ear [American], how could it smell [French]? . . .
>
> So then, the eye [Chinese] cannot say to the hand [Arab], "I don't need you!" Nor can the head [British] say to the foot [Indian], "Well, I don't need you!" [Imagine a functional human being without legs or a head.] On the contrary; we cannot get along without the parts of the body that seem to be weaker, and those parts that we think aren't worth very much are the ones which we treat with greater care; while the parts of the body which don't look very nice receive special attention, which the more beautiful parts of our body do not need
>
> And so *there is no division in the body*, but *all its different parts have the same concern for one another* [they work together and help each other as one]. If one part on the body suffers, all the other parts suffer with it; if one part is praised, all the other parts share its happiness.
>
> All of you, then, are Christ's body, and each one is a part of it. (1 Cor. 12:12–27).

Here we can see, in Christianity, how Saint Paul is concerned with raising people to his awareness of oneness. In a similar way, in Zen tradition the importance of concern for one another and the understanding of the interconnectedness of all creation is expressed by Ga-San through his awareness that, like killing life, there can be similar destruction in killing time, craving power, murdering the economy, and destroying the personal wealth of the country; and through the actions of certain members of the clergy who are not enlightened, and who wreak destruction by preaching nonsense. In *One Hundred and One Zen Stories* Ga-San instructs his followers:

> Those who speak against killing, and who desire to spare the lives of all conscious beings are right. It is good to protect even animals and insects. But what about those persons who kill time, what about those who destroy wealth, and those who murder the economy of their society? We should not overlook them. Again, what of the one who preaches without enlightenment? He is killing Buddhism.

The Self as a "Triumphing Power": Nothing in Themselves, All in God: The Life in which Our Will Is United with God

Aldous Huxley (1894–1963) was a novelist, thinker, and author of *Brave New World* and numerous other works. He was considered, in a number of academic circles, a leader of new thought and a scholar of the highest order. In his profound *The Perennial Philosophy* Huxley states:

> The saint is one who knows that every moment of our human life is a moment of crisis; for at every moment we are called upon to make an all important decision—to choose between the way that leads to death and spiritual darkness and the way that leads towards light and life; between interests exclusively temporal and the eternal order; between our personal will, or the will of some projection of our personality, and the will of God. In order to fit himself to deal with the emergencies of his way of life, the saint undertakes appropriate training

of the mind and body, just as the soldier does. But whereas the objectives of military training are limited and very simple, namely, to make men courageous, cool-headed and co-operatively efficient in the business of killing other men, with whom personally, they have no quarrel, the objective of spiritual training are much more narrowly specialized.

Here the aim is primarily to bring human beings to a state in which, because there are no longer any God eclipsing obstacles between themselves and Reality, they are able to be aware continuously of the divine Ground ['1'] of their own and all other beings; secondarily, as a means to this end, to meet all, even the most trivial circumstances of daily living without malice, greed, self-assertion or voluntary ignorance but consistently with love and understanding. Because its objective are not limited, because, for the lover of God, every moment is a moment of crisis, spiritual training is incomparably more difficult and searching than military training. There are many good soldiers, few saints.

Make the Best Use of Your Life: "Walk the Talk" with Love and Compassion for All Existence

Meister Eckhart maintained that "If I am to know God directly, I must become completely He and He I: so that this He and this I become and are one I." Eckhart shared the following story:

> There was a learned man who, eight years long, desired that God would show him a man who would teach him the truth. And once when he felt a very great longing, a voice from God came to him and said, "Go to the church, and there shalt thou find a man who shalt show thee the way to blessedness." And he went thence, and found a poor man whose feet were torn and covered with dust and dirt: and all his clothes were hardly worth three farthings. And he greeted him, saying:— "God give you good day!"

He answered: "I have never had a bad day."

"God give you good luck."

"I have never had ill luck."

"May you be happy!" "But why do you answer me thus?"

"I have never been unhappy."

"Pray explain this to me, for I cannot understand it."

The poor man answered, willingly. "You wished me good day. I never had a bad day; for if I am hungry I praise God; if it freezes, hails, snows, rains, if the weather is fair or foul, still I praise God; am I wretched and despised, I praise God, and so I have never had an evil day. You wished that God would send me luck. But I never had ill luck, for I know how to live with God, and I know that what He does is best; and what God gives me or ordains for me, be it good or ill. I take it cheerfully from God as the best that can be, and so I have never had ill luck. You wished that God would make me happy. I was never unhappy; for my only desire is to live in God's will, and I have so entirely yielded my will to God's, that what God wills, I will."

"But if God should will to cast you into hell," said the learned man, "what would you do then?"

"Cast me into hell? His goodness forbids! But if He did cast me into hell, I should have two arms to embrace Him. One arm is true humility that I should lay beneath Him, and be thereby united to His holy humanity. And with the right arm of love, which is united with His holy divinity, I should so embrace Him that He would have to go to hell with me. And I would rather be in hell and have God, then in heaven and not have God."

Then the Master understood that true abandonment with utter humility is the nearest way to God.

The Master asked further: "Whence are you come?"

"From God."

"Where did you find God?"

"When I forsook all creatures."

"Where, then, did you leave him, brother?"

"In pure hearts, and in men of good will."

The Master asked: "What sort of man are you?"

"I am a king."

"Where is your kingdom?"

"My soul is my kingdom, for I can so rule my senses inward and outward, that all the desires and power of my soul are in subjection, and this kingdom is greater than a kingdom on earth."

"What brought you to this perfection?"

"My silence, my high thoughts, and my union with God. For I could not rest in anything that was less than God. Now I have found God; and in God have eternal rest and peace."

Living at the Source:
You Can't Improve on God

In this section, we have a treasury of teachings, sayings, and quotations organized into two subdivisions: 1. "Living at the Source: You Can't Improve on God," and 2. "In the Miracle Zone: That Which Is God Is the Best That Can Be."

Arabi, Ibn

When my Beloved appears, with what eye do I see Him? With his eye, not with mine, for none sees Him except Himself. 1 Ch. 9.11.

We ourselves are the attributes by which we describe God; our existence is merely an objectification of His existence. God is necessary to us in order that we may exist, while we are necessary to Him in order that he may be manifested to Himself. 1 Ch. 9.10.

I give Him also life, by knowing Him in my heart. 1 Ch. 9.10.

Ashtavakra

Be constantly engaged in work for the welfare of others. 1 ch. 16:11.

Athanasius, Saint

The Divine Word became human in order that every human being may become God. 1 chs. 9:6, 23:5.

Baba, Meher

Who am I? And to that Question there is only one Answer—I am God! The problem is that people do not know who they really are: you are Infinite. You are really everywhere; but you think you are the body, and therefore consider yourself limited. If you look within and experience your own soul in its true nature, you will realize that you are infinite and beyond all creation. 1 ch. 19:26.

He who has found the Loved One in Him-Self, for him God is not he, nor You, but I. 1 ch. 19:29.

If you find God, then you have found all things! 1 ch. 19:30.

The process of attaining God-realization is a game in which the beginning and the end are identical. The attainment of realization is nevertheless a distinct gain. There are two kinds of advantages. One consists in getting what we did not previously possess; the other consists in realizing what we really are. God-realization is of the second kind. However, there is an infinite difference in the soul that has God-realization and one that does not have it. Though the soul that has God-realization has nothing it did not already possess, its explicit knowledge makes God-realization of the highest significance. The soul that is not God-realized experiences itself as finite and is constantly troubled by the opposites of joy and sorrow. But the soul that has realization is lifted out of them and experiences the Infinite. 1 ch. 22:14.

He who is absent, far away from God—his heart can only say: "God is" somewhere. 1 ch. 19:29.

Just think! If the Creator you do find, can His creation still remain behind? 1 ch. 19:30.

The God-realized knows himself to be God as surely as a man knows himself to be a man. It is for him not a matter of doubt, belief, self-delusion, or guesswork; it is a supreme and unshakeable uncertainty, which needs no external corroboration and remains unaffected by contradiction, because it is based upon self-knowledge. Such spiritual certainty is incapable of being challenged. A man thinks himself to be what in reality he is not; a God-realized knows what in reality he is. 1 ch. 22:8.

Bedrij, Orest
All this time you were me and I was you, and we did not know it. 1 ch. 19.

I am the very people I help, and I am the very people I hurt. 1 ch. 12.

If you improve on the present, you will improve on the past and the future. For that reason, live in the present because it is eternity.

All of us are extraordinary because all of us are the Absolute Infinity.

In sacred marriage wife and husband reflect the spirit of God. One learns lessons of love and compassion, purification of the heart and mind and at the same time expands one's consciousness and joy, equanimity and effortless living.

Bhagavad Gita
Make Me [Krishna, '1'] the ultimate goal of life (6.13). 1 ch. 2:24.

Bible, the
How long, O Lord? Will you hide yourself forever? (Ps. 89:47). 1 ch. 11.

I assure you, as often as you did for one of my least brothers, you did for me (Matt. 25:40). 1 ch. 11.

We, many though we are, are one body (1 Cor. 10:17). 1 ch. 17.

They know not, neither do they understand; they go about in darkness; all the foundations of the earth are shaken. I said: You are gods; all of you are sons of the Most High; yet like men you shall die, and fall like any prince. Rise, O God, judge the earth, for yours are all the nations (Ps. 82:5–8). 1 ch. 19.

For [when] I was hungry and you gave me something to eat, I was thirsty and you gave me something to drink, I was a stranger and you invited me [into your homes], I needed clothes and you clothed me, I was sick and you looked after me, I was in prison and you came to visit me . . . "when did we see you hungry and feed you, or thirsty and give you something to drink? When did we see you a stranger and invite you in, or needing clothes and clothe you? When did we see you sick or in prison and go to visit you?" The King will reply, "I tell you the truth, whatever you did for one of the least [important] of these brothers of mine, you did for me" (Matt. 25:34–40). 1 ch. 22.

We are the temple of the living God (2 Cor. 6:14). 1 ch. 8.

Rise, O God; judge the earth, for yours are all the nations (Ps. 82:8). 1 chs. 8, 19.

Do not give what is holy to dogs or toss your pearls before swine. They will trample them underfoot, at best, and perhaps even tear you to shreds (Matt. 7:6). 1 ch. 5.

The kingdom of God [God's Spirit] is within you (Luke 17:20–21). 1 ch. 19.

It is written in your own Law that God said, "You are gods" (John 10:34). 1 ch. 19.

You are my children, and you put me back in labor pains until Christ [Ultimate Perfection] is formed [realized] in you (Gal. 4:19). 1 ch. 19.

God is love and he who abides in love abides in God, and God in him (1 John 4:16). 1 ch. 19.

Glorify God in your body (1 Cor. 6:20). 1 ch. 19.

Know the truth, and the truth will set you free (John 8:32). 1 ch. 12.

Make every effort to keep the "unity of the Spirit" through the bond of peace. There is one body and one Spirit ['1'] . . . one God and Father of all, who is over all and through all and in all (Eph. 4:3–6). 1 ch. 9.

You shall love the Lord your God with all your heart, soul, and might (Deut. 6:5; Mark 12:30 paraphrased). 1 chs. 2, 8.

You must be made perfect as your heavenly Father is perfect (Matt. 5:48). 1 ch. 25.

Be compassionate as your Father in heaven is (Luke 6:36–42). 1 ch. 7.

If your enemy is hungry, feed him; if he is thirsty, give him something to drink (Rom. 12:20)

I give you a new commandment: Love one another. Such as my love has been for you, so must your love be for each other. This is how all will know you for my disciples; your love for one another (John 13:34–5). 1 ch. 13.

Conquer evil with good (Rom. 12:21).

Strengthen one another (Rom. 14:19).

"Come!" Whoever is thirsty [for God: Love, truth, peace], let him come; and whoever wishes, let him take free gift of the water of life (Rev. 22:17). 1 ch. 15.

Carey, Ken
The Creator and Creation are joined in physical flesh; for it is One Life that pulses within every body. We have only to be joined in consciousness, in awareness, and all will be fulfilled according to the prophecy. 1 ch. 17:2.

Carpenter, Edward
Of all the hard facts of science, I know of none more solid and fundamental than the fact that if you inhibit thought [and persevere], you come to a region of consciousness below or behind thought . . . and a realization of an altogether vaster self than that to which we are accustomed. And . . . the ordinary consciousness with which we are concerned in ordinary life is before all things founded on the little local self, and is in fact self-consciousness in the ordinary self and the ordinary world. It is to die in the ordinary sense, but in another sense, it is to wake up and find that one's real, most intimate self, pervades the universe and all other beings . . . So great, so splendid is this experience, that it may be said that all minor questions and doubts fall away in the face of it; and certain it is that in thousands and thousands of cases the fact of this having come even once

to a man has completely revolutionized his subsequent life and outlook on the world. 1 ch. 12:11.

Catherine of Genoa, Saint
My Me is God, nor do I recognize any other Me except my God himself. 1 ch. 26:20.

Clement of Alexandria
Let us especially remember the words of the master Jesus, which he spoke when he was teaching considerateness and patience. For he spoke in this way: "Show mercy, that you may be shown mercy. Forgive, that you may be forgiven. As you do to others, so will it be done to you. As you give, so will it be given to you. As you judge, so will you be judged. As you show kindness, so will kindness be shown to you. The standard you use will be used back on you." (1 Clement 13:1–2)

Denk, Hans
O my God, how does it happen in this poor old world that Thou art so great and yet nobody finds Thee, that Thou callest so loudly and nobody hears Thee, that Thou art so near and nobody feels Thee, that Thou givest Thyself to everybody and nobody knows Thy name? Men flee from Thee and say they cannot find Thee; they turn they backs and say they cannot see Thee; they stop their ears and say they cannot hear Thee.

Dewey, John
Intelligence has descended from its lonely isolation at the remote edge of things, whence it operated as Unmoved Mover, and ultimate good, to take its seat in the moving affairs of men. 1 ch. 11:10.

Dirac, Paul
All matter is created out of some imperceptible substratum. 1 ch. 10:8.

The creation of matter leaves behind it a "hole" in this substratum which appears as antimatter. Now, this substratum itself is not accurately described as material, since it uniformly fills all space and is undetectable by any observation. In a sense, it appears as nothingness—immaterial, undetectable and omnipresent. But it is a peculiarly material form of nothingness out of which all matter is created. 1 ch. 10:8.

Eckhart, Meister Johann

The seed of God is in us, if the seed had a good, wise, and industrious farmer, it would thrive all the more and grow up to God whose seed it is, and the fruit would be equal to the nature of God. Now the seed of a pear tree grows into a pear tree, a hazel seed into a hazel tree, the seed of God into God. 1 ch. 22:9.

Eddington, Arthur

The mind has but regained from nature that which the mind has put into nature. 1 ch. 9:12.

We have succeeded in reconstructing the creature that made the footprint And Lo! it is our own. 1 chs. 9:12, 35:5.

Einstein, Albert

Our task must be to free ourselves from this prison by widening our circle of compassion to embrace all living creatures and the whole of nature in its beauty. Nobody is able to achieve this completely, but the striving for such achievement is in itself a part of the liberation and a foundation for inner security. 1 ch. 7:11.

Our age is characterized by perfecting the means, while confusing the goals. 1 ch. 1:4.

Place [your] powers freely and gladly in the service of mankind. 1 chs. 2:2, 19:10.

Emerson, Ralph Waldo

All that can be done for you is nothing to what you can do for yourself. 1 ch. 19:4.

The purpose of life seems to be acquainting a man with himself. 1 ch. 11:7.

D'Espagnat, Bernard
This notion of reality existing independently of man has no meaning whatsoever. 1 ch. 7:14.

D'Estaing, Valéry Giscard
The world is unhappy. It is unhappy because it doesn't know where it is going and because it senses that if it knew, it would discover that it was heading for disaster. 1 ch. 1:2.

Francis of Assisi, Saint
Lord, make me a channel of Thy peace
That where there is hatred, I may bring love,
That where there is wrong, I may bring forgiveness,
That where there is discord, I may bring harmony,
That where there is error, I may bring truth,
That where there is doubt, I may bring faith,
That where there is despair, I may bring hope,
That where there is shadow, I may bring Thy light,
That where there is sadness, I may bring joy.

Lord, grant that I may seek to bring comfort
Rather than be comforted;
To understand, rather than be understood;
To love, rather than be loved.

For
It is by giving that one receives;
It is by self-forgetting that one finds;
It is by forgiving that one is forgiven;
It is by dying that one awakens to eternal life.

Gabor, Dennis
Till now man has been up against Nature; from now on he will be up against his own nature. 1 ch. 19:40.

Gandhi, Mahatma

Self-realization comes always through truth, austerity, true knowledge and self-restraint. Seekers who have become free from sins realize the immaculate refulgent spirit within themselves. (39)

To me God is truth and love. God is ethics and morality. God is fearless. God is the source of light and life and yet He is above and beyond all these. God is conscience. He is even the atheism of the atheist. He transcends speech and reason. He is a personal God to those who need His touch. He is the purest essence. He simply *is* to those who have faith. He is long suffering. He is patient but He is also terrible. He is the greatest democrat the world knows, for he leaves us unfettered to make our own choice between evil and good. He is the greatest tyrant ever known for he often dashes the cup from our lips and under cover of free will leaves us a margin so wholly inadequate as to provide only mirth for himself at our expense. Therefore, it is what Hinduism calls all this sport—*Lila*, or calls it an illusion—*Maya*. 1 ch. 19:23.

Gospel of Thomas, The

Jesus said, "I shall give you what no eye has seen and what no ear has heard and what no hand has touched and what has never occurred to the human mind . . . When you come to know yourselves, then you will become known, and you will realize that it is you who are the sons of the living Father" (17). 1 ch. 4:8.

Love your brother as your own soul, guard him as the pupil of your eye. 1 ch. 16:13.

Blessed are the solitary and elect, for you shall find the kingdom; because you come from it (and) you shall go there again. 1 ch. 9.3.

Brother Thomas, while you have time in the world, listen to me and I will reveal to you the things you have pondered in your mind. Now since it has been said that you are my twin and true companion, examine yourself that you may understand who you are, in what way you exist, and how you will come to be. Since you are called my brother, it is not fitting that you be ignorant of yourself. 1 ch. 5:13.

The kingdom is inside of you, and it is outside of you. When you come to know yourselves, then you will become known, and you will realize that it is you who are the sons of the living father ['1']. But if you will not know yourselves, you dwell in poverty and it is you who are that poverty (3). 1 ch. 19:7.

The kingdom of the Father is spread upon the earth and people do not see it (113). 1 ch. 19.

Whoever knows the All but fails (to know) himself lacks everything (65). 1 ch. 7.

Hammarskjöld, Dag

The more faithfully you listen to the voice within you, the better you will hear what is sounding outside. And only he who listens can speak. Is this the starting point of the road towards the union of your two dreams—to be allowed in clarity of mind to mirror life and in purity of heart to mold it?

Give me a pure heart—that I may see Thee, a humble heart—that I may hear Thee, a heart of love—that I may serve Thee, a heart of faith—that I may abide in Thee. 1 ch. 12:18.

Goodness is something so simple: always to live for others, never to seek one's advantage. 1 ch. 20:5.

Herbert, Nick

The world is not objectively real but depends on the mind of the observer. [And,] The observer may be said to partially create the attributes he observes . . . A rainbow appears in a different place for each observer—in fact, each of your eyes sees a slightly different rainbow. Yet the rainbow is an objective phenomenon; it can be photographed. 1 ch. 2:15.

Heschel, Rabbi Abraham Joshua

God is not always silent, and man is not always blind. In every man's life there are moments when there is a lifting of the veil at the horizon of the known, opening a sight of the eternal. Each of us has at least once in his life experienced the momentous reality of God. Each of us has once caught a glimpse of the beauty, peace and power that flow through the souls of those who are devoted to Him. But such experiences are rare events. To some people they are like shooting stars, passing and unremembered. In others they kindle a light that is never quenched. The remembrance of that experience and the loyalty to the response of that moment are the forces that sustain our faith. 1 ch. 3:3

Great is the challenge we face at every moment, sublime the occasion, every occasion. Here we are, contemporaries of God, some of His power at our disposal. 1 ch. 13:18.

We carry the gold of God in our souls to forge the gate of the kingdom. The time for the kingdom may be far off, but the task is plain: To retain our share in God in spite of peril and contempt. There is a war to wage against the vulgar, against the glorification of the absurd, a war that is incessant, universal. Loyal to the presence of the ultimate in the common, we may be able to make it clear that man is more than man, that in doing the finite he may perceive the infinite. 1 ch. 17:4.

Huxley, Aldous
The world is an illusion. 1 ch. 22:11.

Our business is to wake up. We have to find ways in which to detect the whole of reality in the one illusory part which our self-centered consciousness permits us to see. 1 ch. 22:11.

It is only by becoming Godlike that we can know God. And to become Godlike is to identify ourselves with the divine element which in fact constitutes our essential nature. 1 ch. 25:16.

James, William
This overcoming of all the usual barriers between the individual and the Absolute is the great mystic achievement. In mystic states we become one with the Absolute and we become aware of our Oneness. This is the

everlasting and triumphant mystical tradition, hardly altered by differences of clime or creed. In Hinduism, in Neoplatonism, in Sufism, in Christian mysticism, in Whitmanism, we find the same recurring note, so that there is about mystical utterances an eternal unanimity which ought to make a critic stop and think, and which brings about what the mystical classics have, as has been said, neither birthday nor native land, perpetually telling of the unity of man with God, their speech antedates language, and they do not grow old. 1 ch. 14:16.

Jeans, Sir James

Things are not what they seem; it is the general recognition that we are not yet in contact with ultimate reality. We are still imprisoned in our cave, with our backs to the light, and can only watch the shadows on the wall. 1 ch. 19:39.

Jerome, Saint

The most difficult and most obscure of the holy books, Genesis, contains as many secrets as words concealing many things even under each word. 1 ch. 5:20.

John Paul II

The more human beings know reality and the world, the more they know themselves in their uniqueness, with the question of the meaning of things and of their very existence becoming ever more pressing. 1 ch. 2:34.

Kabir

You have slept for millions and millions of years. Why not wake up this morning? 1 ch. 8:7.

Krishna, Gopi

Probably no other spectacle, not even the most incredible supernormal performance of mystics and mediums, so clearly demonstrates the existence of an All-Pervading, Omniscient intelligence behind the infinitely varied phenomena of life as the operations of a freshly awakened Kundalini. 1 ch. 17:14.

Lao-tze
Those who know do not talk. Those who talk do not know.

Knowing harmony is constancy. Knowing constancy is enlightenment.
(55)

Logan, Alastair
Salvation, then, is special knowledge of one's true self, of one's kinship
with the unknown transcendent God and of the true nature of the visible
world . . . the knowledge (gnosis) of our origin, nature and destiny, a
knowledge which tells Gnostics who they really are and frees them from
their present state of ignorance and imprisonment in an alien body and a
hostile world governed by Fate. 1 ch. 3:1.

Mandino, Og
Muscle can split a shield and even destroy life, but only the unseen power
of love can open the hearts of men, and until I master this art, I will remain
no more than a peddler in the market place. 1 ch. 13:3.

Merton, Thomas
God became man in Christ. In becoming what I am, He united me to
Himself and made me His epiphany [appearance or manifestation], so
that now I am meant to reveal Him. 1 ch. 9:7.

Milarepa, Jetsun
It is through resting one's mind at ease [peace] that Buddhahood [the all-
pervading Buddha-nature—Christian "unity of the Spirit"—an experience
of inner enlightenment] is realized. 1 ch. 12:1.

Your inability to drink the nectar [seed of pure pleasure] was because your
central channel was not yet opened. You should practice certain vigorous
bodily exercises. 1 ch. 16:9.

Mozart, Wolfgang Amadeus
A genius without heart is nonsense. 1 ch. 13:15.

Muktananda, Swami
Remember that God himself assumes human forms and lives in the world.
1 ch. 9:9.

All this, indeed, is the Absolute . . . God pervades everywhere . . . This
universe is a true image of the Supreme Reality. 1 ch. 7:1.

Muller, Robert
What is the greatest work of art on Earth? A healthy, beautiful, well-
educated, loving child. Fathers and mothers are the greatest artists there can
be on Earth. A happy, loving family is more precious than any Rembrandt
or Leonardo da Vinci painting. 1 ch. 16:1.

One's family is his foremost church on Earth. The most sacred acts are
conducted in it: Love, the gift of life, care, protection, and education. 1
ch. 7:19.

Life is divine. *Das Leben ist göttlich.* I wish this exclamation of mine as
a child were translated in all languages and displayed in every school on
Earth. 1 ch. 7:20.

To be able to say on the last day of one's life: I loved to live I lived to love
I laughed a lot
I gave much love I left the world a little better than I found it I loved the
world's great beauty I sang life and the universe I looked for the best in
others I gave the best I had.
Thank you, O God, for this miracle of life. 1 ch. 13:10.

Neng, Hui
When not enlightened, Buddhas are no other than ordinary beings; when
there is enlightenment, ordinary beings at once turn into Buddhas. 1 ch.
19:34.

Pasteur, Louis
In the fields of observation, chance favors the mind that is prepared. 1
ch. 14:5.

Patanjali
The causes of suffering are not seeing things as they are.

Peale, Norman Vincent
A vital part of the happiness formula is self-discipline. Whoever conquers himself knows deep happiness that fills the heart with joy.

If you want things different, perhaps the answer is to become different yourself.

Stress the thoughts of plenty. Thoughts of plenty help create plenty.

Optimism, when applied to your life, develops strength and peace within you.

Ramakrishna, Shri
Do not care for doctrines, do not care for dogmas, or sects, or churches, or temples; they count for little compared with the essence of existence in each man, which is spirituality; and the more this is developed in a man, the more powerful is he for good. Earn that first, acquire that, and criticize no one, for all doctrines and creeds have some good in them. Show by your lives that religion does not mean words, or names, or sects, but that it means spiritual realization. Only those can understand who have felt. Only those who have attained to spirituality can communicate it to others, can be great teachers of mankind. They alone are the power of light.

Rumi, Jalaluddin al-
He who knows himself knows his Lord. 1 ch. 20:6.

The sect of lovers is distinct from all others; lovers have a religion and a faith all their own. 1 ch. 13:16.

Sai Baba, Sri Sathya
It is through discrimination and renunciation that man understands who he really is. 1 ch. 22:12.

Santayana, George
Let him clean better, if he can, the windows of his soul, that the variety and beauty of the prospect may spread more brightly before him. 1 ch. 14.

Secret Book of James, The
Listen to the word, understand knowledge, love life, and no one will persecute you and no one will oppress you, other than you yourselves. (9.18–23)

Shankara
The wise man is one who understands that the essence of Brahman and of Atman is Pure Consciousness ['**1**'], and who realizes their absolute identity. The identity of Brahman and Atman is affirmed in hundreds of sacred texts . . .

Supreme, beyond the power of speech to express, Brahman may yet be apprehended by the eye of pure illumination. Pure, absolute and eternal Reality—such is Brahman, and "thou are That."

The truth of Brahman may be understood intellectually. But (even in those who so understand) the desire for personal separateness is deep-rooted and powerful, for it exists from beginningless time. It creates the notion, "I am the actor, I am he who experiences." This notion is the cause of bondage to conditional existence, birth and death. It can be removed only by the earnest effort to live constantly in union with Brahman. By the sages, the eradication of this notion and the craving for personal separateness is called Liberation.

Shipov, Gennady
According to the thinking of ancient philosophers of the Orient, all the material objects emerge from the great emptiness, are its integral part, and, in that sense, are illusionary. In the great emptiness itself acts of creation of real objects continually occur. 1 ch. 10:7.

Singh, Sadhu Sandar
The children of God are very dear but very queer, very nice but very narrow.

Subramuniya
At first you feel light shining within you. 1 ch. 4:19.

As you release desires and cravings through daily meditation, the external mind releases its hold on your awareness and you dive deeper, fearlessly, into the center of this blazing avalanche of light beyond form and formlessness. 1 ch. 4:19.

As you come out of that samadhi, you realize you are the spirit, the life force of all. 1 ch. 4:19.

Sutra, Lankavatara
With the lamp of word and discrimination one must go beyond word and discrimination and enter upon the path of realization. 1 ch. 2:31.

Tauler, Johan
Goodness needeth not enter into the soul, for it is there already, only it is unperceived. 1 ch. 20:4.

Teresa of Avila, Saint
God implants Himself in the interior of that soul in such a way that, when it returns to itself, it cannot possibly doubt that God has been in it and it has been in God. 1 ch. 18:4.

Oh human blindness! How long, how long shall it be before the dust is removed from our eyes? 1 ch. 11.19.

Teresa of Calcutta
The greatest disease in the West today is not TB or leprosy; it is being unwanted, unloved, and uncared for. We can cure physical diseases with medicine, but the only cure for loneliness, despair, and hopelessness is love. There are many in the world who are dying for a piece of bread but there are many more dying for a little love. The poverty in the West is a different kind of poverty—it is not only a poverty of loneliness but also of spirituality. There's a hunger for love, as there is a hunger for God. 1 ch. 13:2.

I always begin my prayer in silence, for it is in the silence of the heart that God speaks. God is the friend of silence—we need to listen to God because it's not what we say but what He says to us and through us that matters. Prayer feeds the soul—as blood is to the body, prayer is to the soul—and it brings you closer to God. It also gives you a clean and pure heart. A clean heart can see God, can speak to God, and can see the love of God in others. When you have a clean heart it means you are open and honest with God, you are not hiding anything from Him, and this lets Him take what He wants from you. 1 ch. 4:15.

Tilopa, Cakrasamvara
Do not imagine, do not think, do not analyze . . . 1 ch. 12:2.

Trungpa, Chogyam
At the beginning, duality is just a way of killing boredom. 1 ch. 11:24.

Tzu, Chuang
A man does not see himself in running water but in still water. 1 ch. 12:6.

Upanishads, the
When they say to a man who sees with his eyes, "Have you seen?" and he says, "I have seen," that is the truth (iv, 1, 4). 1 ch. 2.

In the beginning this world was merely nonbeing. It developed. It turned into an egg. 1 ch. 10:5.

Lonely He felt, and all unsatisfied; so into two He did divide Him-Self, to have a Playmate; Man and Wife He was; all wishes of each other they fulfill. 1 ch. 11:11.

Vivekananda, Swami
Every vicious thought will rebound, every thought of hatred which you may have thought, in a cave even, is stored up, and will one day come back to you with tremendous power in the form of some misery here. If you project hatred and jealousy, they will rebound on you with compound interest.

We reap what we sow. We are makers of our own fate. None else has the blame, none has the praise.

One must work as the dictate comes from within.

When man has seen himself as one with the Infinite Being of the universe, when all separateness has ceased, when all men and women, all gods and angels, all animals and plants, and the whole universe have melted into that Oneness, then all fear disappears.

Wheeler, John Archibald

The unknown is knowable . . . Every darkness can be lighted. 1 ch. 8:13.

The universe does not exist "out there" independent of us. We are inescapably involved in bringing about that which appears to be happening. We are not only observers. We are participators. 1 ch. 7:13.

The universe not only must give rise to life, but once life is created, it will endure forever, become infinitely knowledgeable, and ultimately mold the universe to its will . . . thus, man—or Life—will be not only the measure of things, but their creator as well. 1 ch. 24:15.

White, John

When we finally understand that Great Mystery, we discover our true nature, the Supreme Identity, the Self of all. That direct perception of our Oneness with the infinite, that Noetic realization of our identity with the divine is the source of all happiness, all goodness, all beauty, all truth. The experience is beyond time, space, and causality; it is beyond ego and all socially conditioned sense of I. Knowing ourselves to be timeless, boundless, and therefore cosmically free ends the illusion of separateness and all the painful, destructive defenses we erect, individually and societally, to preserve the ego-illusion at the expense of others. 1 ch. 8:14.

Wu, Joseph
This kind of personality will not be corrupted by wealth or fame, will not be bent by power or force, and will not be moved by poverty or mean conditions. 1 ch. 16.

The phrase "cultivation of *qi*" means almost the same as "development of moral or spiritual power." Such a spiritual power is developed through constant accumulation of righteous deeds and is not to be obtained by occasional moral acts. This is comparative to the Eightfold Path of the Buddha, which integrates right mindfulness and right conduct. 1 ch. 16.

In the Miracle Zone:
That Which Is God Is the Best That Can Be

Basil the Great
Through His aid, hearts are lifted up, the weak are led by the hand, and they who are advancing are brought to perfection . . . Hence comes to them unending joy, abiding in God, being made like unto God, and which is the highest of all, being made God. 1 ch. 25:18.

Bedrij, Orest
When our mind is still and our heart is pure we tune into the '1' and effortless life. We grasp Oneness and the Creator within ourselves. 1 ch. 12.

Purity of Heart = Clear Thinking (wisdom),
　　　　　　　 = Capacity to Reason (intelligence),
　　　　　　　 = Ability to Make Decisions (judgment),
　　　　　　　 = Perception of Truth (understanding); and
　　　　　　　 = Living with Yourself.

When I let the Christ's teachings be my life, I realized that I am, was, and shall always be the Absolute Reality. 1 ch. 11.

Let God in you shine in all its splendor.

Bible, the

He who acts in truth ['1'] comes into the light (John 3:21). 1 ch. 8.

All of us . . . are being transformed from glory to glory into his very image by the Lord who is the Spirit (2 Cor. 3:18). 1 ch. 14.

We are members of one another (Eph. 4:25). 1 chs. 17; 19.

All are one in Christ Jesus (Gal. 3:28). 1 ch. 19.

Your body is a temple of the Holy Spirit, who is within (1 Cor. 6:19). 1 ch. 19.

Live as children of light. Light produces every kind of goodness and justice and truth (Eph. 5:8–9). 1 ch. 8.

Happy are the pure of heart; *they will see* God! (Matt. 5:8). 1 ch. 12.

If your eye be single, your whole body will be full of light (Matt. 6:22). 1 ch. 4.

See! The man has become like one of us, knowing what is good and what is bad! (Gen. 3:22). 1 chs. 7–9, 18.

He that loveth not knoweth not God, for God is love and anyone who lives in love lives in God, and God lives in him. Love will come to its perfection in us when we can face the day of Judgment without fear; because even in this world we have become as He is (1 John 4:13–17). 1 ch. 13.

Be still, and know that I am God (Ps. 46:10). 1 ch. 12.

If you live according to my teaching, you are truly my disciples; then you will know the truth, and the truth will set you free (John 8:31–2). 1 ch. 16.

[Father, I pray . . .] that all may be one as you, Father, are in me, and I in you; I pray that they may be [one] in us . . . I living in them, you living in me—that their unity may be complete (John 17:21–23). 1 ch. 7.

To him who overcomes, I will give some of the hidden manna (Rev. 2:17). 1 ch. 15.

Blake, William

If the doors of perception were cleansed, everything would be seen as it is, infinite. 1 ch. 14:18.

Bohm, David

The entire universe of matter as we generally observe it is to be treated as a comparatively small pattern of excitation. 1 ch. 10:12.

The excitation pattern is relatively autonomous and gives rise to approximately recurrent stable and separable projections into a three dimensional explicate order of manifestation. 1 ch. 10:12.

Catherine of Siena, Saint

If you will arrive at a perfect knowledge and enjoyment of Me, the Eternal Truth, you should never go outside the knowledge of yourself; and by humbling yourself in the valley of humility you will know Me and yourself, from which knowledge you will draw all that is necessary. 1 ch. 18:3.

de Chardin, Teilhard

Someday after mastering the winds and the waves, the tides and gravity, we shall harness the energy of love. And then, for the second time in the history of the world, man will have discovered fire. 1 ch. 19:2.

Confucius

When the personal life is cultivated, the family will be regulated; when the family is regulated, the state will be in order; and when the state is in order, there will be peace throughout the world. 1 ch. 13:1.

Eckhart, Meister
A pure heart is one that is unencumbered, unworried, uncommitted, which does not want its own way about anything but which rather is submerged in the loving of God, having denied self. 1 ch. 12:16.

To gauge the soul we must gauge it with God, for the Ground of God and the Ground of the Soul are one and the same.

Einstein, Albert
There are only two ways to life your life. One is as though nothing is a miracle. The other is as though everything is a miracle.

Emerson, Ralph Waldo
The highest revelation is that God is in everyman . . . know thyself a man and be a God. 1 ch. 19:6.

To believe your own thought, to believe that what is true for you in your private heart is true for all men—that is genius. 1 ch. 15:8.

If we live truly, we shall see truly. 1 ch. 12:17.

Gandhi, Mahatma
The golden rule is to act fearlessly upon what one believes to be right. Constant vigilance under all circumstances is essential.

Gautama, Siddhartha (the Buddha)
All phenomena and their developments are simply manifestations of mind. All causes and effects, from great universes to the fine dust only seen in the sunlight come into apparent existence only by means of the discriminating mind. 1 ch. 12:3.

Gospel of Thomas, The
Jesus says, "Do not worry, from morning [to evening nor] from evening [to] morning, either [about] your [food], what [you will] eat, [or] about [your clothing], what you [will] wear. [You are much] better than the lilies,

which do not card or [spin]. As for you when you have no garment, what [will you put] on? Who might add to your stature? That is the one who will give you your garment." (56)

Hammarskjöld, Dag

The more faithfully you listen to the voice within you, the better you will hear what is sounding outside. And only he who listens can speak. Is this the starting point of the road towards the union of your two dreams—to be allowed in clarity of mind to mirror life and in purity of heart to mold it? 1 ch. 12:7.

Heschel, Rabbi Abraham Joshua

We distinguish between white and black, beautiful and ugly, pleasant and unpleasant, gain and loss, good and evil, right and wrong. The fate of mankind depends upon the realization that the distinction between good and evil, right and wrong, is superior to all other distinctions . . . To teach humanity the primacy of that distinction is of essence to the Biblical message. 1 ch. 12:19.

Living is not a private affair of the individual. Living is what man does with God's time, what man does with God's world. 1 ch. 11:8.

Huxley, Aldous

We must not live thoughtlessly, taking our illusion for the complete reality, but at the same time we must not live too thoughtfully in the sense of trying to escape the dream state. 1 ch. 22:11.

We must continually be on our watch for ways in which we may enlarge our consciousness. We must not attempt to live outside the world, which is given us, but we must somehow learn how to transform it and transfigure it. 1 ch. 22:11.

Irenaeus, Saint

God the Logos became what we are, in order that we may become what He Himself is. 1 chs. 9:1; 1 ch. 23:4.

John of the Cross, Saint

Go forth and exult in your glory, hide yourself in it, and rejoice, and you shall obtain all desires of your heart. 1 ch. 26:4.

Lao-tze

Keep your mouth closed. Guard your senses. Temper your sharpness. Simplify your problems. Mask your brightness.

Be at one with the dust of the Earth. This is primal union.

He who has achieved this state is unconcerned with friends and enemies, with good and harm, with honor and disgrace. This therefore is the highest state of man. (56)

Lincoln, Abraham

I have never had a policy. I have simply tried to do what seemed best each day, as each day came . . . I desire so to conduct the affairs of this administration that if at the end, when I come to lay down the reins of power, I have lost every other friend on earth, I shall at last have one friend left, and that friend shall be down inside of me. 1 ch. 16:5.

Let us have faith that right makes might, and in that faith, let us, to the end, dare to do our duty as we understand it. 1 ch. 16:3.

Maharaj, Tukaram

I went to look for God, but didn't find God. I myself became God. In this very body, God revealed Himself to me. 1 ch. 19:32.

Maharshi, Ramana

Reality is only one and that is the Self, all the rest are mere phenomena in it, of it, and by it. The seer, the objects, and the sight, all are the Self only. Can anyone see or hear, leaving the self aside? . . . If you surrender yourself . . . all is well . . . Only so long as you think that you are the worker, are you obliged to reap the fruits of your actions. If, on the other hand, you surrender yourself and recognize your individual self as only a tool of the Higher Power, that power will take over your affairs along with the fruits of actions. 1 ch. 14:20.

Why should you bear your load on the head when you are traveling in a train? It carries you and your load whether the load is on your head or on the floor of the train. You are not lessening the burden of the train by keeping it on your head but only straining yourself unnecessarily. 1 ch. 14:20.

Mandino, Og

Henceforth will I look on all things with love and I will be born again. I will love the sun for it warms my bones; yet I will love the rain for it cleanses my spirit. I will love the light for it shows me the way; yet I will love the darkness for it shows me the stars. I will welcome happiness for it enlarges my heart; yet I will endure sadness for it opens my soul. I will welcome obstacles for they are my challenge. 1 ch. 13:3.

I will applaud mine enemies and they will become friends; I will encourage my friends and they will become brothers. Always will I dig for reasons to applaud; never will I scratch for excuses to gossip. When I am tempted to criticize, I will bite my tongue; when I am moved to praise, I will shout from the roofs . . . 1 ch. 13:3.

Merton, Thomas

One of the paradoxes of the mystical life is this: that a man cannot enter into the deepest center of himself and pass through that center into God, unless he is able to pass entirely out of himself and empty himself and give himself to other people in the purity of a selfless love. 1 ch. 11:4.

Milarepa, Jetsun

External phenomenal objects: Forms, sounds, smells, tastes, and objects of touch, all these phenomena are no other than the magical tricks of mind. Like a child who builds sand castles, it is mind that fixates on names. Realizing that this is unreal is also mind . . . Know that all manifestations are like reflections of the moon in water. 1 ch. 20:17.

Ming-Dao, Deng
The more you learn, the more you must use your knowledge for others. The wiser you become, the more unselfish you must also become. As your experience deepens, and with it your humility, you will realize unfathomable depths of knowledge. You can never become arrogant and narrow-minded if you perceive how small your abilities are when contrasted to those of the greatest. Remember to use your knowledge in the service of others, but expect nothing in return. 1 ch. 17:3.

Muktananda, Swami
The purer you are, the greater your progress. 1 ch. 12:15.

I see the soft conscious mass of light trembling delicately and shining in all conditions—whether I am eating, drinking, or bathing. It surrounds me even during sleep . . . Thou art That—is, in fact, my own Self—vibrating subtly within me . . . The universe belongs to you. You are its Soul. Different levels of manifestations arise from you. They are your own forms. You are perfect in your aspect as the in dwelling Universal Spirit. Remain continuously aware that the universe is your own splendid glory. 1 ch. 4:25.

Muller, Robert
Decide to live joyfully, exultantly, gratefully, openly, and then miracles will begin to happen. 1 ch. 16:1.

Each human being is a prism in which the whole universe is reflected. 1 ch. 14:9.

Peale, Norman Vincent
Realize you have within yourself what it takes to stand up against anything. Human beings are absolutely undefeatable when they know they are.

Pio, Padre
Lord, lead me each day to a closer relationship with you and help me to appreciate your coming among us as a little child.

Sai Baba, Sri Sathya

When discrimination is keen and mental waves are stilled—and attention is one-pointed as a result of the contemplation of Pure Consciousness, then Divine Splendor is manifested, which can burn away evil and reveal joy. 1 ch. 12:10.

Love all beings—that is enough. Love with no expectation of return; love for the sake of love; love because your very nature is Love; love because that is the form of worship you know and like. When others are happy, be happy likewise. When others are in misery, try to alleviate their lot to the best of your ability. Practice Love through service. By this means, you will realize Unity and dissolve the ego that harms . . . Live in Love, live with love, move with love, speak with love, think with love, and act with love. 1 ch. 13:13.

Santayana, George

Live as much as may be in the eternal. 1 ch. 16:8.

Schrödinger, Erwin

What is it that has called you so suddenly out of nothingness to enjoy for a brief while a spectacle which remains quite indifferent to you? . . . Looking and thinking in that manner you may suddenly come to see, in a flash, the profound rightness of the basic conviction in Vedanta: it is not possible that this unity of knowledge, feeling, and choice which you call your own should have sprung into being from nothingness at a given moment not so long ago; rather this knowledge, feeling, and choice are essentially eternal and unchangeable and numerically one in all men, nay in all sensitive beings. But not in this sense—that you are a part, a piece, of an eternal, infinite being, an aspect or modification of it . . . 1 ch. 15:10.

Shankara

It is ignorance that cause[s] us to identify ourselves with the body, the ego, the senses, or anything that is not the Atman. He is wise man who overcomes this ignorance by devotion to the Atman . . .

Disease is never cured by [pronouncing] the name of medicine, but by taking the medicine. Deliverance is not achieved by repeating the word Brahmam, but by directly experiencing Brahmam . . . The nature of the one Reality must be known by one's own clear spiritual perception; it cannot be known through a pundit. Similarly, the form of the moon can be known only through one's eyes. How can it be known through others? 1 ch. 16:12.

Tampi, R.C.
A man, handicapped by attachment, labors in vain for spiritual progress. The story of the boatman who rowed the boat the whole night is an illustration of this truth. In the morning the boatman found that the boat was just where it was when he began rowing the previous night. Then only did he realize that the rope, which had tied the boat to a peg, had not been cut. As long as one remains attached, he will not make any spiritual progress.

Teresa of Calcutta
Is my heart so clean that I can see the face [image] of God in my brother, my sister, who is that black one, that white one, that naked one, that one suffering from leprosy, that dying one? 1 ch. 7:4.

If sometimes people have had to die of starvation, it is not because God didn't care for them, but because you and I were not instruments of love in the hands of God, to give them bread, because we did not recognize Him when once more the hungry Christ came in distressing disguise. 1 ch. 7:9.

In serving the poorest we directly serve God. 1 ch. 22:2.

Thoreau, Henry David
There is no remedy for love but to love more.

Traherne, Thomas
Your enjoyment of the world is never right till every morning you awake in Heaven; see yourself in your Father's palace; and look upon the skies, the earth and the air as celestial joys; having such a reverent esteem of all, as if you were among the Angels. The bride of a monarch, in her husband's chamber, hath no such causes of delight as you.
You never enjoy the world aright till the sea itself floweth in your veins, till you are clothed with the heavens and crowned with the stars; and perceive

yourself to be the sole heir of the whole world, and more than so, because men are in it who are very one sole heirs as well as you. Till you can sing and rejoice and delight in God, as misers do in gold, and kings in scepters, you can never enjoy the world.

Till your spirit filleth the whole world, and the stars are your jewels, till you are as familiar with the ways of God in all ages as with your walk and table; till you are intimately acquainted with that shady nothing out of which the world was made; till you love men so as to desire their happiness with a thirst equal to the zeal of your own; till you delight in God for being good to all; you never enjoy the world. Till you more feel it than your private estate, and are more present in the hemisphere, considering the glories and the beauties there, than in your own house; till you remember how lately you were made, and how wonderful it was when you came into it; and more rejoice in the palace of your glory than if it had been made today morning.

Yet further, you never enjoyed the world aright, till you so love the beauty of enjoying it, that you are covetous and earnest to persuade others to enjoy it. And so perfectly hate the abominable corruption of men in despising it that you had rather suffer the flames of hell than willingly be guilty of their error.

The world is a mirror of Infinite Beauty, yet no man sees it. It is a Temple of Majesty, yet no man regards it. It is a region of Light and Peace, did not men disquiet it. It is the Paradise of God. It is more to man since he is fallen than it was before. It is the place of Angels and the Gate of Heaven. When Jacob walked out of his dream, he said, God is here, and I wist it not. How dreadful is this place! This is none other than the House of God and the Gate of Heaven.

Upanishads, the

From the unreal lead me to the real, from darkness lead me to light. From death lead me to immortality, 1 ch. 4:10.

Vivekananda, Swami

Each time we suppress hatred, or a feeling of anger, it is so much good energy stored up in our favor; that piece of energy will be converted into the higher powers.

Great work requires great and persistent effort for a long time.

Don't look back—forward, infinite energy, infinite enthusiasm, infinite daring, and infinite patience—then alone can great deeds be accomplished,

All power is within you; you can do anything and everything . . . You can do anything and everything without even the guidance of anyone. All power is there. Stand up and express the divinity within you.

Yahya (ibn Mu'adh ar-Razi)
One mustard seed of love is better than seventy years of worship without love.

IV

Perfections for Living Your Divine Life: My Love and Compassion to You I Give

We bow down in awe and gratitude for the past.
Without all that came before us,
None of us would be awakening now!

—Barbara Marx Hubbard

From truth lead me unto the Absolute Truth.
From light lead me unto the Absolute Light,
From life lead me unto the Absolute Life,

—Orest Bedrij

We Are Children Until We Become Perfect

Let us be the Light of the world that we are,
Advised the Teacher of Righteousness.

Let us be perfect as our Father within us is perfect;
Let us have the love of God in our hearts;
Let us be our best all the time.

How do we become even in this world as He is?
How do we develop this perfection and infinity within us?
How do we nurture the Light of the Most High that we are?

Let us love the Lord our God with all our heart, soul, and might;
Let us love our neighbor as ourselves, for God is in everyone.
Let us bring infinite joy to us and the world with perfections:

1.
The life of the Most High is my life;
The will of the Most High is my will;
The light of the Most High is my light;
The peace of the Most High is my peace;
The purity of the Most High is my purity;
The service of the Most High is my service;
The dedication of the Most High is my dedication.

2.
The being of the Most High is my being;
The altruism of the Most High is my altruism;
The kindness of the Most High is my kindness;
The generosity of the Most High is my generosity;
The abundance of the Most High is my abundance;
The nonconcern of the Most High is my nonconcern;
The perseverance of the Most High is my perseverance;

3
The work of the Most High is my work;
The fidelity of the Most High is my fidelity;
The integrity of the Most High is my integrity;
The gentleness of the Most High is my gentleness;

The magnanimity of the Most High is my magnanimity;
The understanding of the Most High is my understanding.
The trustworthiness of the Most High is my trustworthiness;

4.

The rest of the Most High is my rest;
The health of the Most High is my health;
The humility of the Most High is my humility;
The goodness of the Most High is my goodness;
The excellence of the Most High is my excellence;
The compassion of the Most High is my compassion;
The righteousness of the Most High is my righteousness.

5.

The justice of the Most High is my justice;
The stillness of the Most High is my stillness;
The prudence of the Most High is my prudence;
The willpower of the Most High is my willpower;
The fearlessness of the Most High is my fearlessness;
The self-sacrifice of the Most High is my self-sacrifice;
The noninterference of the Most High is my noninterference.

6.

The grace of the Most High is my grace;
The patience of the Most High is my patience;
The simplicity of the Most High is my simplicity;
The omniscience of the Most High is my omniscience;
The omnipotence of the Most High is my omnipotence;
The effortlessness of the Most High is my effortlessness.
The incorruptibility of the Most High is my incorruptibility;

7.

The mercy of the Most High is my mercy;
The courage of the Most High is my courage;
The freedom of the Most High is my freedom;
The awareness of the Most High is my awareness;

The confidence of the Most High is my confidence;
The transparency of the Most High is my transparency;
The meticulousness of the Most High is my meticulousness.

8.
The beauty of the Most High is my beauty;
The healing of the Most High is my healing;
The knowing of the Most High is my knowing;
The diligence of the Most High is my diligence;
The sacredness of the Most High is my sacredness;
The nonviolence of the Most High is my nonviolence;
The self-expression of the Most High is my self-expression;

9.
The responsibility of the Most High is my responsibility;
The commitment of the Most High is my commitment;
The consistency of the Most High is my consistency;
The forgiveness of the Most High is my forgiveness;
The equanimity of the Most High is my equanimity;
The innocence of the Most High is my innocence;
The foresight of the Most High is my foresight.

10.
The holiness of the Most High is my holiness;
The wisdom of the Most High is my wisdom;
The caring of the Most High is my caring;
The unity of the Most High is my unity;
The truth of the Most High is my truth;
The love of the Most High is my love;
The joy of the Most High is my joy.

So be it.

And now,
Let me bow my head in peace, compassion and omnipresence,
To the Eternal Light in you,
And to the Absolute One in all.

V

Each One Teach One: Living Your Divine Life

How beautiful it would be if all of us, young and old, men and women, devoted ourselves wholly to truth in all that we might do—in our waking hours, whether working, eating, drinking or playing, till pure dreamless sleep claimed us for her own. God as truth has been for me treasure beyond price. May he be so to every one of us!

—Mahatma Gandhi

We Are the Light of the World: It's Time We Came out of the Cave of Pain and Grief to Enjoy Our Sacredness

One might ask: why should we live a godly life? Why should each one of us teach one another about living a divine life?

My answer: if you are a majestic Giant Sequoia tree you should live the life of a majestic Giant Sequoia tree; if you are a magnificent bald eagle you should live the life of a magnificent bald eagle. Conversely, since "You are the light of the world" (Matt. 5:14) you should live and help others to live the life we were all meant to live—as "the light of the world."

The Sermon on the Mount contains some of the central tenets of Jesus' teachings and a comprehensive exposition of what Christians are meant to be. Here, on a hill on the north end of the Sea of Galilee, near Capernaum, the Compassionate One presented to his disciples, to the multitude and to the world in general: the Beatitudes, the Lord's Prayer, the Golden Rule, the Light of the World and other discourses pertaining to the Old Testament, the New Law, and "all about this new life" (Acts 5:20). Addressing the Light of the World and your Infinite Splendor theme Jesus stated:

> You are the light of the world. A city set on a hill cannot be hidden. Men do not light a lamp and then put it under a bushel basket. They set it on a stand where it gives light to all in the house. In the same way your light [of Infinite Splendor] must shine before men so that they may see goodness [decency, kindness, honesty, integrity] in your acts and give praise to your heavenly Father [which is within and outside of you] (Matt. 5:14–16).

What People Know, They Do!
Violence Is Never a Solution:
A Crime against Humanity

Yes, we are the light of the world; yes, we are the Infinite Splendor, as Jesus, the Buddha, Muhammad, Ramana Maharshi, David Bohm, Erwin Schrödinger, and a universe of others have pointed out. Yet that reality has not penetrated into the planetary realization and experience. To borrow from Einstein, the world we have created is a product of the level of thinking we have done thus far.

Francois-Marie Arouet (1694–1778), better known by the pen name Voltaire, was a prolific French writer who produced works in every literary form, and whose topics included the defense of civil liberties, freedom of religion and free trade. Considering the crimes against civil liberties and politics of atrocities, Voltaire observed, "Those who can make you believe absurdities can make you commit atrocities."

Polish-born American political scientist and statesman Zbigniew K. Brzezinski (1928-), professor of American foreign policy at Johns Hopkins University and former United States National Security Advisor to President Jimmy Carter (1971–1981), in his magnificent book *Out of Control* wherein he described how 175 million people were slaughtered in the name of the "politics of organized insanity," writes:

> Contrary to its promise, the twentieth century became mankind's most bloody and hateful century of hallucinatory politics and of monstrous killings. Cruelty was institutionalized to an unprecedented degree; lethality was organized on a mass production basis. The contrast between the scientific potential for good and the political evil that was actually unleashed is shocking. Never before in history was killing so globally pervasive, never before did it consume so many lives, never before was human annihilation pursued with such concentration of sustained effort on behalf of such arrogantly irrational goals.

What was the world doing when millions precious human beings (Jews, Poles, Ukrainians, Russians, Czechs, and Frenchmen) were being slaughtered in the Nazi extermination camps? "Of the 9,600,000 Jews living in Nazi-controlled Europe, at least 5,700,000 disappeared," writes Louis Snyder in *The War, A Concise History, 1935–45,* "most of them put to death in gas chambers. There was ghastly variety in methods—gassing, shooting, hanging, starvation, branding with hot irons, disemboweling, burying alive, injections of poison, 'experimental' surgery, freezing in water." Listen to the *Nazi Conspiracy and Aggression, Official Records of the International Military Tribunal at Nuremberg*:

> Item: There were mass shootings to the accompaniment of music played by incarcerated prisoners.

Item: Concentration-camp officials and guards bleached human skulls for souvenirs and used the skin of prisoners to make lampshades, handbags, and gloves.

Item: Prisoners still alive were thrown indiscriminately into carts loaded with the dead and taken to the crematory.

Item: Bodies of the dead were sent to barbers, who removed the hair, and to the dentists, who extracted gold from the teeth before cremation.

Item: Prisoners who refused to talk were placed in heated asbestos-lined cells until they were cooked beyond endurance.

German news magazine Der Spiegel named Heinrich Himmler (1900-1945) "greatest mass murderer of all time." As head of extermination camps, concentration camps, and special task forces of killing squads, Himmler was Chief of the German Police and Minister of the Interior. Being Reichsfuhrer-SS and one of the most powerful men in Nazi Germany, Himmler supervised all internal and external police and security forces, including the Gestapo. His motto: "The best political weapon is the weapon of terror. Cruelty commands respect. Men may hate us. But we don't ask for their love; only for their fear." Following his arrest in May 1945 by British forces, Himmler committed suicide before he could be interrogated.

Or consider Mao Zedong (1893–1976), the Communist Party of China leader (1949-1976), who according to the Walker Report published by the U.S. Senate Committee of the Judiciary in July 1971, was responsible for the mass murder of 32.2 to 61.7 million people. In 1956 Nikita Khrushchev (1894–1971), First Secretary of the Communist Party of the Soviet Union (1953–1964), tearfully told the Twentieth Party Congress that it was all Joseph Stalin's (1878–1953) fault.

I assume Khrushchev could never have engineered the killing of 45–80 million precious people without help. It was under the guiding leadership of Vladimir Lenin (1870–1924), the first head of the Union of Soviet Socialist Republics, and Stalin, the general secretary of the Communist Party of the Soviet Union (1922–1953), that the Cheka (until 1922), the State Political Directorate (or GPU, 1922–35), the People's Commissariat for International Affairs (or NKVD, 1935–43), the Ministry of Internal Affairs (MVD, 1943–56) and the Committee for State Security (the KGB) were able to implement the Marxist redistribution-of-wealth plan.

Bön Buddhism is one of the world's oldest spiritual traditions and wisdom path for thousands of years before the birth of the Buddha Shakyamuni. It embraces wisdom and measures valid to all parts of life with moral and principled conduct and the growth of love, compassion, bliss and equanimity. Tenzin Wangyal Rinpoche is the founder and resident teacher of Lingmincha Institute in Virginia. He lived and studied with Tibetan masters of Bön Buddhism from the age of 13 and was one of the first lamas to bring the Bön Dzogchen (great completion) wisdom to the West. Like many others, in spiritual traditions, Rinpoche repeats these fundamental considerations in his *Tibetan Sound Healing*:

> Suffering shakes us and brings us opportunity to awaken to a deeper truth. Most of the time when we suffer, we feel we need to change something in order to improve our lives. We change our jobs, relationships, diet, and personal habits, on and on.

Furthermore,

> Our dissatisfaction is useful when it makes us ask new questions, but it is most helpful when we ask the *right* question. According to the highest teaching in my tradition, the question we should be asking is, "Who is suffering? Who is experiencing this problem?" This is a very important question to ask, . . . We have to look directly and clearly into the inner space of our being.

The Russian novelist, dramatist, and historian Aleksandr Solzhenitsyn (1918–2008) was awarded the 1970 Nobel Prize in Literature and was interrogated and tortured in Lubianka prison, the headquarters of the secret police KGB, and imprisoned by the Soviet police state in the Lenin-Stalin forced-labor prison-camp system, known as the Gulag. The imprisonment led him not to hopelessness but to the discovery within himself of his innermost essence, "the first stirrings of good," which ultimately set him free. In the most subversive of all his writings, the monumental three-volume work *The Gulag Archipelago*, Solzhenitsyn recounts:

> If the intellectuals in the plays of Chekhov who spent all their time guessing what would happen in twenty, thirty, or forty years had been told that in forty years interrogation by torture would be practiced in Russia; that prisoners have their skulls squeezed with iron rings; that a human being would be lowered into an acid bath; that they would be trussed up naked to be bitten by ants and bedbugs; that a ramrod heated over a primus stove would be thrust up their anal canal (the "secret brand"); that a man's genitals would be slowly crushed beneath the toe of a jackboot; and that, in the luckiest possible circumstances, prisoners would be tortured by being kept from sleeping for a week, by thirst, and being beaten to a bloody pulp, not one of Chekhov's plays would have gotten to its end because all of the heroes would have gone off to insane asylums . . . In 1944–46 . . . they dumped whole nations down the sewer pipes not to mention millions and millions of others who had been prisoners of war.

Further, Solzhenitsyn's studding visual account of accessing the inner space of our being through "the first stirring of good":

> It was granted to me to carry away from my prison years on my bent back, which nearly broke beneath its load this essential experience: how a human being becomes evil and how good. In the intoxication of youthful successes I felt myself to be infallible, and I was therefore cruel. In the surfeit of power I was a murderer and an oppressor. In my most evil moments I was convinced that I was doing good, and I was well supplied with systematic arguments. It was only when I lay there on rotting prison straw that I sensed within myself the first stirrings of good. Gradually it was disclosed to me that the line separating

good and evil passes not through states, nor between classes, nor between political parties either—but right through every human heart—and through all human hearts . . . . That is why I turn back to the years of my imprisonment and say, sometimes to the astonishment of those about me: "Bless you, prison!" I . . . have served enough time there. I nourished my soul there, and I say without hesitation: "Bless you, prison, for having been in my life!"

Solzhenitsyn's "I sensed within myself the first stirring of good" is the breathless Maharshi's "for the first time, something else arises from the depths of his being and takes possession of him," you read before. Barbara Benjamin in her brilliant "Face to Face" writes, "If you really listen well, you can hear your own heart swell." "The best and most beautiful things in the world," states a prolific Helen Keller, "cannot be seen or even touched. They must be felt with the heart." Moreover, insists Peale:

> The more you venture to live greatly, the more you will find within you what it takes to get on top of things and stay there.

Our Challenges Now:
I Feel Your Pain, I Feel Your Grief

What about now and Voltaire's absurdities and atrocities? Let us explore the human dilemma of our day.

Most of us know the repulsive statistics of our "post-genocidal world." Two out of every three inhabitants on our planet go to sleep hungry each night. One out of every five individuals lives in poverty on $1 a day or less. Five million people on average starve to death each year. Over 2 million humans are dying from diarrhea every year, one million from malaria and two million from AIDS. More than 25 million have passed away from AIDS since 1981; 33 million are infected. Africa alone has 11.6 million AIDS orphans. Women account for 50 percent of all adult infections, and young people (under 25 years old) account for half of all new HIV infections worldwide.

We have over 100 million homeless worldwide. In some countries (i.e., Greece, France, etc.) riots and car torching have become commonplace. We are in a massive global economic crisis, and the social cost is already threatening to topple governments worldwide and incite new waves of terrorism.

Article 2 of the 1944 United Nation Convention on the Prevention and Punishment of the Crime of Genocide (CPPCG) defines *genocide* as killing members of the group, deliberately calculating to bring about its physical destruction, and imposing measures intended to prevent births within the group. Note: almost every third baby conceived in America is killed by abortion.

We see menacing turmoil and the breakdown of the family unit, domestic violence, and a moral and spiritual crisis in education. There is devastation and gang warfare in our inner cities. Each year, federal state and local governments spend billions and billions on the so-called "Drug War," America's longest running war, arresting 1.5 million citizens on drug charges.

We have the growth of government power with a sclerotic and animosity-ridden political reality with astronomical federal deficits. There is a tragic erosion of values in the Christian church (sexual atrocities by bishops and priests, etc.), a general breaking of the social contract between society and worker, declining human rights, high unemployment, and an enormous problem of human sexual violence.

The recent financial meltdown has affected broad sectors of the economy show there is a catastrophe of principles, ethics, and values in the global investment banks, securities trading and brokerage firms, and accounting improprieties in corporate America (e.g., The Bear Stearns Companies, Lehman Brothers Holdings, Arthur Andersen, Enron, Global Crossing, PwG [Pricewaterhouse Cooper], Tyco, WorldCom), that shook world confidence in American business.

Our way of life has fostered reckless proliferation of weapons, environmental pollution, and terrorism in cyberspace, inflicting trillions of dollars of damage. We are all aware of the toxic nuclear waste problem, declining clean water supplies, and water contamination. Lack of clean water in parts of our planet promotes disease and fuels civil conflicts. We see increased harshness of weather patterns, land turning to desert, destruction of vegetation, species extinction, soil depletion and erosion, the punctured ozone layer, environmental degradation, and disappearing forests. There is bloodshed between Israel and the Palestinians. Nuclear-armed Pakistan teeters between extremism and outright war. Systematic campaigns of massacres, mass murder and acts of genocide were perpetrated not only by Mao Zedong, Stalin, and Hitler, but also by leaders in Ukraine (Khrushchev on Stalin's orders created in 1932-1933 artificial famine, deliberate Act of Genicide, 6–11 million deaths by starvation), Japan (6 million), Turkey (2.5–4 million), Cambodia (1.7–3 million), North Korea (1.5–5 million), Ethiopia (1–3 million), Biafra, Afghanistan, Rwanda, Iraq, Iran, and elsewhere. Islamic radicals have called for the destruction of other religions and have stated that the acquisition of weapons of mass destruction is a "religious duty." Many governments are carrying out extra-judicial killings, torture, forced labor, and coerced confessions of prisoners.

The volatility of fiscal prudence, national security, and global relationships makes the edges of the sword seem to get sharper. To carry the analogy further, crime and violence continue to spiral. To relieve nervousness, worry, emotional depletion, physical exhaustion, and even addiction, in an average day Americans puff their way through 1.17 billion cigarettes and 3.5 million joints, pop 2.8 million antidepressants and 145,000 tabs of Ecstasy, and drink 330 million alcoholic drinks. The list goes on and on.

Not long ago it was Hitler who called on the German people to exterminate Jews, Poles, Ukrainians, Russians, Czechs, French people, and so on. Karl Marx—along with Lenin, Stalin, and Mao Zedong—had similar class hatred, redistribution of wealth, and class-war rallying calls with his *The Communist Manifesto* and *Das Kapital*. Now it is Kim Jong-il (North Korea), Hugo Chavez (Venezuela), Raul Castro (Cuba), and Osama bin Laden and his gang of World Islamic Front jihadists. In February 23, 1998, Osama bin Laden in *al-Quds al-Arabi*, an Arabic newspaper published in London, had proclaimed a jihad in the name of the World Islamic Front:

> Kill Americans and their allies, both civil and military . . . By
> God's leave, we call on every Muslim who believes in God and
> hopes for reward to *obey God's command* to kill the Americans

and plunder their possessions wherever he finds them and whenever he can. Likewise we call on the Muslim ulema [the body of scholars and learned men who are authorities on Muslim religion and law] and leaders and youth and soldiers to launch attacks against the armies of the American devils and against those who are allied with them from among the helpers of Satan . . .

The word Islam means "submission" (Jesus' "your will be done"), or complete surrender of oneself to God ('1', Arabic: Allah). A follower of Islam is known as a Muslim, meaning "one who submits" [to Allah]. Thus, for 1.8 billion Muslims, Islam means: submission to God's love, goodness, and compassion: submission to God's life, truth, and service. Osama bin Laden and the World Islamic Front are not Muslims who summit to the God of life, goodness, and love of humanity. They misrepresent the holiness, love, and goodness of Islam and the Muslim community.

Murdering, plundering and the redistribution of wealth may appear like an easy way out of knotty challenges, but it is not the solution. The sun can make you take off your coat more likely than the blustery weather. What Mao Zedong, Stalin, Hitler, Kim Jong-il, Chavez, etc., and Osama bin Laden and his gang of World Islamic Front jihadists did not realize is that the stupendous power of love, compassion, caring, and heartfelt appreciation will make people help you and serve you more readily than all the bluster, robbery, and killing in the world. There is no religion, no science, and no government higher than the Absolute truth, liberty, order, responsibility, and justice. Remember what Lincoln said: "A drop of honey catches more flies than a gallon of gall."

Training in Holiness:
We Need a Sustainable Worldview;
We Must Rise Above Animals and Act Like Gods

Bruce Murray, Professor of Planetary Science and Geology, California Institute of Technology (Caltech) since 1960 and director of the NASA Jet Propulsion Laboratory at Caltech (1976–1982), stated:

We are all desperately in need of a new world-view, consistent with the facts of science but much broader and more encompassing. The new world-view must provide reasonable guides to how men should behave toward one another. We must know how to rise above animals and act like gods. I assert the primary intellectual event of the next several hundred years will be the development of this new world-view.

The suffering and seemingly purposeless disorder and destruction which are the hallmarks of the twentieth century (and perhaps much of the twenty-first as well) will sharpen men's views of themselves and their world. It will create part of the basis of what must truly be a new theology whose effects may be even more enduring than those of previous great religions.

Albert Einstein was of the same opinion as Bruce Murray. Einstein said:

It is not enough to teach man a specialty. Through it he may become a kind of useful machine but not a harmoniously developed personality. It is essential that the student acquire an understanding of and a lively feeling for values. He must acquire a vivid sense of the beautiful and of the morally good. Otherwise he—with his specialized knowledge—more closely resembles a well-trained dog than a harmoniously developed person. He must learn to understand the motives of human beings, their illusions, and their sufferings in order to acquire a proper relationship to individual fellowmen and to the community.

Furthermore, Einstein declared:

The world we have made as a result of the level of thinking we have done thus far creates problems that we cannot solve at the same level of thinking as they were created.

David Bohm, who was painstaking and methodical in the study of our challenge, stated:

What I am proposing here is that man's general way of thinking of the totality, his general world-view, is crucial for overall order of the human mind itself. If he thinks of the totality as constituted of independent fragments, then that is how his mind will tend to operate, but if he can include everything coherently and harmoniously in an overall whole that is undivided, unbroken, and without a border (for every border is a division or break) then his mind will tend to move in a similar way, and from this will flow an orderly action within the whole.

And then you have Mother Teresa of Calcutta. She did not study Bruce Murray, Albert Einstein, or David Bohm, nor had she researched *their* "new worldview," "lively feeling for values," or "man's general way of thinking of the totality." She knew it; she acted upon her knowledge. Like Paul the Apostle and Abraham Lincoln, Mother Teresa was a "humble instrument in the hands of the Almighty." Her life consisted "in accomplishing the will of God with a cheerful heart." She and her compassionate team treated 186,000 victims of leprosy, 126,000 hungry and homeless, and 22,000 forsaken, dying, HIV/AIDS-infected, and destitute individuals. Her compassionate altruism and vision—to make the world a holier place—replaced human abortion, which is reaching genocide proportions, with human adoption:

> I always ask doctors at hospitals in India never to kill an unborn child. If there is no one who wants it, I'll take it. I see God in the eyes of every child—every unwanted child is welcomed by us. We then find homes for these children through adoption.
>
> You know, people worry all the time about innocent children being killed in wars, and they try to prevent this. But what hope is there in stopping it if mothers kill their own children? Every life is precious to God, whatever the circumstances.

See the Glory of God Displayed: Rejoice! This Brother of Yours Was Dead, and Has Come Back to Life

Two thousand years ago with the Lost Son Parable (Luke 15:11), Jesus brings home the heart of the human challenge and the way out. It is the third and concluding set of three parables, following the Parable of the Lost Sheep (Luke 15:4) and the Parable of the Lost Coin (Luke 15:8). Jesus said to them:

> A man had two sons. The younger of them said to his father, "Father, give me the share of the estate that is coming to me." So the father divided up the property. Some days later the younger son collected all his belongings and went off to a distant land, where he squandered his money on dissolute living. After he had spent everything, a great famine broke out in that country and he was in dire need. So he attached himself to one of the propertied class of the place, who sent him to his farm to take care of the pigs. He longed to fill his belly with the husks that were fodder for the pigs, but no one made a move to give him anything. Coming to his senses at last, he said: "How many hired hands at my father's place have more than enough to eat, while here I am starving! I will break away and return to my father, and say to him, Father, I have sinned against God and against you; I no longer deserve to be called your son. Treat me like one of your hired hands."
>
> With that he set off for his father's home. While he was still a long way off, his father caught sight of him and was deeply moved. He ran out to meet him, threw his arms around his neck, and kissed him. The son said to him, "Father, I have sinned against God and against you; I no longer deserve to be called your son." The father said to his servants: "Quick! Bring out the finest robe and put it on him; put a ring on his finger and shoes on his feet. Take the fatted calf and kill it. Let us eat and celebrate because this son of mine was dead and has come

back to life. He was lost and is found." Then the celebration began (Luke 15:11–25).

May God's Face Consciously Shine in You

Our current challenge: we are the Infinite Splendor, "the light of the world" (Matt. 5:14), yet, when we study our history and the current planetary state of affairs, there seems to be a disconnect between what we are, the interconnectedness of all, and what we do. We have two options: 1. Do nothing; "evidence" is irrelevant. Accept what has happened and is happening as good enough; continue as we have been or 2. Like the Lost Son, having experienced a bounty of pain, grief, and misery, decide to go home to a happy, peaceful, and prosperous divine life. The choice is ours. Confucius suggested:

> If there is righteousness in the heart, there will be beauty in the character.
> If there is beauty in the character, there will be harmony in the home.
> If there is harmony in the home, there will be order in the nation.
> If there is order in the nation, there will be peace on earth.

The greatest English poet of the eighteenth century—Alexander Pope (1688–1744)—wrote: "Men must be taught as if you taught them not and things unknown proposed as things forgot."

Sai Baba states:" When the heart is filled with compassion, the hands are dedicated to the service of others, the body is engaged in constant help to others, the life of such a person is sacred, purposeful, and noble."

Over three hundred years ago, an Italian physicist, mathematician, astronomer and philosopher who played a major role in the Scientific Revolution—Galileo Galilei (1564–1642)—stated: "You cannot teach a man anything; you can only help him to find it within himself."

John Archibald Wheeler put it this way:

> Philosophy passes the judgment;
> human idealism raises the flag.

Science shows the possibilities.
Education spreads the motivation.
We, the human species,
can and must take control of our own fate.
How else can we survive over the long haul?

Frank Laubach (1884–1970, please see "The Game with Minutes" in the appendix) was a foremost pioneer of the present-day adult-literacy movement. In 1930, Laubach was deeply troubled about ignorance, poverty, injustice, and illiteracy in the world, and deemed them an impediment to personal empowerment, happiness, prosperity, and world peace. Many of his contemporaries saw poverty as a shameful result of laziness or vice. Laubach maintained that education is the surest way for people to help themselves out of ignorance, poverty, humiliation, mental illness and crime. As an educator, communicator, and organizer, he was looking for a large-scale educational solution without a large-scale capital expenditure.

To achieve this, Laubach developed the "Each One Teach One" literacy curriculum, as the means of disseminating throughout the world. The concept is very simple. In one-on-one mentoring, *those who know how to read teach persons who do not know how to read.* With the "Each One Teach One" method, Laubach brought literacy teaching to 103 countries, helping over 60 million people to learn to read in their own language. Laubach came to be known as "The Apostle to the Illiterates."

Abolition of the World Slavery:
A New Birth of Freedom, Happiness, and Prosperity

Taking into consideration of who we are and what is happening in the world, those of us who understand that we are "the light of the world," using Frank Laubach's Each One Teach One approach, can help others who don't have that understanding. The spread of the message, of living a divine life under the Spirit ('1') direction, will bring inspiration to those seeking new and deeper insights into reality, develop rare powers of concentration, encourage a broader self-confidence, and revolutionize what we know about nature and ourselves.

The leading American statesman during the nation's pre-Civil War Period, Daniel Webster (1782–1852) in the United States Senate stated, "Liberty and Union, one and inseparable, now and forever." Furthermore:

> If we work marble, it will perish;
> If we work upon brass, time will efface it;
> If we rear temples, they will crumble into dust;
> But if we work upon immortal minds
> And instill into them just principles,
> We are engraving upon tablets
> Which no time will efface,
> But will brighten and brighten to all eternity.

Living a divine life, as well as helping others to do the same, will advance us to a new vision of the world and fundamentally alter humanity's view of itself. It will encourage these pioneers of human thought to move ever boldly forward, improving world economies and living conditions, and promoting global health, peace, happiness, and prosperity. At this juncture, I see a new birth and life of freedom. Restating Saint Paul's letter to the Romans:

> Indeed, the whole created world eagerly awaits the revelation
> of the sons of God . . . because the world itself will be freed
> from its slavery . . . and share in the glorious freedom of the
> children of God (Rom. 8:19, 21).

VI

Review: Explore the World from New Perspectives

You are a divine elephant with amnesia
Trying to live in an ant hole.
Sweetheart, O Sweetheart
You are God hiding from yourself.

—Hafiz

Above all else, keep watch over your heart,
For herein lie the wellsprings of life.

—Proverbs 4.23

What Are We Searching For?
Please Share Your Joys with Me

I Am the Absolute,
The sky, the smile, and the sorrow;
I am the little ant and the graceful sparrow.
I am the child you kiss,

The fragrance you love, the beat of your heart,
And the man or woman you hug.
I am everywhere equally:
The beginning, the middle, and the end;
Everyone and everything is me;
And there is no one else but me.
I am gazing out of every face, including yours!
Indeed, I am who I am.
Indeed, I will be what I will be.

Remember my Compassionate Heart;
Before this journey you were in Light and bliss.
There was no time or space, no birth or death.
You decided to celebrate life—
To limit the spectrum of your perception.
You have assumed many forms:
As a flower, a waterfall, or the bright sky,
Your own brother, sister, mother, and father.
Yet, you made certain that the living of effortless life
Takes you back to your original knowledge.
Do not be uneasy, my love,
About this great excursion;
Do not be troubled,
My compassion,
With so many different faces and forms.
They are all carved out of the same One Light of '1'.
They are you!

Grace Be with You:
Find Your Inner Light

Know thyself.
Trust your insights.
Rise to the larger view.
Explore the universe from new awareness.
Be a witness to the world's most important moments.

Press onward to the "unity of knowledge."
Achieve, through self-cultivation, purity of heart,
Love of your neighbor, non-attachment to anything in life,
Stillness of the mind and the omnipotent silence:
Pristine peace, harmony, and freedom.
Rejoice.
Be perfect.
Simplicity is the essence, unity the common binding thread.
Deploy more free will with responsibility.
Cherish each opportunity to serve and to love.
Live with unceasing consciousness in God.
Celebrate effortless life and your divinity.
You will be enraptured in your blissful glory.
Yes my Happiness, yes my Light, and yes my Love;
Dressed in righteousness, kindness, caring and compassion,
You will perceive the Triumphant Splendor in your own being.
Through your personal example,
By your contacts at home, work,
While talking, walking, and serving,
Reading, writing, and traveling,
Bring this message to others.
Promote knowledge of the truth.
Each one teach one to live a divine life.
It is a luminous road of radiant beauty,
Happiness, splendor, and life.
It is a captivating pilgrimage
You have prepared for yourself.
It is unconditional compassion.
It is generosity of spirit.
It is high-mindedness.
It is effortless life.
It is You!

May the Compassion of the Holy One,
Peace, Goodness, Abundance, Freedom,
Love, and Happiness abide with you always.

Thank you so much. I love you very much. God bless you!

Orest

Acknowledgements
and Gratitude
Be to God in Man

The author would like to thank the many who have helped make this work possible:

Absolute compassion, infinite wonder, and heartfelt gratitude to you, O Father, our Love and Light, as Jesus the Christ and the Holy Spirit, Mother of Divine Providence, for your love, wisdom, and perseverance to bring all mankind back home to a state of perfection.

Heavenly love, gratefulness, and appreciation to you, Infinite Wisdom and Goodness, O Father, as contributors, authors, publishers, and the Lords of Light, of this work, and to all who influenced my thinking long before this handiwork was manifest.

Wholehearted compassion, indebtedness and gratitude to you, Infinite Perfection, O Father, as my angelic wife, precious parents, children and grandchildren, treasured coworkers and neighbors, for being caring, loving, and most helpful to all.

Absolute gratitude, brotherly love and compassionate thank you, O Father, as Andrew I. Lenec, Amanda Lowry, Chrystyna Bedrij, Chuck Bubar, Flordeline Silorio, Bill Hungerford, and Jim Lasko for copyediting, reviewing, and suggestions.

Divine love and heartfelt gratitude to you O Father and the Infinite Splendor of Light as my dearest reader of this work.

APPENDIX

Yes it's
Love: your life can be a miracle

_____

Teachers, scientists, sages and saints reveal the living power
of prayer

_____

Orest Bedrij, editor

MAKE YOUR LIFE A MIRACLE

There are as many ways of praying as there are of living, yet the power of prayer to change lives is unique and constant, as this extraordinary collection of worldwide witness proves. Prayer that works speaks a universal language, and that voice of faith is represented here in personal testimony from all corners of the earth: from prominent educators, missionaries, clerics, philosophers, yogis, mystics, sages and saints.

The roads are varied, the possibilities limitless, and the options are yours—progress toward the greatest riches of all: meaningful prayer that yields life's highest possible dividends.

YES IT'S LOVE

Your Life Can Be a Miracle

Edited by

OREST BEDRIJ

E FAMILY LIBRARY   •   NEW YORK

YES IT'S LOVE
Your Life Can Be a Miracle

A FAMILY LIBRARY BOOK

First printing May, 1974

Copyright © 1974 by Orest Bedrij
All Rights Reserved

Library of Congress Catalog Card Number: 73-21089

ISBN: 0-515-03398-7

Printed in the United States of America

FAMILY LIBRARY is published by Pyramid Publications
919 Third Avenue, New York, NY 10022, USA

CONTENTS

DEDICATED TO YOU, MY LOVE

BE LIKE JESUS,
SO THAT YOU MAY ALWAYS
CALL HIM FATHER.

I would like to thank all the authors in this volume for lending their hand—and their ideas—in the preparation and completion of this collection.

And also many thanks to P. Curau, S. B. Lee, and G. Timpano for much valuable help.

I extend my love and thanks to my beautiful wife, who made this book possible.

ACKNOWLEDGMENTS

The authors wish to extend their thanks for permission to use copyrighted material from the following:

> *The New American Bible*, © 1970 by Confraternity of Christian Doctrine (The Catholic Press, Washington, D.C.).
> *Today's English Version of the New Testament*, © 1966, 1967, American Bible Society.
> "Dimensions of Defensive Prayer." From *Quarterly Journal of Spiritual Frontiers Fellowship* by T. N. Tiemeyer (Spiritual Frontiers Fellowship, Inc., Evanston, Illinois).
> *Ena Twigg: Medium* by Ena Twigg with Ruth Hagy Brod (Hawthorn Books, Inc., New York, New York).
> *The Meaning of Prayer* by the Archbishop of Canterbury (A. R. Mowbray & Co. Ltd., London, England).
> *Sermon on the Mount* by Emmet Fox (Harper & Row, Publishers, Inc., New York, New York).

A NOTE TO THE READER

We have made no attempt to fit the authors into any particular theological mold. Each author writes from his own viewpoint, out of his own theological milieu.

The authors have contributed their articles independently of each other. Thus, the appearance of a particular work herein should not be construed as meaning that the author agrees with the theology, approach, or conclusions of any other author.

INTRODUCTION

This book can change your life.

Whether you are rich, poor, peasant, a king, or whoever—you can change your destiny, shape events, perform miracles, heal the sick, become a creative giant, achieve a state of spiritual exaltation, attune your mind to the Creator of the Universe, and be what Socrates, Moses, Saint Paul, Newton, and thousands of other giants were.

The possibilities are limitless. The limitations are only what you make them. By applying the ideas of this book you can tap the mightiest power in the universe. This power is a source of all things that exist. It needs only flow into your being and transform itself into health, inspiration, or anything else you may need or desire. You don't have to be unhappy; you don't have to live in fear or poverty. Your Father created a beautiful universe with all the riches you ever needed to use and enjoy. This power is everywhere. It belongs to all. It is waiting for you to apply it—not merely in crisis but for every occasion, every day of your life.

You will learn about the wisdom of the ages and the essence of the Bible and metaphysics. You will learn about the answers to our world problems. You will find that wars, atrocities, murder, poverty, human slavery, and misery can be eliminated.

By tapping the miracle Love of your Father, you can enjoy peace, love, radiant health, happiness, genius, unlimited knowledge, and much more. Literally you can bend the forces of nature to your will through prayer. You don't have to look for solutions. You have them within your grasp here, now. You can open the doors to life's most profound mysteries. This is not a pie-in-the-sky wish. This is reality. It works miracles.

Prayer has changed my life. It can change yours, too. Through prayer, I have found inner peace, happiness, and a real joy in living. Through prayer, you can find these same things.

When I began to share my thoughts on how to pray, I realized that I knew very little about prayer. In fact, I could share only what was "one man's opinion." Because I wanted people to experience what I had experienced, I knew that I had to ask others to help. Therefore, I asked prayerful people—clergymen and laymen—from many denominations, living in many lands, to share their thoughts.

These thoughts are collected here and presented in the hope that they will in some way prove useful to you.

As you go through these pages, you will find that there is no one perfect way to pray. There are many roads (and forms of prayer) that lead to the Creator. But whatever the road, you must embark and start traveling now. The sooner you realize this, the sooner will your life be what you want it to be.

You probably remember the story of a small boy and a wise old man:

"I have a bird in my hands," said the boy to the wise man. "Is it alive or is it dead?"

"I will trap him," thought the boy. "If he says it is dead I will let the bird fly away. But if he says it is alive I will crush the life out of it."

What is your answer? Will you start living to your fullest? Will you tap the Absolute Love and allow yourself to be what God wants you to be? You have everything to gain and nothing to lose. Do you want to help yourself? Do you want to help others? Test it, experiment, take notes, and verify what Buddha, Mohammed, Pascal, Einstein, and millions of others have found: that prayer is too sacred and too powerful not to be given to the entire human race.

But back to the wise man, who smiled lovingly and said, "His life is in your hands." So is yours. You can be what your Father wanted you to be! Jesus tells us, "It is written in your own Law that God said 'You are gods.'" Then He added, "We know that what the scripture says is true forever" (John 10:34–36). Which will it be? Will you be like the man who found a bag of diamonds while looking for sugar and threw it away because they failed to dissolve in his mouth? Or having found prayer, will you make your life a miracle?

OREST BEDRIJ

SUFFER THE LITTLE ONES

Samuel B. Lee

Praise, thanksgiving, forgiveness, and petition are our side of our conversation with God. In the silence of our hearts, notes Samuel B. Lee, God speaks to us and brings us the joy of His presence.

Samuel B. Lee is a graduate of the Catholic University of America. He is a professional writer who specializes in the area of technical publications. He has been active in the Confraternity of Christian Doctrine for many years. He is currently involved with the Charismatic Renewal and is a member of the Promise of Life Charismatic Community in Hopewell Junction, New York.

When I was very young, I was taught that prayer was the lifting of the mind and heart to God. And I was advised to pray always. So I would try very hard, with eyes tightly shut, to lift my mind and heart to God. But I couldn't do this even for a little while. How, then, was I to pray always?

I soon became discouraged with prayer. True, I wanted to pray, I had been told how to pray, and yet I found I couldn't lift my mind and heart to God. And so my prayer life remained the same until I learned many years later that those old words, which I found so hard to practice, contained the deepest truths about prayer. To lift, or turn, one's mind and heart to someone is to communicate with Him.

Put simply, prayer is conversation with God. And like conversation, prayer is two-sided. We not only speak to God, but we spend time in quiet so that God can speak to us. And how do we speak to God? We speak to Him as the father that He is.

Imagine a father and son playing catch with a baseball in the late fall. And imagine that they lose the ball in the weeds. The father immediately promises to get the boy a new ball in the spring. When spring comes, the son simply reminds the father of the lost ball, and the father's promise is made good. The important point here is that the father's response—answering the son's reminder—is based on the simple words of a son to a father.

And so it must be between our heavenly Father and ourselves. We should talk to Him as the son in our little episode undoubtedly spoke to his earthly father: respectfully, in friendship and love, and with the expectation that He would get what He had been promised.

This is not to say that formal prayer has no place in our prayer life. It has. And most of all we should pray that perfect prayer to the Father taught us by His Son. But we cannot be satisfied to limit ourselves to the set, formal prayers we learned as children. We can no more carry on all our conversations with God using set formulas than business partners can talk over the problems of their business using the ritualism of cocktail party small talk.

The ways of talking to God are as varied as the ways of talking to our friends. But several threads run through all prayer. These threads form the items of mutual interest between our Father and ourselves. They appear most obviously in the prayer that Jesus taught us.

Two of these threads we can call adoration and thankfulness: "Blessed be your name . . . Your kingdom come . . . Your will be done . . . Father in Heaven . . ." Jesus shows us very clearly that we must bless and praise the Father and through our praise and blessing show our thankfulness. Praise and thankfulness should form the bulk of our side of our conversations with God. And praise should be easy for us because we can turn nowhere without encountering Him in His creation: the beauty of His sunset; the coolness of His shade; His fire and hail, snow and frost, mountains and hills; and all His mighty deeds.

We do not need formal prayers to thank our Father for giving us a spouse, a job, children, some measure of success, some small satisfaction in our work, warm days, cool nights, flowers, friends. We do not need formal prayers any more than we need a preset formula in order to thank a friend for a small birthday present. All we need to do is to say "thank you" as it comes to us. Our friend understands; so does our Father.

Another thread is called forgiveness. "Forgive us our sins as we have forgiven those who have sinned against us . . ." And we are asked not only to forgive simply, but also to forgive with that profoundness that includes completely forgetting the offense. We are called upon to put ourselves right with our friends so that no wall or wound stands between us.

After we have adored the Father and been thankful that He is God and forgiven our fellow man, we can then weave the final thread—that of petition—into the tapestry of our prayer. "Give us this day . . . Lead us not . . . Deliver us from evil."

When I was young, I almost never thought of God unless I needed something. Then it was easy to pray, at least for a little while. And I believe that most people turn to God only when they need something. Most of the time, He is like an insurance policy: nice to know it's around, but not really much good until you have an accident. Ah, then how important it suddenly becomes!

But our Father doesn't want to be merely an "insurance policy" God. He wants us to come to Him with thanks and praise and not just with our petitions. He wants to be more like the car—used every day—than the insurance policy—used only "in emergency." Besides, God knows our needs better than we do. Our earthly fathers knew when we needed new shoes, a schoolbook, or a coat; how much more our Heavenly Father knows our needs. If we could truly seek the kingdom of heaven by praising, thanking, and forgiving, we would have, I think, very little need to ask our Father for anything. He would supply it before even we knew we needed it.

Our conversation with God—praise, thanksgiving, forgiveness, and petition—should be like human conversation: Each person speaks, and each listens; and each can enjoy the silent companionship of the other.

God's ways of speaking to us are not our ways. He does not always speak as a voice that we hear. He may speak to us by giving us a new insight into His word as we read it; or He may speak to us through something someone says to us. But most frequently, our Father speaks to us in the silence of our hearts as we come near to Him and silently enjoy being in His presence.

And this is the joy of prayer—to be in the presence of God and know that He loves us, protects us, and guides us. That we can speak to Him who keeps the stars in place and know that He hears us. That we can speak to God, and know that He answers us.

THE PRAYER FACTOR

Marcus Bach

In this selection, Dr. Marcus Bach draws upon his knowledge
of religions from around the world. He finds that from the
diversity of kinds of prayers emerges a common experience:
the elevation to and beyond the moral.

Dr. Bach is a world traveler, author, and popular interpreter
of intercultural relations. *Who's Who* lists him as the foremost
authority on contemporary religious movements and analyst
of the American scene. He holds a PhD from the University of
Iowa and four honorary degrees from other universities; he has
been recognized with numerous awards, has authored twenty
books, has written numerous articles for national periodicals,
and has served as a specialist in the Department of State under
the International Educational Exchange program in Southeast
Asia, India, Pakistan, Korea, and Japan. Dr. Bach is a founder
and director of the Fellowship for Spiritual Understanding,
Palos Verdes, California.

Have you ever wondered what people think of when they pray? What
do they concentrate on, what frame of mind are they in, what happens
when they pray?

I have asked these questions of worshipers in many faiths.

One said, "I fix my mind on thankfulness. Gratitude for my blessings is the key to prayer."

Another told me, "I visualize God as the highest and greatest love imaginable and I see my life as part of that love. I kneel when I pray. I close my eyes and shut out all worldly thoughts. I think of God as a great spiritual Father who created all and who governs all. Then I listen for His voice. His voice comes to me in the form of thoughts and impressions. I actually talk to Him and He talks to me."

Others have confided in me:

"I put all my troubles and problems aside and begin by saying, 'God, I want only to worship Thee.' I keep repeating this until there is no other thought in my mind than this."

"I think of the beauty of nature. I can pray best out of doors, where I feel the fellowship with God."

"I mentally enter a golden tunnel. God is at the far end in a dazzling light. I go farther and farther toward the light until my consciousness merges with His."

"I sit yoga-fashion when I pray. I breathe regularly and say, 'God is my light, God is my life.' I do not ask for anything or expect anything. I just fill myself with the thought that my life is God's life."

"I think of goodness and peace and try to fill my spirit with them."

"I visualize two chambers—one spaceless and eternal, the chamber of God, the Father. The other contains all created things and is ruled over by Christ. I walk through these chambers led by the power of the Holy Spirit. That is how I pray."

"When I pray I make my mind completely receptive to whatever God wants me to know."

"When I pray I mentally hear Jesus saying, 'Come unto me.'"

"Prayer for me is just being still and feeling God's presence."

All of these worshipers had found something; all were still seeking something.

The secret, of course, is to start with ourselves. Someone may intercede for you or pray for you, but no one can truly "find God" for you. It is an inner experience.

You must begin with yourself and develop the inward look.

You must take time for meditation and prayer.

Life is the laboratory. Life is the heart of faith. Life is the great adventure.

You must give God *His* minute. *His* ten minutes. *His* hour. There is no other way. There is no greater secret. *You* are the one who must begin. *You* are the person who matters. *You* in your own faith, whatever the faith may be, *you* are the person to whom God will reveal Himself if you but take time to worship Him.

Right now, if you close your eyes for a moment and think of God—no matter how vague your concept of Him may be—you have already begun an adventure in faith.

An American businessman said to me, "We should not entreat God or force God or beg of God. We should simply become aware in body, mind, and spirit that we are possessed by God fully and completely."

He said when he first set aside a few moments for prayer in his office, his mind was clouded by a rush of thoughts having to do with business, appointments, and problems for the day. His biggest problem was to "keep God in focus." He soon learned that each time he brought his thoughts back to concentrate on the thought of God the thought grew stronger. Each time he warded off worldly thoughts, God became clearer.

I have learned this from many religions around the world. "When you start thinking about the Lord, the Lord starts thinking about you" is the way a Muslim put it.

When the period of meditation or prayer is finished, God should remain as a lingering presence.

When you open your eyes and look upon the world, you should do so with a new inner vision. You are not alone, say those who worship, you are never alone. God and you are one.

An instructor in yoga told me, "If the spiritual exercises leave you exhausted, you are not doing them correctly. They should leave you calm and refreshed."

That is also true of prayer. If your excursion into the "silence" leaves you disquieted or disturbed, you are not worshiping correctly. You have merely sought an escape. Worship and prayer are "finding God," and God is always goodness, peace, and strength.

The "quiet time" or period of meditation, wherever it is sincerely practiced, always develops a feeling of the authority of the moral in God. That is, the immoral becomes opposition to God. The better the worship, the better the man; and, conversely, the better the man, the better the worship. It is an adventure, a quest.

A person can be moral without any specific religious discipline, but he cannot be religious without advancing in morality. Worship always leads beyond the moral. It persuades the worshiper to be critical of himself and to try to be a better person than he was before he worshiped.

JOURNEY TO THE SACRED SELF

Yogi Amrit Desai

How can we find peace, love, and contentment in this harried world? Yogi Amrit Desai affirms that we must turn within and, through prayer and effort, begin the journey of self-realization that is union with God.

Yogi Desai is a close disciple of the great Yogi Guru Swami Kripalvanandji. He is the founder and director of the Yoga Society of Pennsylvania and has recently established Kripalu Ashram-Retreat near Philadelphia, where he lives. Besides his abilities as a teacher, lecturer, and writer, Yogi Desai has a BFA degree and is a recognized artist. His work in the fields of yoga and the arts has brought him many honors and awards.

The Journey Within

Often a man caught up in a hurricane of worldly life, in spite of all earthly efforts, finds himself pushed around helplessly, like a straw, in utter confusion and darkness, leading him to search the infinite power of the Divine. Thus, a man tempered by time and experience humbles himself and accepts the higher self, the divine father, as his savior. He then has the fuel of faith to start his journey within. His spontaneous cries for help under these circumstances are always answered, because they fulfill all the necessary conditions for true prayer. Some are led within only when they

169

experience great suffering in life, while others are led within for the love toward the divine father within.

Prayer

Prayer is the most effective means to start the journey within. The purpose of prayer is to establish communication with God, the father within—to receive guidance, wisdom, and strength to tread the path of self-realization. For prayers to be effective, one must fulfill the necessary conditions. Sometimes such conditions are spontaneously fulfilled, but sometimes man has to prepare his life to bring about right conditions for communication within. All prayers must be accompanied by the corresponding effort. The effort and prayer complement each other like a chariot with two wheels. Prayer without effort is like a chariot with one wheel. A great Indian, Yogi Ramakrishna, says, "The wind of God's grace is always blowing, but we have to put up our sails." It is also said that God helps those who help themselves. This shows that God is everywhere, and that means within us as well. Thus, God works through us but not for us.

In the popular approach, only verbal prayers are offered to God in heaven. But great yogis and masters say that God is within us. Yogis say, "*Tat Twam Asi,*" thou art that; "*Sohum,*" I am that. Jesus says, "The kingdom of heaven is within," and He also says, "Know thyself." If God is omnipresent, omniscient, and omnipotent, He is within us, too. Thus, there is nothing within us that is secret to God. Every thought or action, no matter how secretly or unconsciously performed, is known to the higher self within and has its effect on future actions automatically. This is why verbal, mechanical, ceremonial prayers fail. This is why successful prayer does not depend on careful selection or arrangement of words; such prayers are merely lip service.

Since true prayer is two-way communication with God, verbal prayer should be followed by a silent conscious period. (Conscious verbal prayer without the silent period is like one-way talk, which cannot be called communication.) For successful communication, conscious verbal prayer should lead to silent listening prayer. This listening prayer is called meditation. Listening becomes possible when the mind becomes empty and still.

As long as the mind is striving, expecting, interpreting, or asking, it cannot be empty. In listening prayer, which is far superior, man opens gates to divine inner guidance by placing himself in a state of holy indifference or choiceless awareness and surrendering to the will of the divine. In conscious verbal prayers of petition, praise, supplication, or adoration, man uses his conscious mind, which censors thoughts and feelings according to its own conditioning. In verbal prayers man talks to God, but in listening prayers God talks to man. At this point, through surrender, man becomes one with God. Thus, meditation is a royal path (*raja yoga*) to God.

Our Whole Life Should Become a Prayer

Thus, true prayers are offered not only by our words but also by our most secret thoughts and actions. Under these circumstances, all our desires, expressions, and actions—conscious or unconscious—become our prayers. This is why one must purify one's thoughts, words, and actions to pray. Also, one should pray, at the same time, to receive inner strength and guidance to purify. Consequently, prayer and purity quickly pave the path to progress and the divine. Thus, one must pray with one's whole life. The incongruence in one's thoughts, words, and actions is a basic impurity, and this in turn brings fear, tensions, and imbalance. This blocks the inflow of the universal energy and separates man from the universal orchestra of harmony and unity, leading him further and deeper into disharmony.

To bridge the individual self with the universal self, one must vibrate with the laws of the universe. To accomplish this, man must act in the right direction with all available wisdom, energy, logic, and reasoning, along with prayers. If we consider our verbal prayers as a seed suggestion for our future, our actions are the super-suggestion that supersedes all other prayers. Therefore, prayer is a continuous, spontaneous, effortless flow expressed through our mental, emotional, verbal, and physical actions. Any prayers not coming through our whole being are not answered. This is why we hear the popular expression "Deserve before you demand."

Faith—Surrender

Without faith one cannot truly pray or pursue the higher path with patience. Faith is the fuel that sustains actions in the right direction without distractions. A great yogi of India, Swami Kripalvanandji, says, "A man of faith continues his efforts in one direction with patience for many years, while a man without faith changes many directions in a day." Thus, prayers without faith fail to bear fruit.

Faith means firm inner conviction in the divine self. God within is the sole source of truth consciousness and bliss. This conviction coordinates and focuses all mental, emotional, and physical energies in a singleness of purpose to reach the paramount source of light. With this kind of faith, one naturally and effortlessly renounces all attachments of body, ego, and mind, which represent the lower self. Without such faith there is no way to surrender one's lower self into the hands of the higher self.

To surrender means to surrender all the ego-oriented selfish actions to the divine within and say, "Thy will be done, not mine." As this surrender matures with prayers supported by efforts, one rises above personal insecurities, fears, confusion, and tension. To the extent one surrenders, one begins to see the guiding and comforting light within. This starts the journey toward the heaven within. The surrender lifts man above the narrow, limited, conditioned self and places him in touch with the unlimited source of energy and peace within. He wants nothing for his lower self and becomes merely an instrument or channel of the divine. In such total surrender he lives, moves, and acts in and for divine will. Thus, he emerges from the world of duality, polarity, and contrasts; they exist only for the person whose lower self is active and who says, "My will be done, not Thine." He is a prodigal son who suffers. When the prodigal starts his journey back home to meet His Father with faith and surrender, he feels increasingly contented and at peace within. This is not an ordinary peace but, as Christ says, "Peace that passeth all understanding." Finally when man gives up all his ego-oriented desires and lives fully by the will of His Father, his individuality merges with cosmic consciousness. This union in Sanskrit is called *yoga*, which results in *samadhi*. This mystical union is the direct experience: *"I and my father are one."*

WHAT IS PRAYER?

Sister Cecile Sandra

Prayer, asserts Sister Cecile Sandra, is the enriching intercommunication between God and men. When undertaken with an open heart and an open mind, it becomes the liberating experience that unites mankind.

Sister Cecile Sandra, ICM, OBE, PhD, received her doctorate in psychology from Fordham University and is now a member of the Religious Congregation of the Missionary Sisters of the Immaculate Heart of Mary with headquarters in Rome. She has been engaged in school administration and lecturing in psychology in the Caribbean since 1956 and is presently on the staff of St. Michael's Seminary in Kingston, Jamaica. Sister Cecile Sandra is a member of numerous education and mental health associations in the United States as well as the Caribbean.

Prayer is communication with God and all His people.

Is there any set formula for such communication? There hardly could be any, since communication occurs according to each person's own unique personality. It is with this personality that we have to discover and rediscover our personal God day by day. We discover Him in myriad ways: in the slender palm tree along the winding mountain road, in the angry sea beating the eroding stacks, in the translucent rainbow on a clearing sky, in the "blue light" foreshadowing the daily death of the sun.

We discover Him and, with a touch of His divinity, we are ready to meet men again and find in them another touch of the divine and blend it all in one enriching and refreshing intercommunication.

If we remain attuned to the divine in ourselves and others, we will find God in the sounds all around: in the promising cry of the twins next door, in the dreamy steelband at nighttime, and in the lively guitar chords of the youngsters in church—and—hosanna—have mercy—be merry—let's be proud of the band. We will find Him anew, and thus enriched, we will be able to meet others and enter into that process of mutual enrichment—of true humanization with God ever in the picture.

If we keep our affinity for the divine in our lives, we will see God in the many faces of humanity today: in the charismatic hands of the religious leader, in the restless head of the young radical, in the dynamic smile of the newlywed, in the motionless gaze of the old granny, and in the hungry look of the kid on his way to the tap at the street corner.

We will meet the Lord, and this encounter will stimulate other encounters and lift up humanity while enriching us.

God has many faces in the 1970s. To me His face is one of liberation.

"God, free me," says the young man in the affluent home. Free me! From what? From the deadening comfort, the sophisticated smiles, the artifacts, and the taboos all around me. Free me from role-playing, from enforced acting, from deadening compulsion, from the obsession that I'll never make the grade for the twenty-first century. Free my better self and open it up for You and for others. God, liberate me! God, liberate us, say the young people in the developing countries. We have joined hands, God, because we remain in want, even though the "first world" has it all in abundance. We can't be free if we remain oppressed, Lord!

God, help us to grow to the stature of the others. If only they could liberate us of our dependency on them.

God, why don't the wealthy nations realize that You want them—not as individuals, but as groups? Help us to discover our inner wealth and that of our culture and that of our people everywhere—in what they love to call "the third world."

God, our God, we will discover You fully when they let us grow, when they believe that we too, Your people, have the potential to enrich others because we have suffered more and have been freed from self in the process and will know how to communicate with all others in a positive way, if only they are great enough to meet us with an open mind and an open heart.

UNION WITHOUT CEASING

OREST BEDRIJ

Orest Bedrij has found among Jesus, the apostles and saints, scholars and seers, guidance in achieving the prayer life of union with God through love.

Bedrij, a native of Ukraine, received his education in electrical engineering, physics, and finance in the United States. Professionally he has been involved in the computer sciences and has served the technical director of the California Institute of Technology Jet Propulsion Laboratory, Space Flight Facility. He is president and director of Securities Council, Inc. and founder of a number of corporations.

The world now needs prayer more than any other thing. For ages man has been trying to find solutions to war, genocide, atrocity, poverty, slavery, murder, drug addiction, immorality, and riots, sickness, and so forth.

Have we been successful? Have we come close to the real answer? No, because we have not been using the right tool: we have not been using prayer, the master key to life that our Father has put in our hands. Prayer *can* conquer all problems. Study the history of man's intercession with his Creator and you will find that when properly asked, Your Father will give you whatever you need. All you have to do is ask in Jesus' name and He will provide.

God created you and the universe, with its immensity of splendor and beauty, for you to use and enjoy. Certainly He can help you with your problems. He is waiting and longing to give you much more than the cup you hold up to be filled. But you have to turn to Him. Nobody can do it for you. You have to do it yourself. "He has knocked at the door" (Rev. 3:20). And you have to open the door of your heart and let Him in.

You can read about prayer. You can talk about prayer. You can listen to beautiful sermons. You can attend conferences or help with bazaars. But "let those men of zeal," recommended St. John of the Cross, "who think by their preaching and exterior works to convert the world, consider that they would be much more pleasing to God—to say nothing of the example they give—if they would spend at least one half of their time in prayer."

Some later time, perhaps tomorrow, perhaps next year you will take the next step of prayer. But not now. Now is not the right time. You want the gifts of God without paying the price. Which will it be for you? Will you get involved? Will you do it now? The choice is clearly yours. And the proof is in praying—constantly praying with your heart and your mind and your whole being. You will stop believing in God; you will start seeing Him! You will be consciously walking in Him. He will be your guiding light, your shining perfection, your strength, your courage, and your wisdom. *You will really feel that He dwells in you and you in Him.* Every moment will be His moment. You will drink His life. You will drink His love. You will lose yourself in Him. You and He will be one. You will cry out with a loud voice of Christ: "Eli, Eli, lmana shabachthani! which means, My God, My God, this was my destiny. I was born for this" (Matt. 27:46).[1]*

Here is a list of points you will find helpful as you grow in your prayer life:

1. Make a prayer a definite part of each day.
2. Find a quiet place.

---

[1] *The Gospel Light, Comments on the Teachings of Jesus from Aramaic and Unchanged Eastern Customs,* by George Lansa © 1936, 1939, renewed © 1964 by A. J. Holman Co. Reprinted by permission of A. J. Holman Co., a division of J. B. Lippincott Co.

3. Be comfortable.
4. Be attentive.
5. Ask God to teach you how to pray.
6. Know yourself.
7. Thank God frequently.
8. Pray with your heart.
9. Fast.
10. Have faith.
11. Be still.

Let's look at each one of these and see how they help you attain the union without ceasing that has been called by Dr. R. M. Bucke "cosmic consciousness," by Christian mystics "unitive life" or "beatific vision," by Buddhists "nirvana," and by Hindus "moksha."

1. *Make prayer a definite part of each day.* Set aside a certain time each day, the earlier the better. In the beginning make it five minutes, ten minutes, or whatever your busy schedule permits. Remember: the less you pray, the less you want to pray. No one ever learned how to fly in one easy lesson. It takes time and effort. The great pianist and composer Sergei Rachmaninoff said that when he skipped one day's practice he knew it; when he skipped two days' practice the critics knew it; and after three days, the audience knew it. This is even truer with prayer. Every lapse is a setback and joy lost forever. The goal is to learn to pray always, in all places, without interruption.

2. *Find a quiet place*—any place, outside or inside: an empty room, an attic, a church, a park, a garden, a lakeside bench, a mountain, a bathroom, or a closet. Be certain you will not be disturbed. True, you can pray while scrubbing pots and pans in the kitchen or while driving or on the train. However, the deeper experiences of prayer come in solitude. Jesus advised, "Whenever you pray, go to your room, close your door, and pray to your Father in private. Then your Father, who sees what no man sees, will repay you" (Matt. 6:6).

3. *Be comfortable.* Traditionally Westerners kneel, because kneeling happens to be the accepted gesture of respect before an earthly throne. We know from Matthew that Jesus "threw Himself face down to the ground and prayed fervently" (Matt. 26:39). Easterners seem to feel that sitting

erect with spine straight and the body in equipoise is most conducive to prayer. Possibly there is no "right" posture. You have to pray in the position that suits you best. It's not the position of your body but the state of your heart that counts.

4. *Be attentive.* Keep your mind fixed on God. To do this, you should not be overtired, torpid, overfed, or sleepy. Your body should be tranquil and free from physical and mental tensions. The Swedes have a beautiful proverb that may be used as a guide: "Fear less, hope more; eat less, chew more; whine less, breathe more; talk less, say more; hate less, love more; and all good things are yours."

5. *Ask God to teach you how to pray.* If you think you know how to pray, listen to Saint Teresa: "Those who walk in the way of prayer have the greater need of learning; and the more spiritual they are, the greater is their need."

No matter what you have heard, or read, prayer is no simple task. And it is impossible to pray properly without God's help. "Prayer is the hardest kind of work," confessed German rocket physicist and astronautics engineer Dr. Werner von Braun, "but it is the most important work we can do now." "Here I am, God," tell Him. "Without your help I'm sunk. Holy Spirit, take my weakness, enlighten me, and guide me into all truth." (And He will!) Let Him fill your heart and mind and kindle in you the fire of His love. Let Him make you complete—an overwhelming experience of beauty, love, and joy. Let Him bring you into the exhilarating experience of the presence of God.

6. *Know yourself.* Purify your soul and put your life in order. Search your heart for the sins you have made in thought and deed that have hurt others, as well as yourself. Realize that your sins and failures prevent God's love from working in your life, and unless you remove all barriers, the free flow of His love will be blocked. Jesus recommended, "If you bring your gift to the altar and there recall that your brother has anything against you, leave your gift at the altar, go first to be reconciled, and then come back and offer your gift" (Matt. 5:23, 24). No trespass should be too great for you to forgive. Hanging on the Cross, the Light of Life prayed for those who were killing Him: "Father, forgive them; they do not know what they are doing" (Luke 23:34). A forgiving spirit toward others is required for effective prayer and your own health, and God will forgive you only in the measure in which you forgive. So be merciful—and set yourself free.

Often we are our own debtors. We have trespassed. We have to ask God's forgiveness. Tell Him with the heart of a child in humility and sorrow: "O Father, I am sorry! Forgive me!" And He will forgive you and forget. His forgiveness is the love that completely burns out the past sins. You then have to forgive yourself—not partially but completely. You must not recount over and over your wrongdoing. Bury the garbage of past mistakes; otherwise it is spiritual suicide. It's like opening a wound that is once clean. You will have to make it septic again. Having confessed, turn your back upon your transgressions and be ready in the future to "hate the sin," as the jail inscription at Karnal-India advises, but "not the sinner." Then, "avoid all evil, cherish all goodness," recommended Buddha, and "keep the mind pure." For, as Saint Paul noted, you "are the temple of the living God" (2 Cor. 6:16). And being holy is not only limited to deeds but also to thoughts. Jesus made this clear concerning adultery: "Anyone who looks lustfully at a woman has already committed adultery with her in his thoughts" (Matt. 5:28).

All day long, thoughts that occupy your mind are molding your destiny for good or evil. Once in a vision I saw a good and a bad thought. Chills ran up and down my spine when I realized their great power and the boomerang effect they have. Every thought, I realized then, is a high-frequency energy field that, if viewed with a suitable apparatus, would appear as real as an object you see. Nikola Tesla, for example, who invented the AC motor, transformer, radar, fluorescent light, wireless remote control, and so forth, said he could see his thoughts. They were so vivid and solid that at times it was difficult for him to distinguish between his thought and external reality. While looking at the image, he would construct many desired pieces of machinery completely in every detail and dimension. Sometimes he would test them—still in his mind—over a period of more than a year, observing the parts as they wore, modifying them, as needed.

If you could see your thoughts and their effect on your surrounding, you would be petrified to dwell on anything negative. You would realize that *the whole of your life's experience is but the outer expression of inner thoughts you have chosen to hold.* You would understand that what you think in your mind you will invariably produce in your experience. Think love, and the love energy emanating from your mind will not only surround and modify you but all those about whom you think. Think thoughts of hate, and hate energy will be acting on you and on those about whom you think.

Dr. William Parker demonstrated in the laboratory that if you hold a feeling of hard implacability against life or impulses of unkindness or jealousy, or anger, or hatred (love in reverse) toward someone, you are really slowly killing yourself. It's like grabbing a hot iron to hit someone but in fact hurting yourself instead. The Man of Galilee summarized it very beautifully: "Whatsoever you sow" in your unseen thoughts "that shall you also reap" in that which is seen. Illnesses (cancer, ulcers, heart attacks, and so on), murder, poverty (the list is endless) are self-inflicted thoughts. You have to change the prevailing tenor of your life on love and you will see no darkness. For if you will not take the road of Light you will have to keep on learning by pain. Man cannot break the laws of God; he can only break himself against them. Only by much searching and mining will gold and diamonds be obtained. Therefore concentrate on the right choice and true application of God-like thoughts and deeds and you will grow through love to Love.

So with every breath, with every thought, with every aim, let love be love in you.

7. *Thank God frequently*, joyfully, and eagerly. Thank Him with the deepest affection of your heart for letting you be alive and part of His creation. Praise His goodness and love for you. Recall the many graces of mercy, happiness, joy, wisdom, ability, and health He has given you; the many sins He has forgiven you; your ability to see His glory and drink from the spring of His Spirit. Thank Him always for everything that happens to you during every moment of your life.

"We don't thank God enough for much that He has given us," confessed Robert Woods. "Our prayers are too often the beggar's prayer, the prayer that asks for something. We offer too few prayers of thanksgiving and praise."

Remember when Jesus healed the ten lepers? Why did only one return to give thanks to God? Were not ten cleansed (Luke 17:14–19)?

"When I look at your heavens," cried David in Psalms 8:3–4, which "the work of thy fingers, the moon and the stars you have established; what is man that thou art mindful of Him?" We are so small, our life so short, our knowledge so limited, we begin to feel with Tennyson that the life of men is but "murmur of gnats in the gleam of a million suns." Thank God; adore Him because "Thou has made us for Thyself," sang St. Augustine, "and our hearts can find no rest outside of Thee."

8. *Pray with your heart.* When you pray, realize that you are addressing the Maker of all. He is the love of loves, the Creator who is infinitely bigger to our universe than the universe is to an atom. The Absolute Beauty, Gentleness, Wisdom, Goodness, and Power. Do not address Him while you are thinking of other things. Show your gratitude to Him for allowing you to come near Him. Remember, before you can really pray with sincerity you must begin to know the greatness and holiness of God. And the greater the depth and extent of the knowledge, the more love there will be. The more easily the heart will soften and lay itself open to the love of God.

God knows before you open your lips what you will say. You must pray with your mind, your heart, and your whole life. You must seek to know His will, be eager to offer yourself to Him, and be ready to be filled with His Holy Spirit. You must pray in your own words, just the way you talk to friends. The cry from the heart of the most illiterate is just as welcome to God as the perfectly formed prayer of a great scholar. But it is not the utterances of the lips that God hears; rather it is the song and joy of the heart. If your heart does not speak, you are silent to God. Love God and He will hear you.

9. *Fast.* Deliberately abstain from food for spiritual purposes. Why fast? Isn't a good life adequate? Why did Jesus fast? Why did Moses, Samuel, David, Elijah, Daniel, Isaiah, Cornelius, Paul, Socrates, Plato, Buddha, Gandhi, Pythagoras, Luther, Lincoln . . . fast? Did they know something we don't know? Christ did not have to fast! He is the Light of Life and Perfection. Yet He taught, fasted, performed miracles, was crucified, died, and arose not for exhibition but to teach us how to grow. In His Sermon on the Mount, Jesus did not say *"if* you pray . . . *if* you fast . . . *if* you give alms" but *"when* you pray . . . *when* you fast . . . *when* you give alms." His language for prayer and fast is identical. He expects us unambiguously, and without qualification, to pray, to fast, and to give when the occasion demands it. There is one requirement, however: when you fast, please God and not the eyes of other people. "Appear not to men that you are fasting, but to your Father who is unseen: and your Father, who sees what is hidden

will reward you" (Matt. 6:18). The shameful hypocrisy, the egocentric piety, and showy acts of fasting of the Pharisees had no place in Jesus' life and must be curbed in your life. Fasting should be inconspicuous, noncompetitive, and uninjurious to your health. A fast of one to three days is easy and does not fall into this last category. But if you embark on a longer fast (seven to forty days) be sure that God is leading you to do this and that you understand how to go about it. If you have an illness or doubts as to the physical advisability of fasting, consult your own doctor and follow his advice. (For additional reading we have listed some of the books you may consider.)

So why are you afraid to fast? Why are you not doing what Jesus has instructed you to do? Very simply: the evil spirits (earthbound, unenlightened individuals) that Christ had to deal with are working against you. Every opportunity the dark forces get, every roadblock they can set up (chaos, disruption, fear, hatred, worry, aggression, separation) goes into action. Fasting clears the doors of perception and removes the impediments to holiness. It helps to crucify self-love and self-will and allows God's overwhelming power to shape the real, eternal you. It breaks down that which stands between God and you and *tunes your mind and body to be a better instrument for love.*

Both the Old and the New Testament very clearly state (74 times) that prayer and fasting are a must, that "man cannot live by bread alone" (Matt. 4:4), that some evil spirits can only be driven out by prayer and fasting (Matt. 17:21). People who have fasted will testify that it constitutes one of the most powerful tools God has put in your hands. When you fast you bring a note of urgency to your prayer. You are telling God that you are truly in earnest, that you do not intend to take no for an answer, that you want a miracle.

The great prophet Isaiah (740–700 BC), who vividly foretold the suffering and death of Jesus, listed some of the benefits of fasting: answer to prayer, health, guidance, healing, inspiration, and that the Glory of the Lord shall be your reward (Isaiah 58:1–14). Can you wish for more? Individuals who fast claim many other benefits: Daniel—improvement of his prophetic ability; Elijah—spiritual direction; Socrates, Plato, Plutarch, Pythagoras, and Galileo—sharpening of intellect and mental clarity; the people of Israel—divine intervention; the apostles—spiritual enrichment;

Krishna, Buddha, Shankara, Confucius, Gandhi—understanding of truth; the 8,000 (1948 through the present) patients under Dr. Yurij Nikolayev at Moscow's Gannushkin Institute—treatment of sluggish forms of schizophrenia.

The famous physical fitness authority Dr. Paul Bragg testifies that "you purify your body physically, mentally, and spiritually and therefore enjoy super vitality and super health. Greatest of all are the inner peacefulness and tranquility that make life worth living. You come into harmony with that power higher than yourself. You learn the meaning of the truth that 'your body is the temple of the living God.'" How to start? Very simply:

A. You have to believe that fasting is good for you.
B. If this is your first, don't start on a long fast. Learn to walk before you run.
C. Have fruit for your last meal.
D. Abstain completely (initially for twenty-four hours) from eating and drinking everything except water.
E. Drink as much boiled, warm water as you wish.
F. The first time you fast you might get a headache, especially if you are used to drinking coffee, tea, or alcohol. This is one of the signs that your body is undergoing detoxification. It is unpleasant but good for you. You might consider stopping coffee, tea, or alcohol a few days before the fast.
G. To fight discouragement (evil spirit attacks), praise God.
H. Break fast with fruit or vegetable juices (apple, tomato, or citrus).
I. At the following mealtime have fresh salad (without dressing) or homemade vegetable soup (no fat). Avoid pastries, biscuits, and starchy foods.
J. At first sensation of fullness stop eating.
K. To avoid pain and discomfort after a longer fast, Dr. Herbert Shelton (who has supervised over 30,000 healing fasts) advises that after the fast you discipline yourself and control your appetite and food intake.

10. *Have faith* that God will solve your problems. Realize that all things come from Him out of His love for us. "Ask, and you will receive," recommended the Man of Nazareth. "Seek, and you will find. Knock, and it will be opened to you. For the one who asks, receives. The one who seeks, finds. The one who knocks, enters" (Matt. 7:7–8). Jesus' words

assure you that the door is wide open to receive whatsoever you desire for yourself or your loved ones. Just lay before Him the needs of your soul and body, *believing that you have already received them.* Open your heart reverently and wholeheartedly, and He will bestow the richest blessing. "Would one of you hand his son a stone when he asks for a loaf, or a poisonous snake when he asks for a fish?" further taught Jesus. "If you, with all your sins, know how to give your children what is good, how much more will your Heavenly Father give good things to anyone who asks Him" (Matt. 7:9–11).

Your Father, the Ultimate Spring of Living Water, is longing to help you with your needs. Therefore, *be always alert and attuned to Him for inner guidance, direction and support.* But once you know what has to be done, you have to get up and do it. Suppose your house were in darkness, yet there is a power line directly outside. All you have to do is bring that electric line into your home. You have a choice: you can curse the darkness or you can link the Eternal Light into your life. However, if you assume that the purpose of prayer is only to get what you want in material things from God, then you may never rise far. There is a deeper purpose and meaning to prayer. Pray with humility for spiritual strength, help in avoiding sin, guidance, wisdom, understanding, and love. Pray for others, and hold them up into the light of God's presence.

"There is nothing that makes us love a man so much as praying for Him," confessed William Law. "By considering yourself as an advocate with God for your neighbors and acquaintances, you would never cease to be at peace with them yourself . . . such prayers as these amongst neighbors and acquaintances would unite them to one another in the strongest bonds of love and tenderness."

Pray for those who hate you; pray for those who persecute you. Pray, love, and serve men in utter selflessness. Be a channel through which God may act. We do not live alone, and we do not die alone. "We are members of one another" (Eph. 4:25); "I am the vine, you are the branches" (John 15:5), taught the Light of Life. *Everything we say or do has some influence on everyone in the human community.*

The best petition is not to reach out in your own way for what you don't understand completely but to leave yourself in the arms of your Father and *let His will be your will.* Let His law be your law. Let "not I, but Christ in me" be your motto. Remember, when Jesus prayed in the garden of Gethsemane, He asked to be relieved of the cross—"Abba [oh, Father], you have the power to do all things. Take this cup away from me. But *let it be as you would have it, not as I*" (Mark 14:36).

11. *Be still*, and listen to God within. If you were with a king or a president, would you be talking all the time? Would you be asking without stopping—especially if the ruler could read your mind and know your heart's desires before you opened your lips? "Your Father," said Jesus, "knows what you need before you ask Him" (Matt. 6:8). Having done your talking and petitioning, wait before Him in love, joy, adoration, and devotion, and listen to Him.

God speaks to your heart in silence. Silence means more than ceasing to speak with your lips; it means also practicing and *maintaining stillness in your mind* (when you turn within, leave the problem outside). Sometimes when you are praying, you may not speak at all with your lips, but your mind is boiling over with emotions and fears so that you cannot hear the "still small voice" of God within you.

Dom John Chapman captured the essence of silence when he stated that "you can't make silence—you can make noise. But you can only make silence by stopping the noise." The prophet Habakkuk testified: "But the Lord is in His holy temple: let all the earth keep silence before Him" (Hab. 2:20). We should not let our cries for our earthly needs disturb the inner peace of God's temple.

"A man does not see himself in running water," confirmed the sage Chuang Tzu, "but in still water." So, make the stillness your own. Turn your creative faculties into a receiving station and start listening not only with your ears but with your entire being to the still, small voice of God's whisper. As you listen and rest in His love you may come to feel as though the whole world were vibrating with the presence and love of God, with absolute peace and stillness and yet with an intense and ceaseless energy. *IN THIS STILLNESS YOU WILL LEARN WHO YOU REALLY ARE.* You will learn of love. You will learn of patience, humility, peace, joy, and life. You will learn of Him. This learning you have to do yourself. No book or teacher can tell you the feeling of quietness, clearness, stillness, love, or beauty. You have to experience it yourself. There is no other way. The teacher can show you the direction, but you have to throw your whole self into the journey. You have to "be still and know that I am God" (Ps. 46:11).

An unknown writer expressed: "Wait still upon God. Open your heart to Him, let the light and warmth of His love flood your mind and heart and soul as silently as the flower opens itself to, and drinks in, the light and warmth of the sun, and becomes itself truly beautiful, and thereby rest in the conscious thought of your living union with Christ."

The eleven points discussed above have one purpose: To help us achieve *union without ceasing*. Webster defines union as "an act of joining together, or a state of being united." What actually takes place, said Saint Teresa of Avila, is that "your soul becomes one with God." Saint Paul defined union in similar way: "Whoever is joined to the Lord becomes one spirit with Him" (1 Cor. 6:17). The great Indian (Hindu) philosopher Radhakrishnan elaborates further, "The oldest wisdom in the world tells us that we can consciously unite with the divine while in this body, for this is man really born. If he misses his destiny Nature is not in a hurry; she will catch him someday and compel him to fulfill her secret purpose.

We know that Our Father is within. He is also without. Just like all the TV and radio programs. To hear or see them we need a tuner. *That tuner to our Father is* purity (in thought, word, and deed), *stillness and love.*

Incidentally, if you are not perfectly aligned on your radio or TV dial you will also be getting noise. Your program will be disturbed. The same is true here. *Your mind has to be emptied of sensations, images, and thoughts.* You have to forget yourself. You have to concentrate on love of God, the Light within your soul, all universe and beyond. *Be still* and *love Him* with all your heart, *be still* and *love Him* with all your soul, *be still* and *love Him* with all your power, *be still* and *love Him* with all your mind (lose yourself in the Beloved) and nothing else.

In this loving embrace and bliss your spirit will be absorbed into Eternal Love. All will become One. Like one light merged in the ocean of Light. You will transcend the uttermost bounds of anticipation or desire. You will have reached a fountain of Holy Joy and Peace so overpowering that it transcends all other joys and passes all understanding. You will have returned to Your Father's heart. Similarly you may also concentrate on His will. Let the Father's will permeate all of you. Let Him make you complete. Let Him exhilarate you. Let Him make you One. In this splendor of joy you will notice that you as such have disappeared. Only His will, His love, His light, has remained.

Initially the state of rapturous union could be momentary, with exhilarating joy and exultation—later on of longer durations (lasting for hours) and extending even into sleep. And eventually you could establish a permanent conscious (living) union with God. The impact of each experience is most overpowering. It "penetrates to the very marrow of your bones," testified Saint Teresa. "Your senses could be fused into one ineffable act of perception. Differences between time, space, and motion will cease to exist. You will understand the profound truth that there is only God, the I Am Who Am" (Ex. 3:14), that "The Father and I are one" (John 10:30), that "I am in the Father and the Father is in me" (John 14:11), that "the life I live now is not my own; Christ is living in me" (Gal. 2:20), that "My Me is God, nor do I recognize any other Me except my God Himself" (Saint Catherine of Genoa), that "whoever has seen me has seen the Father" (John 14:9).

You might find yourself in the center of stillness and living glow so pronounced that the distinction between you and your surroundings will disappear. You will see that you and the rest of the surroundings are one and the same light and stillness, one and the same joy of shimmering conscious glory and love. You will be moving, sitting, and working in it. It is a fantastic and indescribable splendor of delightful stillness and peace. The mind thinks—but for some reason all of you ceases to exist as a separate entity but becomes a part of one infinite Light and Love. You might dive into an ocean of knowledge (truth, basic concepts of science, works of art, inventions) where all that was obscured is now explained, where all problems are solved, and all that is or will be knowable is known. All knowledge of that which is above all reason and beyond all thought is nearer to you than you are to yourself. You have tuned in to Your Father's heart.

"This is the way," said the voice of God to Saint Catherine of Siena. "If you will arrive at a perfect knowledge and enjoyment of Me, the Eternal Truth, you should never go outside the knowledge of yourself; and by humbling yourself in the valley of humility you will know Me and yourself, from which knowledge you will draw all that is necessary."

Saint Teresa of Avila, who drank God's wine of union, similarly related: "There will suddenly come to it (soul) a suspension in which the

Lord communicates most secret things, which it seems to see within God Himself.... The brilliance of this vision is like that of infused light or of a sun covered with some material of the transparency of a diamond.... For as long as such a soul is in this state, it can neither see nor hear nor understand: the period is always short and seems to the soul even shorter than it really is. God implants Himself in the interior of that soul in such a way that, when it returns to itself, it cannot possibly doubt that God has been in it and it has been in God; so firmly does this truth remain within it that, although for years God may never grant it that favor again, it can neither forget it nor doubt that it has received it."

Saint Catherine of Genoa, who was one of the most penetrating gazers into the secrets of Eternal Light, stated: "When the loving kindness of God calls a soul from the world, He finds it full of vices and sins; and first He gives it an instinct for virtue, and then urges it to perfection, and then by infused grace leads it to true self-naughting, and at last to true transformation. And this noteworthy order serves God to lead the soul along the Way; but when the soul is naughted and transformed, then of herself she neither works nor speaks nor wills, nor feels nor hears nor understands, neither has she of herself the feeling of outward or inward, where she may move. And in all things it is God who rules and guides her, without the mediation of any creature. And the state of this soul is then a feeling of such utter peace and tranquility that it seems to her that her heart, and her bodily being, and all both within and without is immersed in an ocean of utmost peace; from when she shall never come forth for anything that can befall her in this life. And she stays immovable, imperturbable, impassable. So much so, that it seems to her in her human and her spiritual nature, both within and without, she can feel no other thing than sweetest peace. And she is so full of peace that though she press her flesh, her nerves, her bones, no other thing comes forth from them than peace."

Having immersed yourself in Perfect Love for a new life and a new purpose, you can't stop here. You have to go on. You have to bring forth your fruits in good deeds. You have to serve others. You have to *treat every person as you would treat Jesus* (see Him in every heart and every face. For He said it Himself and we shall hear it again in a day of judgment: "I assure you, as often as you did it for one of my least brothers, you did it for me" (Matt. 25:40). Say nothing, do nothing, think nothing that is not love-directed. If what you do, be it in thought, word or deed does not create love, don't do it. Remember, you are not just rendering it to a mortal man but unto God who is within that man.

A note of caution: As you are journeying onward and upward to God (growing in goodness and love), you may come upon many "wine cellars," "fireworks," and "beautiful scenery" full of surprises. As the Bible shows (1 Cor. 12:9, 10; 2 Cor. 12:1), these by-products could exhibit themselves in many forms:

1. You may speak or interpret tongues.
2. You may experience "visions and revelations," "prophecy," and have the "power to distinguish one spirit from another."
3. You may acquire a new kind of perception where the whole cosmic panorama may appear magnified and full of light and grandeur.
4. Your body sweat may emanate perfume-like fragrance.
5. You may acquire the "healing" touch.
6. You may exhibit bilocation (go to distant places with your body instantaneously—(John 20:26–9; Acts 8:39–40). This is possible because as you concentrate on God, His forces dematerialize the body. It becomes less solid and more flexible (your body frequencies increase) and therefore can be more easily acted on by your thought. For additional reading, read about people who had this quality: Saint Ignatius, Saint Clement, Saint Francis of Assisi, Saint Anthony of Padua, Saint Francis Xavier, Joseph Cupertino, Saint Martin de Porres, Saint Alphonsus Liguori, Padre Pio.

These and similar diversions may so overpower you that you will become arrested at this level of growth. True, the dramatic phenomenon is fascinating, but it should *never* become for you the circumference of your horizon. Similarly it is highly dangerous to one's soul and health to seek gifts of this nature for their own sake or for personal enhancement. Let the scenery be there (use it in a constructive way), *but keep in mind your destination is the living union with Your Heavenly Father* and nothing less.

And at the union you have to arrive not by expending consciousness with drugs, chemicals, and hallucinogens, but through the way of Jesus. With drugs and chemicals you are not improving yourself, you are drowning yourself. You are letting yourself be possessed by saboteur and insidious spirit entities, with results that are far worse after the trip than before the trip.

Listen to what the Son of Man had to say about this: "I tell you the truth: whoever does not enter the sheepfold by the door, but climbs in some other way, is a thief and a marauder. To get there," said He, "I am the door. Whoever enters through me will be safe. He will go in and out and find pasture" (John 10:9). Similarly Jesus reproached the Pharisees, most of who were ignorant of union yet deliberately obstructed the helpless masses: "Woe to you lawyers! You have taken away the key of knowledge. You yourselves have not gained access, yet you have stopped those who wish to enter!" (Luke 11:52) The key to union you will find only through crucifying your self-love and self-will. Jesus demonstrated this with His death on the cross and demanded that we do the same: "Whoever wishes to be my follower must *deny his very self,* take up his cross each day" (not the cross of suffering, but the self-crucifixion), and "and follow in my steps" (Luke 9:23).

True, the lower self doesn't want to die, it wants to live; it wants Father to take that cup away, but your conscious self knows that "for he who wishes to save his life must lose it," he must destroy the lower self so that it will not be the deciding guide, but the higher will, the Father's will, will be the way.

You have to consciously live in God's presence, a life of Jesus Christ (make iron determination to be pure within), a life of "be perfect just as your Father in heaven is perfect" (perfect in love), continuously a life of *love in action* (love everything because it needs love like you; your Father has programmed "the branches" that way, so "that all may be one . . . as we are one") . . . one day at a time—now. The reward of this type of life is union without ceasing, where Eternal Love and you will be One, where heaven and all glory will exist here and now, where the state of joy, splendor, bliss, tranquility, and overpowering peace will be with you every moment, where with tears in your eyes, you the Prodigal Son will be embraced by your Beloved Father on your welcome home, where with a might of Christ you will proclaim: "Eli, Eli, Imana shabachthani! . . . My God, My God, this was my destiny. I was born for this."

Then you will know this chapter "is finished." Now a new chapter of Resurrection, Light and Unity is upon you.

I LOVE YOU!

BASIC SOURCES

Biblical references in italics are from the *New American Bible;* others are from *Good News for Modern Man.*—Editor

The New American Bible, © 1970 by Confraternity of Christian Doctrine
 (The Catholic Press, Washington D.C.)
Good News for Modern Man
Today's Version of the New Testament, © 1966, 1971, American Bible Society

THE LORD'S PRAYER

Our Father, which art in heaven, Hallowed be thy name. Thy kingdom come.
Thy will be done, on earth as it is in heaven. Give us this day our daily bread.
And forgive us our trespasses, as we forgive them that trespass against us. And
lead us not into temptation; but deliver us from evil: For thine is the kingdom,
the power, and the glory, for ever and ever.

Amen.

Emmet Fox

The Lord's Prayer is a distillation of all Christian theology.
Here, Dr. Emmet Fox examines this concise vehicle for progress
through the whole of spiritual life.

Dr. Fox was one of the outstanding spiritual teachers of
our times. While he lived, he addressed some of the largest
audiences ever gathered to hear his on the religious meaning
of life. He published extensively, and some of his best-known
works are *The Sermon on the Mount*, *The Ten Commandments*,
Alter Your Life, *Power through Constructive Thinking*, *Make Your
Life Worth-while*, and *Find and Use Your Inner Power*.

The Lord's Prayer is the most important of all the Christian documents. It
was carefully constructed by Jesus with certain, very clear ends in view. That
is why, of all His teachings, it is by far the best known and the most often

quoted. It is, indeed, the one common denominator of all the Christian churches. Every one of them, without exception, uses the Lord's Prayer; it is perhaps the only ground upon which they all meet. Every Christian child is taught the Lord's Prayer, and any Christian who prays at all says it almost every day. Its actual use probably exceeds that of all other prayers put together. Undoubtedly, everyone who is seeking to follow along the way that Jesus led should make a point of using the Lord's Prayer and using it intelligently every day.

In order to do this, we should understand that the prayer is a carefully constructed organic whole. Many people rattle through it like parrots, forgetful of the warning that Jesus gave us against vain repetitions, and, of course, no one derives any profit from that sort of thing.

The Great Prayer is a compact formula for the development of the soul. It is designed with the utmost care for that specific purpose; so that those who use it regularly, with understanding, will experience a real change of soul. The only progress is this change, which is what the Bible calls being born again. It is the change of soul that matters. The mere acquisition of fresh knowledge received intellectually makes no change in the soul. The Lord's Prayer is especially designed to bring this change about, and when it is regularly used it invariably does so.

The more one analyzes the Lord's Prayer, the more wonderful is its construction seen to be. It meets everyone's need just at his own level. It not only provides a rapid spiritual development for those who are sufficiently advanced to be ready, but in its superficial meaning it supplies the more simple-minded and even the more materially minded people with just what they need at the moment, if they use the prayer sincerely.

This greatest of all prayers was designed with still another purpose in view, quite as important as either of the others. Jesus foresaw that, as the centuries went by, His simple, primitive teaching would gradually become overlaid by all sorts of external things that really have nothing whatsoever to do with it. He foresaw that men who had never known Him, relying, quite sincerely, no doubt, upon their own limited intellects, would build up theologies and doctrinal systems, obscuring the direct simplicity of the spiritual message, and actually erecting a wall between God and man. He designed His prayer in such a way that it would pass safely through those ages without being tampered with. He arranged it with consummate skill, so that it could not be twisted or distorted, or adapted to any man-made system; so that, in fact, it would carry the whole "Christ message" within it and yet not have anything on the surface to attract the attention of the restless, managing type of person. So it has turned out that, through all the changes and chances of Christian history, this prayer has come through to us uncorrupted and unspoiled.

The first thing that we notice is that the prayer naturally falls into seven clauses. This is very characteristic of the Oriental tradition. Seven symbolizes individual completeness, the perfection of the individual soul, just as the number twelve in the same convention stands for corporate completeness. In practical use, we often find an eighth clause added— "Thine is the kingdom, the power, and the glory"—but this, though in itself an excellent affirmation, is not really a part of the prayer. The seven clauses are put together with the utmost care, in perfect order and sequence, and they contain everything that is necessary for the nourishment of the soul. Let us consider the first clause:

Our Father

This simple statement in itself constitutes a definite and complete system of theology. It fixes clearly and distinctly the nature and character of God. It sums up the Truth of Being. It tells all that man needs to know about God, and about himself, and about his neighbor. Anything that is added to this can only be by way of commentary, and is more likely than not to complicate and obscure the true meaning of the text. Oliver Wendell Holmes said: "My religion is summed up in the first two words of the Lord's Prayer," and most of us will find ourselves in full agreement with Him.

Notice the simple, clear-cut, definite statement—"Our Father." In this clause Jesus lays down once and for all that the relationship between God and man is that of father and child. This cuts out any possibility that the Deity could be the relentless and cruel tyrant that is often pictured by theology. Jesus says definitely that the relationship is that of parent and child; not a despot dealing with groveling slaves, but parent and child. Now we all know perfectly well that men and women, however short they may fall in other respects, nearly always do the best they can for their children. Unfortunately, cruel and wicked parents are to be found, but they are so exceptional as to make a paragraph for the newspapers. The vast majority of men and women are at their best in dealing with their children. Speaking of the same truth elsewhere, Jesus said: "If you, who are so full of evil, nevertheless do your best for your children, how much more will God, who is altogether good, do for you;" and so He begins His prayer by establishing the character of God as that of the perfect Father dealing with His children.

Note that this clause, which fixes the nature of God, at the same time fixes the nature of man, because if man is the offspring of God, he must partake of the nature of God, since the nature of the offspring is invariably similar to that of the parent. It is a cosmic law that like begets like. It is not possible that a rosebush should produce lilies or that a cow should give birth to a colt. The offspring is and must be of the same nature as the parent; and so, since God is Divine Spirit, man must essentially be Divine Spirit too, whatever appearances may say to the contrary.

Let us pause here for a moment and try to realize what a tremendous step forward we have taken in appreciating the teaching of Jesus on this point. Do you not see that at a single blow it swept away 99 percent of all the old theology, with its avenging God, its chosen and favored individuals, its eternal hellfire, and all the other horrible paraphernalia of man's diseased and terrified imagination. God exists—and the eternal, all-powerful, all-present God is the loving father of mankind.

If you would meditate upon this fact until you had some degree of understanding of what it really means, most of your difficulties and physical ailments would disappear, for they are rooted and grounded in fear. The underlying cause of all trouble is fear. If only you could realize to some extent that Omnipotent Wisdom is your living, loving Father, most of your fears would go. If you could realize it completely, every negative thing in your life would vanish away, and you would demonstrate perfection in every phase. Now you see the object that Jesus had in mind when He placed this clause first.

Next we see that the prayer says not "My Father" but "Our Father," and this indicates, beyond the possibility of mistake, the truth of the brotherhood of man. It forces upon our attention at the very beginning the fact that all men are indeed brethren, the children of One Father; and that "there is neither Jew nor Greek, there is neither bond nor free, there is neither chosen nor unchosen" because all men are brethren (Gal. 3:28). Here Jesus, in making His second point, ends all the tiresome nonsense about a "chosen race," about the spiritual superiority of any one group of human beings over any other group. He cuts away the illusion that the members of any nation, or race, or territory, or group, or class, or color, are, in the sight of God, superior to any other group. A belief in the superiority of one's own particular group, or "herd," as the psychologists call it, is an illusion to which mankind is very prone, but in the teaching of Jesus it has no place. He teaches that the thing that places a man is the spiritual condition of his own individual soul, and that as long as he is upon the spiritual path it makes no difference whatever to what group he belongs or does not belong.

The final point is the implied command that we are to pray not only for ourselves but also for all mankind. Every student of truth should hold the thought of the "truth of being" for the whole human race for at least a moment each day, since none of us lives to himself nor dies to himself; for indeed we are all truly—and in a much more literal sense than people are aware—limbs of one body.

Now we begin to see how very much more than appears on the surface is contained in those simple words "Our Father." Simple—one might almost say innocent—as they look, Jesus has concealed within them a spiritual explosive that will ultimately destroy every man-made system that holds the human race in bondage.

Which art in heaven

Having clearly established the fatherhood of God and the brotherhood of man, Jesus next goes on to enlarge upon the nature of God, and to describe the fundamental facts of existence. Having shown that God and man are parent and child, he goes on to delineate the function of each in the grand scheme of things. He explains that it is the nature of God to be in heaven, and of man to be on earth, because God is Cause, and man is manifestation. Cause cannot be expression, and expression cannot be cause, and we must be careful not to confuse the two things. Here heaven stands for God or Cause, because in religious phraseology heaven is the term for the presence of God. In metaphysics it is called the "absolute," because it is the realm of pure unconditioned being, of archetypal ideas. The word "earth" means manifestation, and man's function is to manifest or express God, or Cause. In other words, God is the Infinite and Perfect Cause of all things; but Cause has to be expressed, and God expresses Himself by means of man. Man's destiny is to express God in all sorts of glorious and wonderful ways. Some of this expression we see as his surroundings; first his physical body, which is really only the most intimate part of his embodiment; then his home; his work; his recreation—in short, his whole expression. To express means to press outward, or bring into sight that which already exists implicitly. Every feature of your life is really a manifestation or expression of something in your soul.

Some of these points may seem at first to be a little abstract; but since it is misunderstandings about the relationship of God and man that lead to all our difficulties, it is worth any amount of trouble to understand correctly that relationship. Trying to have manifestation without Cause is atheism and materialism, and we know where they lead. Trying to have Cause without manifestation leads man to suppose himself to be a personal God, and this commonly ends in megalomania and a kind of paralysis of expression.

The important thing to realize is that God is in heaven and man is on earth and that each has his own role in the scheme of things. Although they are One, they are not one-and-the-same. Jesus establishes this point carefully when He says, "Our Father which art in heaven."

Hallowed be thy name

In the Bible, as elsewhere, the "name" of anything means the essential nature or character of that thing, and so, when we are told what the name of God is, we are told what His nature is, and His name or nature, Jesus says, is "hallowed." Now, what does the word "hallowed" mean? Well, if you trace the derivation back into Old English, you will discover a most extraordinarily interesting and significant fact. The word "hallowed" has the same meaning as "holy," "whole," "wholesome," and "heal," or "healed;" so we see that the nature of God is not merely worthy of our veneration, but is complete and perfect—altogether good. Some very remarkable consequences follow from this. We have agreed that an effect must be similar in its nature to its cause, and so, because the nature of God is hallowed, everything that follows from that Cause must be hallowed or perfect, too. Just as a rosebush cannot produce lilies, so God cannot cause or send anything but perfect good. As the Bible says, "the same fountain cannot send forth both sweet and bitter water." From this it follows that God cannot, as people sometimes think, send sickness or trouble or accidents—much less death—for these things are unlike His nature. "Hallowed be thy name" means "Thy nature is altogether good, and thou art the author only of perfect good." Of purer eyes than to behold evil, and canst not look on iniquity.

If you think that God has sent any of your difficulties to you, for no matter how good a reason, you are giving power to your troubles, and this makes it very difficult to get rid of them.

Thy kingdom come;
Thy will be done, on earth as it is in heaven

Man, being manifestation or expression of God, has a limitless destiny before Him. His work is to express, in concrete, definite form, the abstract ideas with which God furnishes Him; and in order to do this, he must have creative power. If he did not have creative power, he would be merely a machine through which God worked—an automaton. But man is not an automaton; he is an individualized consciousness. God individualizes Himself in an infinite number of distinct focal points of consciousness, each one quite different; and therefore each one is a distinct way of knowing the universe, each a distinct experience. Notice carefully that the word "individual" means undivided. The consciousness of each one is distinct from God and from all others, and yet none are separated. How can this be? How can two things be one, and yet not one and the same? The answer is that in matter, which is finite, they cannot; but in spirit, which is infinite, they can. With our present limited, three-dimensional consciousness, we cannot see this; but intuitively we can understand it through prayer. If God did not individualize Himself, there would be only one experience; as it is, there are as many universes as there are individuals to form them through thinking.

"Thy kingdom come" means that it is our duty to be ever occupied in helping to establish the kingdom of God on earth. That is to say, our work is to bring more and more of God's ideas into concrete manifestation upon this plane. That is what we are here for. The old saying "God has a plan for every man, and He has one for you" is quite correct. God has glorious and wonderful plans for every one of us; He has planned a splendid career, full of interest, life, and joy, for each, and if our lives are dull, or restricted, or squalid, that is not His fault, but ours.

If only you will find out the thing God intends you to do, and will do it, you will find that all doors will open to you; all obstacles in your path will melt away; you will be acclaimed a brilliant success; you will be most liberally rewarded from the monetary point of view; and you will be gloriously happy.

There is a true place in life for each one of us, upon the attainment of which we shall be completely happy and perfectly secure. On the other hand, until we do find our true place we never shall be either happy or secure, no matter what other things we may have. Our true place is the one place where we can bring the kingdom of God into manifestation, and truly say, "Thy kingdom cometh."

We have seen that man too often chooses to use his free will in a negative way. He allows himself to think wrongly, selfishly, and this wrong thinking brings upon him all his troubles. Instead of understanding that it is his essential nature to express God, to be ever about his Father's business, he tries to set up upon his own account. All our troubles arise from just this folly. We abuse our free will, trying to work apart from God; and the very natural result is all the sickness, poverty, sin, trouble, and death that we find on the physical plane.

We must never for a moment try to live for ourselves, or make plans or arrangements without reference to God, or suppose that we can be either happy or successful if we are seeking any other end than to do His will. Whatever our desire may be, whether it be something concerning our daily work, or our duty at home, our relations with our fellow man, or private plans for the employment of our own time, if we seek to serve self instead of God, we are ordering trouble, disappointment, and unhappiness, notwithstanding what the evidence to the contrary may seem to be. Whereas, if we choose what, through prayer, we know to be God's will, we are insuring for ourselves ultimate success, freedom, and joy, however much self-sacrifice and self-discipline it may involve at the moment.

Our business is to bring our whole nature as fast as we can into conformity with the will of God, by constant prayer and unceasing—though unanxious—watching. "Our wills are ours to make them thine."

"In His Will is our peace," said Dante. And the *Divine Comedy* is really a study in fundamental states of consciousness, the inferno representing the state of the soul that is endeavoring to live without God, the paradiso representing the state of the soul that has achieved its conscious unity with the divine will, and the purgatorio the condition of the soul that is struggling to pass from the one state to the other. It was this sublime conflict of the soul which wrung from the heart of the great Augustine the cry "Thou hast made us for Thyself, and our hearts are restless until they repose in Thee."

Give us this day our daily bread

Because we are the children of a loving Father, we are entitled to expect that God will provide us fully with everything we need. Children naturally and spontaneously look to their human parents to supply all their wants, and in the same way we should look to God to supply ours. If we do so, in faith and understanding, we shall never look in vain.

It is the will of God that we should all lead healthy, happy lives, full of joyous experience; that we should develop freely and steadily, day by day and week by week, as our pathways unfold more and more unto the perfect day. To this end we require such things as food, clothing, shelter, means of travel, books, and so on; above all, we require freedom; and in the prayer all these things are included under the heading of bread. Bread, that is to say, means not merely food in general, but all things that man requires for a healthy, happy, free, and harmonious life. But in order to obtain these things, we have to claim them—not necessarily in detail—but we have to claim them, and we have to recognize God and God alone as the source and fountainhead of all our good. Lack of any kind is always traceable to the fact that we have been seeking our supply from some secondary source, instead of from God Himself, the author and giver of life.

People think of their supply as coming from certain investments, or from a business, or from an employer, perhaps; but these are merely the channels through which that supply comes—God being the source. The number of possible channels is infinite, the Source is one. The particular channel through which you are getting your supply is quite likely to change, because change is the cosmic law for manifestation. Stagnation is really death; but as long as you realize that the Source of your supply is the one unchangeable Spirit, all is well. The fading out of one channel will be but the signal for the opening of another. If, on the other hand, like most people, you regard the particular channel as being the source, then when that channel fails, as it is very likely to do, you are left stranded, because you believe that the source has dried up—and for practical purposes, on the physical plane, things are as we believe them to be.

Consider, for instance, a man who thinks of his employment as the source of his income, and for some reason he loses it. His employer goes out of business, or cuts down the staff, or they have a falling out. Now, because he believes that his position is the source of his income, the loss of the position naturally means the loss of the income, and so he has to start looking about for another job, and perhaps he has to look a long time, meanwhile finding himself without apparent supply. If such a man had realized, through regular daily treatment, that God was his supply, and his job only the particular channel through which it came, then upon the closing of that channel he would have found another, and probably a better, opening immediately. If his belief had been in God as his supply, then since God cannot change or fail or fade out, his supply would have come from somewhere and would have formed its own channel in whatever was the easiest way.

In precisely the same way the proprietor of a business may find himself obliged to close down for some cause outside of his control; or one whose income is dependent upon stocks or bonds may suddenly find that source dried up, owing to unexpected happenings on the stock market, or to some catastrophe to a factory or a mine. If he regards the business or the investment as his source of supply, he will believe his source to have collapsed, and will in consequence be left stranded; whereas, if his reliance is upon God, he will be comparatively indifferent to the channel and so that channel will be easily supplanted by a new one. In short, we have to train ourselves to look to God, Cause, for all that we need; and then the channel, which is entirely a secondary matter, will take care of itself.

In its inner and most important meaning, "our daily bread" signifies the realization of the Presence of God—an actual sense that God exists not merely in a nominal way, but as the great reality; the sense that he is present with us; and the feeling that because He is God—all-good, all-powerful, all-wise, and all-loving—we have nothing to fear; that we can rely upon Him to take every care of us; that He will supply all that we need to have; teach us all that we need to know; and guide our steps so that we shall not make mistakes. This is Emanuel, or "God with us;" and remember that it absolutely means some degree of actual realization—that is to say, some experience in consciousness, and not just a theoretical recognition of the fact; not simply talking about God, however beautifully one may talk, or thinking about Him—but some degree of actual experience.

We must begin by thinking about God, but this should lead to the realization, which is the daily bread or manna. That is the gist of the whole matter. Realization, which is experience, is the thing that counts. It is realization that marks the progress of the soul. It is realization that guarantees the demonstration. It is realization, as distinct from mere theorizing and fine words, which is the substance of things hoped for, the evidence of things not seen. This is the Bread of Life, the hidden manna; and when one has that, he has all things in deed and in truth. Jesus several times refers to this experience as bread because it is the nourishment of the soul, just as physical food is the nourishment of the physical body. Supplied with this food, the soul grows and waxes strong, gradually developing to adult stature. Without it, she, being deprived of the essential nourishment, is naturally stunted and crippled.

The common mistake, of course, is to suppose that a formal recognition of God is sufficient, or that talking about divine things, perhaps talking very poetically, is the same as possessing them; but this is exactly on a par with supposing that looking at a tray of food, or discussing the chemical composition of sundry foodstuffs, is the same thing as actually eating a meal. It is this mistake that is responsible for the fact that people sometimes pray for a thing for years without any tangible result. If prayer is a force at all, it cannot be possible to pray without something happening.

A realization cannot be obtained to order; it must come spontaneously as the result of regular daily prayer. To seek realization by willpower is the surest way to miss it. Pray regularly and quietly—remember that in all mental work, effort or strain defeats itself—then presently, perhaps when you least expect it, like a thief in the night, the realization will come. Meanwhile it is well to know that all sorts of practical difficulties can be overcome by sincere prayer without any realization at all. Good workers have said that they have had some of their best demonstrations without any realization worth speaking about; but while it is, of course, a wonderful boon to surmount such particular difficulties, we do not achieve the sense of security and well-being to which we are entitled until we have experienced realization.

Another reason why the food or bread symbol for the experience of the presence of God is such a telling one is that the act of eating food is essentially a thing that must be done for oneself. No one can assimilate food for another. One may hire servants to do all sorts of other things for Him; but there is one thing that one must positively do for himself, and that is to eat his own food. In the same way, the realization of the presence of God is a thing that no one else can have for us. We can and should help one another in the overcoming of specific difficulties—"bear ye one another's burdens"—but the realization (or making real) of the presence of God, the "substance" and "evidence," can, in the nature of things, be had only at first hand.

In speaking of the "bread of life, Emanuel," Jesus calls it our daily bread. The reason for this is very fundamental—our contact with God must be a living one. It is our momentary attitude to God that governs our being. "Behold now is the accepted time; behold now is the day of salvation." The most futile thing in the world is to seek to live upon a past realization. The thing that means spiritual life to you is your realization of God here and now.

Today's realization, no matter how feeble and poor it may seem, has a million times more power to help you than the most vivid realization of yesterday. Be thankful for yesterday's experience, knowing that it is with you forever in the change of consciousness that it brought about, but do not lean upon it for a single moment for the need of today. Divine Spirit is and changes not with the ebb and flow of human apprehension.

The manna in the desert is the Old Testament prototype of this. The people wandering in the wilderness were told that they would be supplied with manna from heaven every day, each one always receiving abundant for his needs, but they were on no account to try to save it up for the morrow. They were on no account to endeavor to live upon yesterday's food, and when, notwithstanding the rule, some of them did try to do so, the result was pestilence or death.

So it is with us. When we seek to live upon yesterday's realization, we are actually seeking to live in the past, and to live in the past is death. The art of life is to live in the present moment and to make that moment as perfect as we can by the realization that we are the instruments and expression of God Himself. The best way to prepare for tomorrow is to make today all that it should be.

Forgive us our trespasses, as we forgive them that trespass against us

This clause is the turning point of the prayer. It is the strategic key to the whole treatment. Let us notice here that Jesus has so arranged this marvelous prayer that it covers the entire ground of the unfoldment of our souls completely and in the most concise and telling way. It omits nothing that is essential for our salvation, and yet so compact is it that there is not a thought or a word too much. Every idea fits into its place with perfect harmony and in perfect sequence. Anything more would be redundant; anything less would be incomplete, and at this point the prayer takes up the critical factor of forgiveness.

Having told us what God is, what man is, how the universe works, how we are to do our own work—the salvation of humanity and of our own souls—Jesus then explains what our true nourishment or supply is, and the way in which we can obtain it; and now He comes to the forgiveness of sins.

The forgiveness of sins is the central problem of life. Sin is a sense of separation from God and is the major tragedy of human experience. It is, of course, rooted in selfishness. It is essentially an attempt to gain some supposed good to which we are not entitled in justice. It is a sense of isolated, self-regarding, personal existence, whereas the "truth of being" is that all is one. Our true selves are at one with God, undivided from Him, expressing His ideas, witnessing to His nature—the dynamic thinking of that mind. Because we are all one with the great Whole of which we are spiritually a part, it follows that we are one with all men. Just because in Him we live and move and have our being, we are, in the absolute sense, all essentially one.

Evil, sin, and the fall of man, in fact, are essentially the attempt to negate this truth in our thoughts. We try to live apart from God. We try to do without Him. We act as though we had life of our own; as separate minds; as though we could have plans and purposes and interests separate from His. All this, if it were true, would mean that existence is not one and harmonious, but a chaos of competition and strife. It would mean that we are quite separate from our fellow man and could injure him, rob him, hurt him, or even destroy him, without any damage to ourselves, and, in fact, that the more we took from other people the more we should have for ourselves.

It would mean that the more we considered our own interests, and the more indifferent we were to the welfare of others, the better off we should be. Of course it would then follow naturally that it would pay others to treat us in the same way, and that accordingly we might expect many of them to do so. Now, if this were true, it would mean that the whole universe is only a jungle, and that sooner or later it must destroy itself by its own inherent weakness and anarchy. But, of course, it is not true, and therein lies the joy of life.

Undoubtedly, many people do act as though they believe it to be true, and a great many more, who would be dreadfully shocked if brought face to face with that proposition in cold blood, have, nevertheless, a vague feeling that such must be very much the way things are, even though they, themselves, are personally above consciously acting in accordance with such a notion. Now this is the real basis of sin, of resentment, of condemnation, of jealousy, of remorse, and all the evil brood that walk that path.

This belief in independent and separate existence is the arch sin, and now, before we can progress any further, we have to take the knife to this evil thing and cut it out once and for all. Jesus knew this, and with this definite end in view He inserted at this critical point a carefully prepared statement that would compass our end and his, without the shadow of a possibility of miscarrying. He inserted what is nothing less than a trip clause. He drafted a declaration that would force us, without any conceivable possibility of escape, evasion, mental reservation, or subterfuge of any kind, to execute the great sacrament of forgiveness in all its fullness and far-reaching power.

As we repeat the Great Prayer intelligently, considering and meaning what we say, we are suddenly, so to speak, caught off our feet and grasped as though in a vise, so that we must face this problem—and there is no escape. We must positively and definitely extend forgiveness to everyone whom it is possible that we can owe forgiveness; namely, to anyone who we think can have injured us in any way. Jesus leaves no room for any possible glossing of this fundamental thing. He has constructed His prayer with more skill than ever yet lawyer displayed in the casting of a deed. He has so contrived it that once our attention has been drawn to this matter, we are inevitably obliged either to forgive our enemies in sincerity and truth or never again to repeat that prayer. It is safe to say that no one who reads this essay with understanding will ever again be able to use the Lord's Prayer unless and until he has forgiven. Should you now attempt to repeat it without forgiving, it can safely be predicted that you will not be able to finish it. This great central clause will stick in your throat.

Notice that Jesus does not say, "Forgive me my trespasses and I will try to forgive others," or "I will see if it can be done," or "I will forgive generally, with certain exceptions." He obliges us to declare that we have actually forgiven, and forgiven all, and He makes our claim to our own forgiveness to depend upon that. Who is there who has grace enough to say His prayers at all, who does not long for the forgiveness or cancellation of his own mistakes and faults. Who would be so insane as to endeavor to seek the kingdom of God without desiring to be relieved of his own sense of guilt? No one, we may believe. And so we see that we are trapped in the inescapable position that we cannot demand our own release before we have released our brother.

The forgiveness of others is the vestibule of heaven, and Jesus knew it and has led us to the door. You must forgive everyone who has ever hurt you if you want to be forgiven yourself; that is the long and the short of it. You have to get rid of all resentment and condemnation of others, and, not least, of self-condemnation and remorse. You have to forgive others, and having discontinued your own mistakes, you have to accept the forgiveness of God for them, too, or you cannot make any progress. You have to forgive yourself, but you cannot forgive yourself sincerely until you have forgiven others first. Having forgiven others, you must be prepared to forgive yourself too, for to refuse to forgive oneself is only spiritual pride. "And by that sin fell the angels." We cannot make this point too clear to ourselves; we must forgive. There are few people in the world who have not at some time or other been hurt, really hurt, by someone else; or been disappointed, or injured, or deceived, or misled. Such things sink into the memory where they usually cause inflamed and festering wounds, and there is only one remedy—they have to be plucked out and thrown away. And the one and only way to do that is by forgiveness.

Of course, nothing in the world is easier than to forgive people who have not hurt us very much. Nothing is easier than to rise above the thought of a trifling loss. Anybody will be willing to do this, but what the Law of Being requires of us is that we forgive not only these trifles, but also the very things that are so hard to forgive that at first it seems impossible to do it at all. The despairing heart cries, "It is too much to ask. That thing meant too much to me. It is impossible. I cannot forgive it." But the Lord's Prayer makes our own forgiveness from God, which means our escape from guilt and limitation, dependent upon just this very thing. There is no escape from this, and so forgiveness there must be, no matter how deeply we may have been injured or how terribly we have suffered. It must be done.

If your prayers are not being answered, search your consciousness and see whether there is not someone whom you have yet to forgive. Find out whether there is not some old thing about which you are very resentful. Search and see whether you are not really holding a grudge (it may be camouflaged in some self-righteous way) against some individual, or some body of people, a nation, a race, a social class, some religious movement of which you disapprove, perhaps a political party or whatnot. If you are doing so, then you have an act of forgiveness to perform; and when this is done, you will probably make your demonstration. If you cannot forgive at present, you will have to wait for your demonstration until you can, and you will have to postpone finishing your recital of the Lord's Prayer, too, or involve yourself in the position that you do not desire the forgiveness of God.

Setting others free means setting yourself free, because resentment is really a form of attachment. It is a cosmic truth that it takes two to make a prisoner: the prisoner and a gaoler. There is no such thing as being a prisoner on one's own account. Every prisoner must have a gaoler, and the gaoler is as much a prisoner as his charge. When you hold resentment against anyone, you are bound to that person by a cosmic link, a real, though mental chain. You are tied by a cosmic tie to the thing that you hate. The one person perhaps in the whole world whom you most dislike is the very one to whom you are attaching yourself by a hook that is stronger than steel.

Is this what you wish? Is this the condition in which you desire to go on living? Remember, you belong to the thing with which you are linked in thought, and at some time or other, if that tie endures, the object of your resentment will be drawn again into your life, perhaps to work further havoc. Do you think that you can afford this? Of course, no one can afford such a thing; and so the way is clear. You must cut all such ties by a clear and spiritual act of forgiveness. You must loose him and let him go. By forgiveness you set yourself free; you save your soul. And because the law of love works alike for one and all, you help to save his soul, too, making it just so much easier for him to become what he ought to be.

But how, in the name of all that is wise and good, is the magic act of forgiveness to be accomplished when we have been so deeply injured that, though we have long wished with all our hearts that we could forgive, we have nevertheless found it impossible; when we have tried and tried to forgive but have found the task beyond us?

The technique of forgiveness is simple enough and not very difficult to manage when you understand how to do it. The only thing that is essential is willingness to forgive. Provided you desire to forgive the offender, the greater part of the work is already done. People have always made such a bogey of forgiveness because they have been under the erroneous impression that to forgive a person means that you have to compel yourself to like him. Happily this is by no means the case—we are not called upon to like anyone whom we do not find ourselves liking spontaneously, and, indeed, it is quite impossible to like people to order. You can no more like to order than you can hold the winds in your fist, and if you endeavor to coerce yourself into doing so, you will finish by disliking or hating the offender more than ever. People used to think that when someone had hurt them very much, it was their duty as good Christians to pump up, as it were, a feeling of liking for him; and since such a thing is utterly impossible, they suffered a great deal of distress, and ended, necessarily, with failure and a resulting sense of sinfulness. We are not obliged to like anyone; but we are under a binding obligation to love everyone, love, or charity as the Bible calls it, meaning a vivid sense of impersonal goodwill. This has nothing directly to do with the feelings, though it is always followed, sooner or later, by a wonderful feeling of peace and happiness.

The method of forgiving is this: Get by yourself and become quiet. Repeat any prayer or treatment that appeals to you, or read a chapter of the Bible. Then quietly say, "I fully and freely forgive X (mentioning the name of the offender); I loose him and let him go. I completely forgive the whole business in question. As far as I am concerned, it is finished forever. I cast the burden of resentment upon the Christ within me. He is free now, and I am free too. I wish him well in every phase of his life. That incident is finished. The Truth of Christ has set us both free. I thank God." Then get up and go about your business.

On no account repeat this act of forgiveness, because you have done it once and for all, and to do it a second time would be tacitly to repudiate your own work. Afterward, whenever the memory of the offender or the offense happens to come into your mind, bless the delinquent briefly and dismiss the thought. However, do this many times and the thought may come back. After a few days it will return less and less often until you forget it altogether. Then, perhaps after an interval, shorter or longer, the old trouble may come back to memory once more, but you will find that now all bitterness and resentment have disappeared, and you are both free with the perfect freedom of the children of God. Your forgiveness is complete. You will experience a wonderful joy in the realization of the demonstration.

Everybody should practice general forgiveness every day as a matter of course. When you say your daily prayers, issue a general amnesty, forgiving everyone who may have injured you in any way and on no account particularize. Simply say: "I freely forgive everyone." Then in the course of the day, should the thought of grievance or resentment come up, bless the offender briefly and dismiss the thought.

The result of this policy will be that very soon you will find yourself cleared of all resentment and condemnation, and the effect upon your happiness, your bodily health, and your general life will be nothing less than revolutionary.

Lead us not into temptation, but deliver us from evil

This clause has probably caused more difficulty than any other part of the prayer. For many earnest people it has been a veritable stumbling block. They feel, and rightly, that God could not lead anyone into temptation or into evil in any circumstances, and so these words do not ring true.

For this reason, a number of attempts have been made to recast the wording. People have felt that Jesus could not have said what He is represented to have said, and so they look about for some phrasing which they think would be more in accordance with the general tone of His teaching. Heroic efforts have been made to wrest the Greek original into something different. All this, however, is unnecessary. The prayer in the form in which we have it in English gives a perfectly correct sense of the true inner meaning. Remember that the Lord's Prayer covers the whole of the spiritual life. Condensed though the form is, it is nevertheless a complete manual for the development of the soul, and Jesus knew only too well the subtle perils and difficulties that can and do beset the soul when once the preliminary stages of spiritual unfoldment have been passed. Because those who are yet at a comparatively early stage of development do not experience such difficulties, they are apt to jump to the conclusion that this clause is unnecessary; but such is not the case.

The facts are these: the more you pray, the more time you spend in meditation and spiritual treatment, the more sensitive you become. And if you spend a great deal of time working on your soul in the right way, you will become very sensitive. This is excellent; but like everything in the universe, it works both ways. The more sensitive and spiritual you become, the more powerful and effective are your prayers, you do better healing, and you advance rapidly. But, for the same reason, you also become susceptible to forms of temptation that simply do not beset those at an earlier stage. You will also find that for ordinary faults, even things that many men and women of the world would consider to be trifling, you will be sharply punished, and this is well, because it keeps you up to the mark. The seemingly minor transgressions, the "little foxes that spoil the vines," would fritter away our spiritual power if not promptly dealt with.

No one at this level will be tempted to pick a pocket or burgle a house, but this does not by any means imply that one will not have difficulties, and because of their subtlety, even greater difficulties to meet.

As we advance, new and powerful temptations await us on the path, ever ready to hurl us down if we are not watchful—temptations to work for self-glory and self-aggrandizement instead of for God; for personal honors and distinctions, even for material gain; temptations to allow personal preferences to hold sway in our counsels when it is a sacred duty to deal with all men in perfect impartiality. Above and beyond all other sins the deadly sin of spiritual pride, truly "the last infirmity of noble mind," lurks on this road.

Many fine souls who have triumphantly surmounted all other testing have lapsed into a condition of superiority and self-righteousness that has fallen like a curtain of steel between them and God. Great knowledge brings great responsibility. Great responsibility betrayed brings terrible punishment in its train. Noblesse oblige is preeminently true in spiritual things. One's knowledge of the truth, however little it may be, is a sacred trust for humanity that must not be violated. While we should never make the mistake of casting our pearls before swine nor urge the truth in quarters where it is not welcome, we must do all that we wisely can to spread the true knowledge of God among mankind, that not one of "these little ones" may go hungry through our selfishness or our neglect. "Feed my lambs, feed my sheep."

The old occult writers were so vividly sensible of these dangers that, with their instinct for dramatization, they spoke of the soul as being challenged by various tests as it traversed the upward road. It was as though the traveler were halted at various gates or turnpike bars and tested by some ordeal to determine whether he were ready to advance any further. If he succeeded in passing the test, they said, he was allowed to continue upon his way with the blessing of the challenger. If, however, he failed to survive the ordeal, he was forbidden to proceed.

Now, some less experienced souls, eager for rapid advancement, have rashly desired to be subjected immediately to all kinds of tests, and have even looked about, seeking difficulties to overcome; as though one's own personality did not already present quite enough material for any one man or woman to deal with. Forgetting the lesson of Our Lord's own ordeal in the wilderness, forgetting the injunction "Thou shalt not tempt the Lord thy God," they have virtually done this very thing, with sad results. And so Jesus has inserted this clause, in which we pray that we may not have to meet anything that is too much for us at the present level of our understanding. And, if we are wise, and work daily, as we should—for wisdom, understanding, purity, and the guidance of the Holy Spirit—we never shall find ourselves in any difficulty for which we have not the understanding necessary to clear ourselves. Nothing shall by any means hurt you. *Behold, I am with you always* (Matt. 28.20).

Thine is the kingdom, and the power, and the glory for ever and ever

This is a wonderful gnomic saying that sums up the essential truth of the omnipresence and the all-ness of God. It means that God is indeed "all in all," the doer, the doing, and the deed, and one can say also the spectator. His "kingdom" in this sense means all creation, on every plane, for that is the presence of God—God as manifestation or expression.

The "power," of course, is the power of God. We know that God is the only power, and so, when we work, as when we pray, it is really God doing it by means of us. Just as the pianist produces his music by means of, or through his fingers, so may mankind be thought of as the fingers of God. His is the power. If, when you are praying, you hold the thought that it is really God who is working through you, your prayers will gain immeasurably in efficiency. Say, "God is inspiring me." If, when you have any ordinary thing to do, you hold the thought, "Divine intelligence is working through me now," you will perform the most difficult tasks with astonishing success.

The wondrous change that comes over us as we gradually realize what the omnipresence of God really means, transfigures every phase of our lives, turning sorrow into joy, age into youth, and dullness into light and life. This is the glory—and the glory which comes to us is, of course, God's, too. And the bliss we know in that experience is still God Himself, who is knowing that bliss through us.

In recent years, the Lord's Prayer has often been rewritten in the affirmative form. In this style, for instance, the clause "Thy Kingdom come, thy will be done," becomes, "Thy kingdom is come, thy will is being done." All such paraphrases are interesting and suggestive, but their importance is not vital. The affirmative form of prayer should be used for all healing work, but it is only one form of prayer. Jesus used the invocatory form very often, though not always, and the frequent use of this form is essential to the growth of the soul. It is not to be confused with supplicatory prayer, in which the subject begs and whines to God as a slave pleading with His master. That is always wrong. The highest of all forms of prayer is true contemplation, in which the thought and the thinker become one. This is the unity of the mystic, but it is rarely experienced in the earlier stages. Pray in whatever way you find easiest, for the easiest way is the best.

WITH GOD IN A
DEVELOPING COUNTRY

Archbishop Emmanuel Milingo

Prayer, for Archbishop Emanuel Milingo, is the heartbeat of the lover for the beloved, of the child for his Father. Through prayer comes the intense joy of being in the presence of the beloved.

His eminence was born to a poor shepherd family. He received his education in Zambia, Rome, and Dublin. In 1969 he was consecrated by Pope Paul VI at Kampala, Uganda, as archbishop. Since 1965 he has been responsible for all religious broadcasting for the Catholic Church in Lusaka, Zambia. He is also a founder of the Zambia Helpers Society movement, author of "Communist Dialectics and Tactics in Developing Countries," "Patronado and Apartheid: Easter Message," and "Amace-Joni."

I want to speak to you about simple things. I am certain that you like to listen to simple things so that they can enter the mind quickly. But when I say that I am going to speak about "prayer," you might say, "But that is not a simple thing." Often in our catechism classes or during a sermon someone spoke to us about prayer in such a complicated way that we ended up by saying, "Prayer must be very difficult indeed!"

I consider prayer as a simple exercise. To me, prayer is a natural channel of communication between a creature and his Creator. When a creature feels life in Him, when he sees a wonderful world around Him, he cannot but start a conversation with the One who is the cause of it all. He likes to thank, to wonder, to enjoy, and to adore. He suddenly loves the One who made him part of all this beauty. That is why I would rather say: prayer is the palpitation of the heart of the lover for the beloved. The beloved is never absent from the lover. He sees Him, he talks with Him, he wishes Him well, and he is ashamed of any misdemeanor against Him. That is why it is wrong to say that God is only with us when we are celebrating the Eucharist or when we enter a church. If God is truly my beloved, He is everywhere, wherever I am. He is with me, and He accompanies me as the beloved.

May I reduce the nature of prayer to a still simpler example? Take the case of the lover and the beloved: the separation of the two does not change the power of their love for each other. The intensity of their love grows even more. They long to be together, and their imagination develops into pictures of possibilities as to how He is now and where He might be, how He looks since I saw Him last and how I should write Him a love letter. Their longing for reunion grows from day to day. The separation of the lover from the beloved increases the fondness between them.

God, my dear brothers and sisters, is not separated from us, though we often think He is. In fact, He is not far from us: He is with us but in a form our poor minds are unable to perceive. His presence is felt by all those who really believe in Him. Just like the two blind friends, walking beside one another, supporting one another: though they do not see each other, they believe in and feel the presence of each other. In this way should every son and daughter of God feel His presence at all times—as he or she awakens, washes, goes to work, says his daily prayers, is busy with the children, or just walks around in the fields. God is not an uninterested spectator of our actions, but both the coach and the aim of our actions. He wants us to act as His sons and daughters should act. He anticipates the success of our actions, and He rejoices when there is no disappointment. Prayer therefore is the palpitation of a child's loving heart for his Father, for God, the beloved.

Formal Prayer

Now, sometimes we hear the words "formal prayer." By this is meant our set prayers, which we recite so often: the rosary, the prayers during mass, morning and evening prayers, and the prayer before meals. These are prayers everybody knows, and in times of great stress or when someone asks us to lead the prayers, we just start reciting an "Our Father" or "Hail Mary." But we must never forget that without the understanding of the true relation between the creature and the Creator, about which I spoke just now, this kind of formal prayer may become a habit and just a cold law, which we must obey. Often we do like the husband whose wife complained that he did not return from his work as quickly as he used to do and that his love was finished. He bought a tape recorder, filled a complete tape with the words "I love you, dear," and told his wife to play it when she felt lonely in the evenings. We must remember that we are lovers of God and everything we do must be the unfolding of that love to Him.

The formal prayers should be considered, in our African context, as "chewing the cud." That is to say, during formal prayer we "regrind" the spiritual food that is needed for ourselves and for all those we pray for. I think another example could be that formal prayer is an oasis, where we draw our strength and where we are always ready—after being refreshed—to start again. In this way we have to consider whether our actions have been as high as we expected or desired. If we have failed, we ask for pardon of God, who is the receiver of our actions. We talk with Him and ask advice as to how to proceed.

Importance of Prayer

"We should always pray." I wonder whether we have the same simple belief in this line that Saint Paul had. We cannot persevere in our apostolic work without prayer. We cannot share the benefits of our faith with others unless we know how to pray. Throughout my years of pastoral work, I have been involved in social activities, which by themselves could have been sufficient to satisfy my ego. But I must confess that it often happened that I could not sleep till I had said my prayers. Never have I been so satisfied by carrying out projects of service to my fellow man that I found that this work actually replaced my personal prayer. I always felt that I had to go to the reference library, that is, to Jesus Christ Himself, the perfect Son of God, in order to sit with Him and to talk to our common Father. Though I believe in being recollected in God's presence, wherever I am, I still feel the importance of reserving a time exclusively for my Beloved. I enjoy being alone with Him, my Savior, who is the truth, the way and the light.

"Teach Us How to Pray"

Now, you might ask me to show you some ways of prayer, of being with the Beloved. Again we must say that this is very simple. For me, one of the best ways is surely to sit with Him, to be with Him, and to relax completely in His presence. Prayer should be moments of intense joy, and we should not try to heap one word upon the other. "Come here and relax a bit," said Jesus to the apostles, after a full day's work.

Often we enter a church or a small room with many worries and many frustrations. We are angry with people and we are tired. But when we are just with Him, we should shake everything from ourselves as does a dog when it comes out of the water. Then we shall remain high and dry with Him. And we then realize that all these frustrations or worries or feelings of discontent come from our pride or from attempts to make our ego triumphant over others. In fact, we let ourselves fill with the warm love of Our Creator, while all the ill feelings toward our fellow men gurgle away into the waste. Coming away from such moments of intense silence before the Origin of All Good, we are as refreshed as if we had taken a cool bath in the clear river. We then notice that our attitude toward our fellow men has changed and taken the attitude of the loving God.

The apostles, we know, asked the same question of Jesus: "Lord, teach us how to pray," and Jesus pronounced the wonderful words of the "Our Father." When we pray for something we should try to pray for the things that Jesus, Our Savior, prayed for: "May your kingdom come." Yes, may our prayer extend God's kingdom on earth: may His love be known. Someone who loves and is loved wants to communicate his happiness to others. You know how it happens with a youngster. He might be very sulky and difficult, but one day he is just radiant and nice toward others. We then quickly say, "He must be in love," because you can almost read it in his face. So in our prayers we should want to communicate our love toward others: May your kingdom come. May your love be felt by others. May they realize the happiness of being the sons and daughters of God. May they be with us, O Lord.

My dear brethren, God is not a punisher but a rewarder. To refer to punishment is the last thing that God will do. God is knocking on the door of our hearts, so often closed. When He speaks to us today, "let us listen to Him and let us not harden our hearts like stones." He sent His son to redeem man, not to punish him. Sometimes we do sin, but honestly it is hard for me to imagine myself sinning outside God—without still remembering that I am His son. The temptations, the moral weaknesses, all these sufficiently help me to realize how weak I am by myself. Then I am obliged to look back to my God and He fills my hollow heart with Himself. The immensity of my sorrow for my sins will wipe away the dirt on my soul. God Himself uplifts me from the pitfall and once more helps me to walk again in His presence.

My brothers and sisters, may this genuine spirit of prayer be always with you.

MAN IS PRAYER

Archbishop Joseph Tawil

Archbishop Joseph Tawil finds in prayer the well of joy that encompasses praise, hope, repentance, and glory. His excellency, the Titular Archbishop of Myra, is apostolic exarch for the Melkites in the United States. He has been director of the Patriarchal College, Cairo, and publisher of the patriarchal bulletin *Le Lien*. He has also served as patriarchal vicar at Alexandria, Egypt, and patriarchal vicar at Damascus, Syria.

Prayer—a constantly renewed joy: Prayer is not a pious occupation that is learned in books but an intimate and personal experience that no one can have in our place and that gives meaning to our whole life, to our entire existence. Man lives but once, and so it is of the utmost importance that he make of his life not a success or a triumph—that does not always depend on him and besides does not amount to much—but rather a wellspring of ever-renewed joy.

Doxological prayer (Prayer of Glorification): Why, as a matter of fact, should we not overflow with joy at the sight of so marvelous a world, made for our happiness and enchantment? How can man refrain from rejoicing at the idea that from the very moment of our creation we have been the object of God's loving kindness? Did not God place the first man in Eden? And didn't He converse with him at eventide as friend to friend? Like Adam[1] we discover anew every day this exhilarating world of wonders which reveals itself to us in its own language. Does not the smallest plant speak to us of God's grandeur, the least flower, of His beauty? Is not the slightest smile capable of throwing us into ecstasy at His infinite and exquisite goodness? Really, man has lost this sense of wonder before the beauty of the visible world. The hectic pace of life does not leave time to devote to contemplation and reflection. His whole life could be a "doxology" without end, praise and glorification of God, who though unique in grandeur and dwelling in the highest heavens yet agrees to become a pilgrim for and with us, just as He did with the disciples at Emmaus:[2] accepting the invitation to share our table and by the incarnation becoming one of us. Such is His intimacy with man.

For this reason, mirroring the shepherds who, after having seen the Firstborn lying in the manger, "returned, glorifying and praising God for all they had heard and seen" (Luke 2:20), the first cry to well up in our hearts, the first name which we ought to stammer as a baby learning to talk, is the name of our heavenly Father, for He envelops us with His presence, with His love, with His glory. For all eternity He has loved us, even before He formed us in our mothers' wombs.

The great sadness of modern man: Is it not the sense of wonder lacking in man that has caused him to turn in on himself, choking on his limitations and becoming the prey of sorrow? Who will deny man's great sadness? No matter how much, no matter how hard he tries to avoid it by sating himself with distractions, amusements, frivolities, and pastimes, it pursues him everywhere. You can even see the traces of sadness' pursuit on his face. Man has cause for seeing everything as dull and insipid beyond words. While he has received the world from God's hands, he has turned away from the Giver to cling to the gift, instead of returning it to Him in "doxology," thanksgiving.

Man has forgotten that every perfect gift comes from the Father of Lights to whom he owes a debt of gratitude. That is why he is held in thrall to so great a sadness that devours the little *joie de vivre* that he has left. Man forgets that he does not live by bread alone but by every word that comes from the mouth of God. Still, this very sadness can ripen into joy and become a gateway to salvation by means of repentance. For God knows that we were fashioned out of clay, but he also knows that he has imprinted His image on us. Even sin itself cannot destroy that image, for it is destined to eventual self-perfection until it achieves the Divine Likeness. Only then does it reach its full measure, the fulfillment of the Gift of Christ.

Prayer billowing with hope: Discouragement resulting from our miserable failures is the soul's worst affliction. We have to recognize that despite the scars of sin, "within us we bear the brilliance of His ineffable glory."[3] Nor can we ever forget that God in His infinite guidance has loved us despite our deficiencies precisely "in order to cause to shine on our faces the light of His countenance."[4] In fact, couldn't we say that the Creator fell in love with His creation to the point of giving it His only son "so that whoever believes in Him might not perish but have eternal life"?[5] Isn't this what Saint Paul means when he speaks of the folly of the cross? So away with discouragement in face of our sins![6] Let us adopt the attitude of Saint Isaac the Syrian: "All the sins of mankind amount to but a grain of sand in the ocean of His love."

Renewed by the tears of the joy of repentance: Of course, this ought not lead us to take sin lightly—that would be to tempt God—but ought rather to bring us to repentance of our faults, to a genuine conversion of heart and spirit to Him who alone is deserving of our love. How can it be that we do not fear that sin will forever separate us from that ocean of goodness and beauty? But such is the mystery of free will that enables man to lose God's friendship and to flounder on the rocks of his destruction. Thus Saint Isaac the Syrian offers as a definition of all prayer: "the quaking of the soul before the gates of Paradise." This explains the character of loving, confident repentance: as we abandon ourselves in the arms of the Father, no sooner does he hear the cry for forgiveness of his prodigal son than he throws his arms around him, presses him to his breast, covers him with kisses, and gives the order for festivities. Herein also lies the clearly paschal character of repentance, which can be defined as a "return to Paradise" at which the very angels of heaven rejoice.

The spirit of the Father prays in us: It is the Spirit of the Father dwelling in us that makes us cry out, "Abba, Father," and this gives our prayer its validity. This same Spirit causes our hearts to flutter, the voice to well up in our throats, and our ears to perk up. He animates all our senses and grants understanding to our faculties and to our whole person.

Nothing can be done without Him; for it is He who renders our prayer efficacious. Thanks to Him it is transformed and drenches the world in a rain of graces.

Formerly, at the moment of ordination to the ministry, the deacon solemnly commanded the assembly to pay strict attention and to keep silent, because the Spirit who was being invoked was about to descend on the candidate for Holy Orders. This Spirit whom we have received in baptism empowers us by his sanctifying might to receive in communion the body and blood of Our Lord Jesus Christ into whose image we are transformed. Thus do we become the temple of the Holy Spirit and the members of the body of Christ, which is the church. This same Spirit makes present the risen Christ and manifests His power in the church and the sacraments. Finally it is He who brings history to its fulfillment because, since Pentecost, the world has been veering toward its end.

Seek first the kingdom of God and His justice: Prayer of petition constitutes the second objective of the Lord's Prayer and concerns our needs. For many it occupies the first place, since for them prayer means asking God to fulfill their needs. In reality we can and should do so, in the conviction that our heavenly Father knows our needs before we formulate them and grants us His grace before we even ask for it. We ought to seek first the kingdom of God and His justice and everything else will be added unto us.[7] But God has a need for men: if He gives, it is, in fact, in order that we may give; if He has mercy on us, it is so that we may share in the misery of others. To do otherwise would be to enclose God's gift within the limits of our egotism and keep the waters of grace from flowing.

Created for glory: All prayer is the intimate experience of the discovery of God, beginning with the signs and symbols of the language of creation wherein He is hidden. Since the incarnation, God has a human face who is the Christ, the Son of the Living God. "For we do not come to Him; it is rather He that inclines the heavens in search of us, and when He did not find Adam on earth He descended into Hell itself to free him from his chains" to enable him to climb from the abyss into which he had fallen from the bosom of the Glory of the Father.

If He asks us to carry His cross, it is because He has destined us for glory, and it is not too much to partake of His sufferings here below before entering His kingdom, "for His commandments are not burdensome" (John 5:3). And we know that "His yoke is sweet and His burden is light" (Matt. 2:30) with the assistance of His grace, as He Himself assures us. And His generosity is beyond imagining: He who knows how to reward a glass of water given in His name. For when He rewards, He exceeds all hope, all expectations. He crosses the frontiers of generosity; He knows no limits. He does it infinitely, divinely.

You are gods: The image of God that He has imprinted on us must be polished to the point of completely reflecting the archetype. The polishing is brought about by prayer and the sacraments of the church, particularly by the Eucharist, which plunges our entire being into the fire of Christ's divinity, making it become fire in its turn.

From the beginning, man was promised life with God, life in God. As Saint Peter said, "To share in the divine Life."[9] Now what else does sharing in the divine nature mean if not being deified? We will be by participation what God is by nature. Plunged into the fire iron becomes fire itself; but once removed from the fire it becomes iron, or something else, once more. Just as the firmament which receives the light of the sun reflects and diffuses it, so it will be with the just, "who will shine like suns in the kingdom of their Father."[10]

Only when one has read the entire book can one judge its contents; only when one has seen the film through to the end can one judge its value. So it is with each one of us: only at the end of one's life can one estimate its worth. Woven by the hand of the Divine Artist, it will unfold to bedazzled eyes the shimmering of the pearls of grace that have gained for us the kingdom of glory. To Him be glory and adoration, now and always and forever and ever!

---

[1] Gen. 3:8
[2] Luke 24:13
[3] Service for the Dead
[4] Ibid.
[5] John 3:14
[6] 1 Cor. 1:18
[7] Matt. 6:33
[8] Office of Holy Friday
[9] Peter 1:4
[10] Matt. 13:43

NO TIME FOR GOD

Lubomyr Husar

Through prayer we acknowledge our dependence on God
and express our convictions. But, notes Lubomyr Husar, in
our preoccupation with our worldly business we are often so
"busy" that we exclude the loving presence of God.

Lubomyr M. Husar, a native of Ukraine, received his
licentiate in theology from the Catholic University of America
in Washington, D.C. He engaged in pastoral ministry and
teaching at the St. Basil's Ukrainian Seminary in Stamford,
Connecticut. In 1967 he received his master's degree in
philosophy from Fordham University, and in 1972 he received
his doctor of sacred theology at the Pontificia Universita
Urbaniana in Rome. At present he is assistant professor of
fundamental theology at that university. Father Husar is
a monk of the St. Theodore Studite Monastery in Castel
Gandolfo, Italy, near Rome.

A friend of mine, a city pastor—a very active and wise administrator–
–suffered a heart attack. When he came to himself, he was a different
man. He recovered his strength sufficiently to retain his pastorship, but
his interests were no longer the same. Now he has time for prayer and
the spiritual needs of his people. From a widely admired administrator of
church property he has become a true pastor of his flock.

This happy metamorphosis—so he himself says—came over him as a result of his coming close to death. Somehow in the course of his near-fatal illness he understood that there is more to life than meets the eye. Man himself is very weak, but engulfed in the love of his Creator and heavenly Father he is strong and secure. This understanding made the successful and certainly well-intentioned worldling into a man of God, a man of prayer, and a brother to his fellow men as he should have been all the time.

That story had a very happy ending. It repeats itself often enough, but its lesson, unfortunately, is usually restricted to the person involved. We others who did not undergo such a critical experience fail to see its implications for us.

It is no secret that most of us absolutely do not have the time for prayer. From morning till night we are caught up in various activities, all of which lay a just claim on our time. When we manage to snatch a free moment we have to relax—our health demands that from us. When vacation time comes around it is usually a hectic race from the minute we turn the key of our house door in good-bye until, totally exhausted, we turn it again two or three weeks later. Vacation time, so precious and so short, is time free from all our normal engagements; consequently, free also from prayer, if such were our habit during our working days. There is, of course, Sunday, the official day of prayer. But how well do we observe it? The prayer part is somehow submerged under all the social bustle.

Let us stop! Let us not wait for a heart attack to slow us down beyond repair. Why is it that we do not have time for prayer? Really, the chronic lack of time for prayer is only a symptom of an unhealthy state of mind.

Prayer is the conscious acknowledgment of our dependence on God expressed in some way. This description contains all the important elements of prayer. The fundamental truth from which prayer takes all its meaning is the fact of our dependence on God. We have been created; we do not exist of ourselves. There was a time when we were not; there will be a time when no trace of our existence on this earth will be left. We are a passing reality. Our existence is ultimately from God, who alone exists through Himself and through no other. Not only we but the whole universe comes from the same hand of God. No matter how extensive it is, the same laws govern it, as our attempts to travel through space have so amply demonstrated.

Our dependence on God is totally peculiar. He Himself tells us that our relationship to Him is that of children to a father. He has chosen to set us into being, not as mineral stones, not as lovely plants, not as swift animals, but as rational beings to whom He communicates Himself as a Father to His children. This relationship, which men would never even presume to suspect, has been revealed to us by God Himself. He asks that we address Him as Father, and he in turn bountifully showers His gifts on us. The father-child character of the relationship that comes to exist between God and ourselves is of utmost importance for us. If it did not exist we still would have to admit our dependence, but that would be a purely mechanical, totally impersonal, heartless, joyless affair. Even then we would be obligated by the sheer fact of our existence to acknowledge that we have taken our origin from some other, superior being. As things stand, however, we are children in a very real sense: God is our Father.

Every page of the sacred scriptures tells us of our heavenly Father. How is it possible that we overlook such a basic truth in our daily life? Obviously we do not read and meditate on God's revealed word. The life that we lead can easily distort our vision. All that we have and use is man-made. We hardly ever reflect that the finest things in life—as Mark Twain is said to have observed—sun, air, water, and life, are given to us free. We take them completely for granted. We have learned to survive grave natural disasters, we have taken great strides into the universe, we are repeatedly made proud by new technological achievements. Our preachers and prophets often enough these days cater to our sense of pride. It is usually only when we come into a critical situation, not unlike that of my friend, that the whole truth begins to dawn on us: we are fragile creatures.

Once we come to realize our dependence on God we begin to pray. Prayer can take various forms—asking for favors, or begging forgiveness, or adoration unencumbered by any other sentiment. The form is not important. The central idea is that we as rational beings, creatures endowed with reason, knowingly and willingly acknowledge our dependence on God.

To this many people—I myself have met scores of them—say, of course, "I know that God is my creator." But, pray, they do not. What is lacking? A realization that man must somehow give an expression to his convictions. Mere rational cognition does not suffice.

Let's take a case like this: a young couple gets married. The husband immediately goes away to another city where he can earn much more money, which he duly sends to his spouse. This is his way of loving and caring. Grateful as she may be for this, the woman has good grounds to wonder whether they are really a married couple. Does she have a husband? Legal documents and the financial support seem to prove it, but who would want such a life? True meaningful companionship is completely lacking. Similarly, the person who knows that God is his creator and sustainer but refuses or neglects to give that relationship its proper expression is somehow not living up to his belief.

To see better how prayer is an external expression of our dependence on God, let us take an example of a special kind of a religious act, a pilgrimage. Nowadays, a pilgrimage no longer entails many of the hardships of past days. We get into a car or bus, speed to our destination, spend several hours there, then hurry back. Generally not more than one day is spent, and even that is spent in cushioned comfort. But even under these circumstances we perceive that two things that we prize very highly, time and money, have been spent to seemingly no good purpose. A person who does not believe in God would never "waste" his time and money in such a foolish way. To consider a one-week pilgrimage to Lourdes, let us say, surpasses even the imagination of "busy" people. What good, they ask, can come of it?

That same question is asked many times over when someone dares to suggest daily prayer. Are not the ten or five minutes better spent in learning something or recovering our strength for better effort in our normal work? The answer, of course, depends on our understanding of our existence. If we take ourselves as the ultimate reality, then no amount of persuasion or reasoning can succeed in making us pray. And logically so. The case is quite different if we permit our faith to set the tone of our lives. Then prayer becomes a necessity. The question in the long run is not how do I find time for prayer, but do I believe that God is my Father? We always find time for eating and sleeping—time is not the real problem.

What is the state of prayer to which we should aspire? Our Lord has told us to remain in prayer always. Is that possible? Yes, it certainly is. Must we then close ourselves into monasteries, and give up all work and activity? How few could do this, and yet the Gospel speaks to all, not just a chosen few. Have you ever considered a child at play? He seems to be completely preoccupied with his toys and games. He is, however, constantly conscious of his mother's presence. He lifts his head to look when she is leaving the room, no matter how quietly she may open the door. A feeling similar to that must be developed in regard to God. A person who meditates and reflects much on his relationship, on his dependence on God, and often turns his attention to his loving Father acquires a special sense for Him—a consciousness of God that does not cease.

THE GAME WITH MINUTES

Frank C. Laubach

Spiritual growth is a process of becoming increasingly close to God. Dr. Frank C. Laubach tells us how to abet that growth—how to practice the presence of God and find exhilaration, strength, and peace in bringing Him into every minute of our lives.

Dr. Laubach during his lifetime brought literacy programs to 103 countries and taught over 60 million people to read. He started in 1929 with the Moro tribesmen of the Philippines, when he translated their unwritten Maguindanao language into a roman alphabet. In a very short time, 70,000 Moros became literate. When the Great Depression forced the cutting of U.S. aid, the Moros continued teaching, using the "Each One Teach One" method. His work went beyond the field of literacy to that of the religious when he wrote *Prayer—the Mightiest Force in the World*. The Laubach Literacy Organization, which he founded before his death, is carrying on his "War of Amazing Love" against ignorance and poverty.

Christ Is the Only Hope of the World

"Disillusioned by all our other efforts, we now see that the only hope left for the human race is to become like Christ." That is the statement of a famous scientist, and it is being repeated among ever more educators, statesmen, and philosophers. Yet Christ has not saved the world from its present terrifying dilemma. The reason is obvious: Few people are getting enough of Christ to save either themselves or the world. Take the United States, for example. Only a third of the population belongs to a Christian church. Less than half of this third attend service regularly. Preachers speak about Christ in perhaps one service in four—thirty minutes a month! Good sermons, many of them excellent, but too infrequent in presenting Christ.

Less than ten minutes a week given to thinking about Christ by one-sixth of the people is not saving our country or our world; for selfishness, greed, and hate are getting a thousand times that much thought. What a nation thinks about, that it is. We shall not become like Christ until we give Him more time. A teachers' college requires students to attend classes for twenty-five hours a week for three years. Could it prepare competent teachers or could a law school prepare competent lawyers if they studied only ten minutes a week? Neither can Christ, and he never pretended that he could. To His disciples he said, "Come with me, walk with me, talk and listen to me, work and rest with me, eat and sleep with me, twenty-four hours a day for three years." That was their college course: "he chose them," the Bible says, "that they might be with Him"—168 hours a week!

All who have tried that kind of abiding for a month know the power of it—it is like being born again from center to circumference. It absolutely changes every person who does it. And it will change the world that does it.

How can a man or woman take this course with Christ today? The answer is so simple a child can understand it. Indeed, unless we "turn and become like children" we shall not succeed.

1. We have a study hour. We read and reread the life of Jesus recorded in the Gospels thoughtfully and prayerfully at least an hour a day. We find fresh ways and new translations, so that this reading will never be dull, but always stimulating and inspiring. Thus we walk with Jesus through Galilee by walking with Him through the pages of His earthly history.

2. We make Him our inseparable chum. We can try to win a high percentage of His minutes with as little do not need to forget other things nor stop our work, but we invite Him to share everything we do or say or think. Hundreds of people have experimented until they have found ways to let Him share every minute that they are awake. In fact, it is no

harder to learn this new habit than to learn the touch system in typing, and in time one can win a high percentage of His minutes with as little effort as an expert needs to write a letter.

While these two practices take all our time, they do not take it from any good enterprise. They take Christ into that enterprise and make it more fruitful. They also keep a man's religion steady. If the temperature of a sick man rises and falls daily the doctor regards him as seriously ill. This is the case with religion. Not spiritual chills and fevers, but an abiding faith which gently presses the will toward Christ all day, is a sign of a healthy religion.

Practicing the presence of God is not on trial. It has already been proven by countless thousands of people. Indeed, the spiritual giants of all ages have known it. Christians who do it today become more fervent and beautiful and are tireless witnesses. Men and women who had been slaves of vices have been set free. Catholics and Protestants find this practicing the presence of God at the heart of their faith. Conservatives and liberals agree that here is a reality they need. Letters from all parts of the world testify that in this game multitudes are turning defeat into victory and despair into joy.

Somebody may be saying, "All this is very orthodox and very ancient." It is indeed, the secret of the great saints of all ages. "Pray without ceasing," said Paul. "In everything make your wants known unto God. As many as are led by the Spirit of God, these are the sons of God."

How We Win the Game with Minutes

Nobody is wholly satisfied with himself. Our lives are made up of lights and shadows, of some good days and many unsatisfactory days. We have learned that the good days and hours come when we are very close to Christ, and that the poor days come whenever we push Him out of our thoughts. Clearly, then, the way to a more consistent high level is to take Him into everything we do or say or think.

Experience has told us that good resolutions are not enough. We need to discipline our lives to an ordered regime. The "Game with Minutes" is a rather lighthearted name for such a regime in the realm of the spirit. It is a new name for something as old as Enoch, who "walked with God." It is a way of living that nearly everybody knows and nearly everybody has ignored. Students will at once recognize it as a fresh approach to Brother Lawrence's "Practice of the Presence of God."

We call this a "game" because it is a delightful experience and an exhilarating spiritual exercise, but we soon discover that it is far more than a game. Perhaps a better name for it would be "an exploratory expedition," because it opens out into what seems at first like a beautiful garden; then the garden widens into a country; and at last we realize that we are exploring a new world. This may sound like poetry, but it is not overstating what experience has shown us. Some people have compared it to getting out of a dark prison and beginning to *live*. We still see the same world, yet it is not the same, for it has a new glorious color and a far deeper meaning. Thank God, this adventure is free for everybody, rich or poor, wise or ignorant, famous or unknown, with a good past or a bad—"Whosoever will, may come." The greatest thing in the world is for everybody!

You will find this just as easy and just as hard as forming any other habit. You have hitherto thought of God for only a few seconds or minutes a week, and he was out of your mind the rest of the time. Now you are attempting, like Brother Lawrence, to have God in mind each minute you are awake. Such drastic change in habit requires a real effort at the beginning.

Many of us find it very useful to have pictures of Christ where our eyes will fall on them every time we look around. A very happy hobby is to collect the friendliest-looking pictures of Christ, pocket size, so that we can erect our own shrine in a few seconds.

How to Begin

Select a favorable hour; try how many minutes of the hour you can remember God at least *once* each minute; that is to say, bring God to mind at least one second out of every sixty. It is not necessary to remember God every second, for the mind runs along like a rapid stream from one idea to another.

Your score will be low at first, but keep trying, for it constantly becomes easier, and after a while it is almost automatic. It follows the well-known laws of forming habits. If you try to write shorthand you are at first very awkward. This is true when you are learning to play a piano, or to ride a bicycle, or to use any new muscles. When you try this "game with minutes" you discover that spiritually you are still a very weak infant. A babe in the crib seizes upon everything at hand to pull himself to His feet, wobbles for a few seconds and falls exhausted. Then he tries again, each time standing a little longer than before. We are like that babe when we begin to try to keep God in mind. We need something to which we can cling. Our minds wobble and fall, then rise for a new effort. Each time we try we shall do better until at last we may be able to remember God as much as 90 percent of the whole day.

How to Try the Experiment in Church

You have a good chance of starting well if you begin in church—provided the sermon is about God. When our congregation first tried it, we distributed slips of paper that read:

GAME WITH MINUTES

Score Card

During this hour I thought of God at least once each minute for _____ different minutes. Signed _____

At the opening of the service the pastor made this announcement: "Everybody will be asked to fill in this score card at the end of one hour. In order to succeed, you may use any help within reach. You may look at the cross, or you may leaf through your hymn book or Bible, looking for the verses that remind you of God."

The sermon that Sunday explained how to play the game. At the end of the hour, the scorecards were collected. The congregation reported scores ranging from five to sixty minutes. The average was forty-four minutes, which meant 73 percent of the hour. For beginners this was excellent. Such an experiment, by the way, will encourage the congregation to listen better than usual and will remind the preacher to keep his sermon close to God.

If you score 75 percent in church, you can probably make a rather good score for the rest of the day. It is a question of being master of every new situation.

Never use a scorecard more than an hour and not that long if it tires you. This is a new delight you are learning, and it must not be turned into a task.

While Going Home from Church

Can you win your game with minutes while passing people on the street? Yes! Experiments have revealed a sure way to succeed: offer a swift prayer for the people at whom you glance. It is easy to think an instantaneous prayer while looking people straight in the eye, and the way people smile back at you shows that they like it! This practice gives a surprising exhilaration, as you may prove for yourself. A half-hour spent walking and praying for all one meets, instead of tiring one, gives Him a sense of ever-heightening energy like a battery being charged. It is a tonic, a good way to overcome a tired feeling.

Some of us walk on the right side of the pavement, leaving room for our unseen friend, whom we visualize walking by our side, and we engage in silent conversations with Him about the people we meet. For example, we may say: "Dear Companion, what can we do together for this man whom we are passing?" Then we whisper what we believe Christ would answer.

Where to Look for Christ

We have a right to use any aid that proves useful. One such aid is to think of Christ as in a definite location. To be sure, He is a spirit, everywhere at once—and therefore anywhere we realize Him to be. Many of us win our game nearly all of some days by realizing His unseen presence sitting in a chair or walking beside us. Some of us have gazed at our favorite picture of Him until it floats before our memories whenever we glance at His unseen presence, and we almost see Him. Indeed, many of us do see Him in our dreams. Others, like Saint Paul, like to feel Him within the breast; many, like Saint Patrick, feel Him all around us, above, below, before, behind, as though we walked in His kindly halo. We may have our secret ways of helping us to realize that He is very near and very dear.

On a Train or in a Crowd

We whisper "God" or "Jesus" or "Christ" constantly as we glance at every person near us. We try to see double, as Christ does—we see the person as he is and the person Christ longs to make of Him. Remarkable things happen, until those in tune look around as though you spoke—especially children. The atmosphere of a room changes when a few people keep whispering to Him about all the rest. Perhaps there is no finer ministry than just to be in meetings or crowds, whispering "Jesus," and then helping people whenever you see an opportunity. When Dr. Chalmers answers the telephone, he whispers: "A child of God will now speak to me." We can do that when anybody speaks to us.

If everybody in America would do the things just described above, we should have a "heaven below." This is not pious poetry. We have seen what happens. Try it during all this week, until a strange power develops within you. As messages from England are broadcast in Long Island for all America, so we can become spiritual broadcasters for Christ. Every cell in our brain is an electric battery that He can use to intensify what He longs to say to people who are spiritually too deaf to hear Him without our help.

While in Conversation

Suppose when you reach home you find a group of friends engaged in ordinary conversation. Can you remember God at least once every minute? This is hard, but we have found that we can be successful if we employ some reminders. Here are aids that have proven useful:

1. Have a picture of Christ in front of you where you can glance at it frequently.
2. Have an empty chair beside you and imagine that your Unseen Master is sitting in it; if possible reach your hand and touch that chair, as though holding His hand. He is there, for He said: "Lo, I am with you always."

3. Keep humming to yourself a favorite prayer hymn—for example "Have Thine Own Way, Lord, Have Thine Own Way."
4. Silently pray for each person in the circle.
5. Keep whispering inside: "Lord, put thy thoughts in my mind. Tell me what to say."
6. Best of all, tell your companions about the "Game with Minutes." If they are interested, you will have no more trouble. You cannot keep God unless you give Him to others.

When at the Table

All the previous suggestions are useful at mealtime. If possible, have an empty chair for your Invisible Guest, who said, "Wherever two or three are gathered together, I am in the midst." Another useful aid is to recall what the Quakers believe about every meal. Jesus told us: "Eat this in remembrance of me." They think that He meant not only consecrated bread, but all food so that every mouthful is His "body broken for you."

While Reading a Book

When we are reading a newspaper or magazine or book, we read it to God! We often glance at the empty chair where we visualize Him, or at His picture, and continue a running conversation with Him inwardly about the pages we are reading. Kagawa says scientific books are letters from God telling how He runs His universe.

Have you ever opened a letter and read it with Jesus, realizing that He smiles with us at the fun, rejoices with us in the successes, and weeps with us at life's tragedies? If not, you have missed one of life's sweetest experiences.

When Thinking

If you lean back and think about some problem deeply, how can you remember God? You can do it by forming a new habit. All thought employs silent words and is really conversation with your inner self. Instead of talking to yourself, you will now form the habit of talking to Christ. Many of us who have tried this have found that we think so much better that we never want to try to think without Him again. We are helped if we imagine Him sitting in a chair beside us, talking with us. We say with our tongue what we think Christ might say in reply to our questions. Thus we consult Christ about everything.

No practice we have ever found has held our thinking so uniformly high and wholesome as this making all thought a conversation with God. When evil thoughts of any kind come, we say, "Lord, these thoughts are not fit to discuss with thee. Think thy thoughts in my mind." The result is an instantaneous purification.

When Walking Alone

If you are strolling out of doors alone, you can recall God at least once every minute with no effort if you remember that "beauty is the voice of God." Every flower and tree, river and lake, mountain and sunset, is God speaking. "This is my Father's world, and to my listening ears all nature sings." "So as you look at each lovely thing, you may keep asking: 'Dear Father, what are you telling me through this, and this and this?'"

If you have wandered to a place where you can talk aloud without being overheard, you may speak to the Invisible Companion inside you or beside you. Ask Him what is most on His heart and then answer back aloud with your voice what you believe God would reply to you.

Of course, we are not always sure whether we have guessed God's answer right, but it is surprising how much of the time we are very certain. It really is not necessary to be sure that our answer is right, for the answer is not the great thing—he is! God is infinitely more important than His advice or His gifts; indeed, He Himself is the great gift. The youth in love does not so much prize what his sweetheart may say or may give Him as the fact that she is his and that she is here. The most precious privilege in talking with God is this intimacy which we can have with Him. We may have a glorious succession of heavenly minutes. How foolish people are to lose life's most poignant joy—seeing it may be had while taking a walk alone!

But the most wonderful discovery of all is, to use the words of Saint Paul, "Christ liveth in me." He dwells in us, walks in our minds, reaches out through our hands, speaks with our voices, *if* we obey His every whisper.

Be My Last Thought

We make sure that there is a picture of Christ, or a Bible, or a cross or some other object where it will meet our closing eyes as we fall asleep. We continue to whisper any words of endearment our hearts suggest. If all day long we have been walking with Him, we shall find Him the dear companion of our dreams. Sometimes after such a day, we have fallen asleep with our pillows wet from tears of joy, feeling His tender touch on our foreheads. Usually we feel no deep emotion, but always we have a "peace that passeth all understanding." This is the end of a perfect day.

Monday Morning

If on Sunday we have rated over 50 percent in our game with minutes, we shall be eager to try the experiment during a busy Monday. As we open our eyes and see a picture of Christ on the wall, we may ask: "Now, Master, shall we get up?" Some of us whisper to Him our every thought about washing and dressing in the morning, about brushing our shoes and choosing our clothes. Christ is interested in every trifle, because He loves us more intimately than a mother loves her babe, or a lover his sweetheart, and is happy only when we share every question with Him.

Men at Work

Countless thousands of men keep God in mind while engaged in all types of work, mental or manual, and find that they are happier and get better results. Those who endure the most intolerable ordeals gain new strength when they realize that their Unseen Comrade is by their side. To be sure, no man whose business is harmful or whose methods are dishonest can expect God's partnership. But if an enterprise is useful, God eagerly shares in its real progress. The carpenter can do better work if he talks quietly to God about each task, as Jesus certainly did when He was a carpenter. Many of us have found that we can compose a letter or write a book better when we say: "God, think thy thoughts in my mind. What dost thou desire written? Here is my hand; use it. Pour thy wisdom through my hand." Our thoughts flow faster, and what we write is better. God loves to be a coauthor!

Merchants and Bankers

A merchant who waits on his customers and prays for them at the same time wins their affection and their business. A salesman who prays for those with whom he is dealing has far more likelihood of making a sale. A bookkeeper or banker can whisper to God about every column of figures and be certain that God is even more interested in the figures than he is. The famous astronomer Sir James Jeans calls God the "super-mathematician of the universe, making constant use of mathematical formulae that would drive Einstein mad."

In the Home

Many women cultivate Christ's companionship while cooking, washing dishes, sweeping, sewing, and caring for children. Aids that they find helpful are:

1. Whispering to God about each small matter, knowing that He loves to help.
2. Humming or singing a favorite prayer hymn.
3. Showing the children how to play the game with minutes, and asking them to share in playing it. Children love this game and develop an inner control when they play it that renders discipline almost needless.
4. Having pictures of Christ about the house as a constant reminder.
5. Saying to God, "Think thy thoughts in my mind."

When in School

An increasing army of students in school who are winning this game tell us how they do it. Here is their secret:

When in study period, say: "God, I have just forty precious minutes. Help my wavering thoughts to concentrate so that I may not waste a moment. Show me what is worth remembering in this first paragraph"— then read the lesson to God instead of reading it to yourself.

When going to recitation, whisper: "Make my mind clear so that I will be able to recall all I have studied. Take away fear."

When rising to recite before a group, say: "God, speak through my lips."

When taking an examination, say all during the hour, "Father, keep my mind clear, and help me to remember all that I have learned. How shall we answer this next question?" Visualize Him looking over your shoulder every minute you are writing. God will not tell you what you have never studied, but He does sharpen your memory and take away your stage fright when you ask Him. Have you not discovered that when you pray about some forgotten name it often flashes into your memory?

To be sure, this prevents us from being dishonest or cheating, for if we are not honest we cannot expect His help. But that is a good reason for playing the game with minutes. Character is a hundred times more valuable than knowledge or high grades.

To be popular with the other students, acquire the habit of breathing a momentary prayer for each student you meet while you are in conversation with Him. Some instinct tells Him you are interested in His welfare and He likes you for it.

Praying Horseshoes

A very powerful way to pray is for a group of friends to join hands while seated in the shape of a horseshoe. Some of us have an altar at the open end of the horseshoe, with a cross or a picture of Jesus, or a Bible, or a globe of the world. The horseshoe opens toward the cities, countries, and people most in need of prayer.

This horseshoe of prayer reminds us of the great magnets that can lift a locomotive when the electric power is turned on. We are seeking to be used by the in-pouring Holy Spirit to lift the world and to draw all men to Christ.

It also reminds us of the radio broadcast that, when the power is on, leaps around the world. We offer ourselves as God's broadcasting station.

The gentle tingle that we usually feel reminds us of the glow and soft purr in the tubes of a radio when the power is on.

Every Christian family at mealtime can form a prayer radio broadcast by joining hands. Young people's societies will love it. It will vitalize every

Sunday school class to spend ten minutes in broadcasting. Defunct prayer meetings will come to life when they become horseshoe magnets of prayer. Schools and colleges, public or private, will find prayer horseshoes popular with the students. Here is something that Christians and Jews can do together. Worship can thus be made the most thrilling experience of their lives.

The group may prepare a list of the most urgent world needs and of key persons. An excellent plan at breakfast is for someone to read from the newspaper the problems and persons that are most in need of prayer that morning.

The leader may say words like these: "Lord, in this terribly critical hour we want to do everything we can. We pray thee, use us to help the president to be hungry for thee, to listen and hear and obey thee. We lift our president into thy presence."

Then all may raise their clasped hands toward heaven. And so with the entire list.

After the prayer list is completed, the globe of the world may be lifted toward God while somebody prays the Lord's Prayer.

During Play Hours

God is interested in our fun as much as we are. Many of us talk to Him during our games. Some of the famous football players long ago discovered that they played better if they prayed all during the game. Some of the famous runners pray during races. If a thing brings health and joy and friendship and a fresh mind, God is keenly interested, because He is interested in us.

While on the playground, do not ask to win, but whisper: "God, get thy will done exactly. Help us all to do our best. Give us what is far more important than defeating our opponents—make us clean sportsmen and make us good friends."

God and Love

Sweethearts who have been wise enough to share their love with God have found it incomparably more wonderful. Since "God is Love" He is in deepest sympathy with every fond whisper and look. Husbands and wives, too, give rapturous testimony of homes transformed by praying silently when together. In some cases where they had begun to give each other "nerves," they have found, after playing this game when they are alone together by day or by night that their love grew strangely fresh, rich, beautiful—"like a new honeymoon." God is the maker of all true marriages, and He gives His highest joy to a man and wife who share their love for each other with Him, who pray inwardly each for the other when they are together looking into one another's eyes. Married love becomes infinitely more wonderful when Christ is the bond every minute, and it grows sweeter as the years go by to the very last day. Imagine, too, what this does for the children!

Troubles

Troubles and pain come to those who practice God's presence, as they came to Jesus, but these seem trivial as compared to their new joyous experience. If we have spent our days with Him, we find that when earthquakes, fires, famines, or other catastrophes threaten us, we are not terrified any more than Paul was in time of shipwreck. "Perfect love casteth our Fear."

The game with minutes is good for people suffering from illness at home or in hospitals. Nurses remind us that the thoughts of people turn toward God when sick as at no other time. Patients who are convalescing have many idle hours when their minds reach up toward God. Playing this game produces a perfect mental state for rapid recovery.

Those who are seeking awareness of God constantly have found that their former horror at death has vanished. We may have a new mystic intimacy with our departed loved ones for though unseen to us, they are with Christ and since He is with us they are with us as well.

Some Prices We Must Pay to Win This Game

The first price is pressure of our wills, gentle but constant. What game is ever won without effort and concentration?

The second price is perseverance. A low score at the outset is not the least reason for discouragement; everybody gets a low score for a long while. Each week grows better and requires less strain.

The third price is perfect surrender. We lose Christ the moment our wills rebel. If we try to keep even a remote corner of life for self or evil and refuse to let God rule us wholly, that small worm will spoil the entire fruit. We must be utterly sincere.

The fourth price is reaching out and telling others. When anybody complains that he is losing the game, we flash this question back at Him: "Are you telling your friends about it?" For you cannot keep Christ unless you give Him away.

The fifth price is sacrificing personal time to be in a group. We need the stimulus of a few intimate friends who exchange their experiences with us.

The Prizes We Win

It is obvious that this is unlike other games in many respects. One difference is that we all win. We may not win all or even half of our minutes but we do win a richer life, which is all that really matters. There are no losers except those who quit. Let us consider some of the prizes:

1. We develop what Thomas à Kempis calls a "familiar friendship with Jesus." Our Unseen Friend becomes dearer, closer, and more wonderful every day until at last we know Him as "Jesus, lover of my soul" not only in songs, but in blissful experiences. Doubts vanish; we are more sure of Him being with us than of anybody else. This warm, ardent friendship ripens rapidly until people see its glory shining in our eyes—and it keeps on growing richer and more radiant every month.

2. All we undertake is done better and more smoothly. We have daily evidence that God helps our work, piling one proof upon another until we are sure of God, not from books or preachers, but from our own experience.

3. When we are playing this game our minds are pure as a mountain stream every moment.

4. The Bible and Christian hymns seem like different books, for they begin to sparkle with the beautiful thoughts of saints who have had

glorious experiences with God. We begin to understand their bliss for we share it with them.

5. All day long we are content, whatever our lot may be, for He is with us. "When Jesus goes with me, I'll go anywhere."

6. It becomes easy to tell others about Christ because our minds are flooded with Him. "Out of the fullness of the heart the mouth speaketh."

7. Grudges, jealousies, hatred, and prejudices melt away. Little hells turn into little heavens. Communities have been transformed where this game was introduced. Love rises like a kindly sea and at last drowns all the demons of malice and selfishness. Then we see that the only hope for this insane world is to persuade people to "practice the presence of God."

8. "Genius is 90 percent concentration." This game, like all concentration upon one objective, eventually results in flashes of new brilliant thought that astonish us and keep us tiptoe with expectancy for the next vision which God will give us.

Infinite Variety

The notion that religion is dull, stupid, and sleepy is abhorrent to God, for He has created infinite variety and He loves to surprise us. If you are weary of some sleepy form of devotion, probably God is as weary of it as you are. Shake out of it, and approach Him in one of the countless fresh directions. When our minds lose the edge of their zest, let us shift to another form of fellowship as we turn the dial of a radio. Every tree, every cloud, every bird, every orchestra, every child, every city, every soap bubble is alive with God to those who know His language.

It Is for Anybody

Humble folk often believe that walking with God is above their heads, or that they may "lose a good time" if they share all their joys with God. What tragic misunderstanding to regard Him as a killer of happiness! A growing chorus of joyous voices round the world fairly sing that spending their hours with God is the most thrilling joy ever known and that beside it a baseball game or a horse race is stupid.

Radiant Religion

This game is not a grim duty. Nobody need play it unless he seeks richer life. It is a delightful privilege. If you forget to play it for minutes or hours or days, do not groan or repent, but begin anew with a smile. It is a thrilling joy—don't turn it into a sour-faced penance. With God, every minute can be a fresh beginning. Ahead of you lie limitless anticipations. Walt Whitman looked up into the starry skies and fairly shouted:

> "Away, O Soul, hoist instantly the Sail!
> O daring joy but safe!
> Are they not all the seas of God?
> O farther, farther, farther sail!"

What Is Meant by Winning

You win your minute if during that minute you

1. pray;
2. recall God;
3. sing or hum a devotional hymn;
4. talk or write about God;
5. seek to relieve suffering of any kind in a prayerful spirit;
6. work with the consciousness of God's presence;
7. whisper to God;
8. feel yourself encompassed by God;
9. look at a picture or a symbol of Christ;
10. read a scripture verse or poem about God;
11. give somebody a helping hand for the Lord's sake;
12. breathe a prayer for the people you meet;
13. follow the leading of the Inner Voice;
14. plan or work for the kingdom of God;
15. testify to others about God, the church, or this game;

16. share suffering or sorrow with another; and
17. hear God and see Him in flowers, trees, water, hills, sky.

We never attempt to keep a minute-by-minute record (excepting perhaps occasionally for an hour), since such a record would interfere with normal life. We are practicing a new freedom, not a new bondage. We must not get so tied down to score-keeping that we lose the glory of it and its spontaneity. We fix our eyes upon Jesus, not upon a clock.

THE MEANING OF PRAYER

Archbishop Michael Ramsey

We must submit our wills to God, declares Archbishop Michael Ramsey, so that through our good actions and prayers we may become the channels of God's goodness. Moreover, our prayers become ultimate assertions of the God/man relationship.

His Grace was educated at Repton School, Magdalene College, and Cuddesdon Theological College. He is a world traveler in support of the Anglican Communion and ecumenical movement throughout the Americas, Asia, Africa, and Europe. He is a noted lecturer and author and was the chairman of the National Committee of Commonwealth Immigrants. Dr. Ramsey holds over fourteen honorary degrees from some of the most prominent colleges and universities in the world. Presently, he is the archbishop of Canterbury.

Prayer is not a kind of pious chatter—indeed it is neither pious nor chatter—but a realizing of ourselves and God in right relation.

Let me first clear away some debris from our path: misleading ideas. One of the most misleading ideas is that prayer is a sort of bombardment. We want certain things for ourselves or for others, and so we bombard God with requests for what we want, sometimes with the idea that if a lot of us keep up the bombardment simultaneously something will happen. And when the result does not happen as we had hoped, we can be very disillusioned. The trouble was that the exercise started with ourselves and our own wishes—even though our wishes might be partly right—and also that this image of a bombardment suggests that God is some distance away from us, a kind of target away across the fields.

No, prayer is God and ourselves: near, together, sharing, conversing. An analogy: if it is your father or mother and you, or some great friend and you, the relationship is far deeper than one of you asking for things and the other saying "yes" or "no." The relation is one of being together, enjoying, loving, listening, talking, thinking, receiving the whole impress that passes from one to the other and back again. Something like that is the relation of God and ourselves, which is what prayer means.

Now you may react. You may say: "Oh, but I don't feel God to be near like that; I just don't get the sort of religious feeling which some people get; the prayers and hymns and all that—to me it is just blank."

Well, leave out any idea of feeling pious; no one wants you to feel pious. Leave out the word *God*, if you like. It is you and the realities you know. Deep down in you there is a sense perhaps of tremendous obligation, things that are a "must" for you because they are right. So, too, in the lives of others there are things that you admire tremendously, with reverence and awe. Then, from time to time there is the horrid sense of guilt: something I am meant to be and I have willfully failed to be. Then in some of the crises of the world you remember a conviction in you that something is right and is therefore meant to prevail. And with all these experiences there is often a sense of wonder, wonder at something, someone, intimate with you in the depths of your being, and yet beyond, far beyond. It is all this which, for me, adds up to the word *God*, especially when I consider the person of Jesus as gathering up the whole. But perhaps for you, though it all means so much to you, though the heart of the matter is in you, there is a kind of emptiness, a blank, a hunger.

Now, it is just this emptiness, this blank, this hunger that can find any of us nearer to God than a spate of consciously religious feelings and phrases can. No one is nearer to God than the man who has a hunger, a want—however tiny and inarticulate. And that is where prayer can begin, the prayer of simply being oneself in utter sincerity. One can pray like this: "O my God, I want thee, help me to want thee more." "O my God, I love thee so little, help me to love thee as thou lovest me." "O my God,

I scarcely believe in thee, increase my tiny faith." "O my God, I do not really feel sorry for my sin, but I want to—give me a true sorrow for it."

We don't find God by trying to be more religious than we are or can be. No, we are near God by being true to ourselves in all the experiences such as I described just now, and then God can begin to find us, to fill our emptiness, and some of the old phrases of religion can be near to what is in the heart.

"O Lord, thou hast searched me out and known me. Whither shall I go then from thy presence?" God finding me.

"Make me a clean heart, O God." God making me fit to be near Him.

"O God, thou art my God, early will I seek thee." Wanting God more than you ever thought you did.

"Praise the Lord, O my soul, and all that is within me, praise His holy name." Being grateful for all this and wanting to say how grateful you are.

Fifty-five years ago Dietrich Bonhoeffer, a pastor of the Lutheran Church in Germany, was put to death by the Nazis. Many years hence his *Letters from Prison* are, I think, likely to be read as a classic of Christian faith and spirituality. In his loneliness and privation, he found that God was there. He reacted against much of the religion of his time, but many of the letters show Him still drawing upon psalms, hymns, and prayers—the old language of religion.

We were using the analogy of ourselves and a friend conversing. God is the friend of man, and in any exchange between God and man, God will be the one who is giving far more, giving so much that what man gives seems feeble, tiny, almost nothing. It is God who searches, finds, gives, and what He gives is Himself. That is the meaning of Christmas, Good Friday, Easter—God giving Himself in generous self-giving to mankind, so that He is near us, with us, in us in ways beyond our imagining. God and us—, yes, God and us together, and together in a wonderful nearness. And when we pray we will not be bombarding God with our own desires. We will be starting far nearer to God, sharing a little of His heart and mind and putting our will at His disposal to serve His good purpose to the world.

I said earlier that prayer doesn't mean bombarding God with requests. If we think of it like that, we are putting God wrongly at a distance from us like a target across the fields, and are starting with our own wills. No, prayer is a kind of intercourse between God and ourselves, ourselves and God, in which we soak our minds and hearts and wills in His, and so put ourselves at His disposal to become channels of His loving purposes towards the world, toward this or that person or affair.

But how do we soak ourselves in God's heart and mind? It is like the overwhelming impact of person upon person when two are together, listening, loving, pondering, assimilating. Now this can be put in religious language, the language of psalm and hymn and devotion. Perhaps you find that language unreal to you and are shy of it. Very well, do not force yourself into it. And yet there may be ways in which, haltingly, inarticulately, you find God real to you: in the sense of supreme moral obligation that you sometimes feel, in the reverence of lovely qualities in people that seem to be somehow beyond and to give meaning to human existence, in the sense of guilt, in the sense of wonder at the world and its meaning. There you find the reality that has the name of God. But just because He is supreme and majestic and you are not, it is not you finding Him so much as He finding you. "Before I sought thee, thou didst find me."

It is this that Christianity puts into words of religion. God made the world, God made man in His own likeness, God is the giver of all good, and because God is the giver He gives no less a gift than Himself to us. That is the meaning of Christmas, Good Friday, Easter. That is the center of our gratitude. And what would be just gratitude if it were between one man and another man, between a creature and a fellow creature, becomes praise, adoration, worship when it is between us who are creatures and sinners and one who is our creator and our god. Worship means a kind of self-forgetfulness as we lose ourselves in praise and wonder, ascribing nothing to ourselves and all to Him, the good giver.

Now prayer. Our starting place is not our own will, but God's. We find ourselves with Him, so to speak, or rather realize He is near to us. And in our own words, or the words of the Bible, or other words given to us by Christians, or in no words—we praise, thank, wonder, love, confess sorrow for our sins, lift up our heart to God. We may specially dwell upon the image of God given to us in the story of Jesus—reading, seeing, reflecting: Jesus the image of the unseen God. So we are drawn inside the heart, the mind, the purpose of God. Our wills can begin to be attuned to His.

Now God's purpose is like a stream of goodness flowing out into the world and all its needs. But it is our privilege as God's children to help this stream of goodness to reach other people, becoming ourselves like channels. Our good actions can be channels of God's goodness, and so too can our prayers. We do not bombard God with our desires; no, we bring our desires into tune with His, so that He, waiting upon our cooperation and using the channel of our prayers, brings the stream of His good purpose into the parched deserts of human need.

Isn't this what Jesus tells us when He gives us the "Our Father" as the model prayer? Jesus meant not only "pray in these words," but "pray with this sequence of thought and desire." God first, the Father, the heavenly Father, hallowed be Thy name. His name is His character and glory, to be dwelled upon, honored, loved, our hearts and minds to be soaked in it. And then we ask that His reign may come and His will be done. With our wills first surrendered to His we bring the affairs of the world to Him in our requests.

There is in all of us a genuine freedom of will, and that freedom of will is the condition of a moral universe, a universe of moral beings and not automata.

Palm Sunday is the beginning of the week when Christians everywhere commemorate the crucifixion of Jesus. Its significance rests upon the belief that Jesus was, and is, divine, and that the event is a universal symbol of the conflict between the self-giving love of God and the deep pride and selfishness which is in man. Seen in the historical event, the conflict could know no compromise. The selfishness of man, resisting and hating the self-giving love of God, destroyed Jesus by crucifixion. But there was another side to the story. The self-giving love of God on its part cannot tolerate the selfishness of man and sets out to destroy it—by the only weapon that can destroy it, namely love itself. The event is thus a symbol; more than that, it is an enactment of God's love invading the life of the world. It is to that love that we try to submit our wills to become its channels in our deeds and our prayers.

Prayer means God and us, near, together, conversing, so that our mind and heart become filled with God's desires and purposes. Then, submitting our desires to God's, we become a sort of channel of His good purpose towards humanity and its needs.

So the Christian in his prayers, and his actions, is looking constantly toward the world and its needs and looking with something of God's own care and love. In that way we serve and love humanity here, now. But there is another aspect of the matter. The God-and-man relation exists because our existence is intrinsically concerned with God. Each one of us is His child and creature. He created us in order that we might have a fellowship with Him lasting forever, with heaven as its goal. That is the deep, lasting meaning of the God-and-man relation.

Think how this is so. Each of us is created in God's own image, and it means that, though you are a creature full of sins and defects, there is a deep-down likeness between us and God, and your destiny is to be with Him. When we say that God loves us we mean that He cares for each single one of us as if there is no one else for Him to care for; He cares for you in all that unique individuality that is yours. He wants you to be with Him forever, to share with you all He has to share. That is heaven. It is the perfection of the God-and-man relation. And it cannot be selfish in any way, because it implies the plural, and heaven includes the mutual love and service of all who share it together, a love and service totally integrated with the love of God and the vision of God.

If that is our goal, how does it affect our present daily existence? In this way: our prayer, while it is a channel of God's good purposes in the world around, is also the assertion of that God-and-man relation that has heaven as its goal. Indeed it is already a little anticipation of heaven in the present life. And it is a good thing for the world that this is so. It is good that there should be, in the midst of all this world's work and turmoil, men and women who love and serve humanity with their hearts set upon that goal of heaven which is God's final purpose for every one of us.

Easter Sunday is the day when we commemorate the resurrection of Jesus. I recall a painting of the risen Christ by Piero della Francesca that has been called "a monument of contemplation, in which the current of life seems to flow with the deliberation of eternity." For the resurrection is an event that confirms and sets its seal upon the belief of which we have just been thinking: that the goal of men is fellowship with God for eternity. That is the meaning of our infinite worth to God, and of those longings that we express, sometimes in words or religion and sometimes in a hunger that finds no words at all, because God made us for Himself and our heart is restless until it finds rest in Him.

PRAYING FOR ONE ANOTHER

Paul L. Higgins

In this selection Paul L. Higgins explores the power of intercessory prayer—both the objective good that comes to others and the subjective value to the person of faith who prays for others.

Reverend Higgins, a minister of the United Methodist Church and cofounder and first president of Spiritual Frontiers Fellowship, has served pastorates in California and Illinois, including nine years at Hyde Park, Chicago, and twelve years at Richards Street Church in the Chicago suburb of Joliet. A devotee of the Christian mystical tradition, he conducts religious retreats and seminars and lectures on psychical and spiritual subjects. He is the author of several books, including *Preachers of Power, John Wesley: Spiritual Witness, Encountering the Unseen*, and *Mother of All*, and is a contributor to anthologies, magazines, and journals. He resides in Rockport, Massachusetts, and is the founder-director of the Rockport Colony.

In our Christian heritage, the power of intercessory prayer is clearly expressed. Effective prayer is being in communion with the all-powerful and all-merciful God, who hears the requests of the faithful and who answers according to His good and perfect will.

Saint James writes in the New Testament, saying: "If any is afflicted, let him pray. If any is merry, let him sing psalms and be thankful. If any is sick, let him call for the elders of the Church, that they might come, pray over him, and anoint him with oil in the name of the Lord." Then he says that the prayer of faith shall heal the sick. If he has committed sins, he shall be forgiven. "Pray one for another, that ye may be healed. The effectual fervent prayer of a righteous man availeth much."

The effectiveness of prayer is discovered through our practice of prayer. The proof we find is in the individual experience of those who pray. As Martin Luther said: "None can believe how powerful prayer is, and what it is able to effect, but those who have learned it by experience."

Dr. Alexis Carrel, the French physician and surgeon, who later became famous for his discoveries in physiology and medicine and became a Nobel Prize winner, had a patient in his earlier years who was apparently dying. There was nothing more he could do for her. She wanted to go to the Shrine of Our Lady at Lourdes. Dr. Carrel was skeptical about religion at that time, but being a kind man, he accompanied her. He later confessed that as they approached the shrine, he wondered in his heart what would happen in his own life if she should be cured. The young woman was healed almost immediately, in one of the miracles of faith. Dr. Carrel's life was changed; he always counted this experience the most important in his whole life. He became a man of great faith and one of the modern world's greatest exponents of the prayer life.

Intercessory prayer has both subjective and objective values. The main purpose, of course, is objective—that is, to be of help to someone else. But a word should be said for the subjective value, too. It has been said that you cannot really hate another person when you begin to pray for him. William Law, the English mystic, tells the story of Susurrus, a pious man who had one serious fault—he loved to gossip. One day he whispered some choice bit of gossip into the ear of a friend. The latter told him he should go home at once and pray for the man about whom he was spreading a tale. Susurrus was upset by this advice but went home and prayed for the man. He was never the same again. His heart was changed, and he promised God he would never again gossip; in fact, he named one day a week as a day of penance, to confess his sorrow to God over his former guilt. He kept the weekly day of penance the rest of his life.

The grand value of intercession is the objective good that actually comes to the lives of those for whom we pray. Intercessory prayer is far more powerful than most of us ever dream possible. As Gerald Heard says, "It is good we do not always know how widespread is the influence of our prayers, lest we become too proud in the good that is accomplished."

"Pray one for another that ye may be healed." This is to pray for the wholeness of the individual, that in mind and body and soul he might be what God wants him to be. We are reminded how Our Lord Jesus set the example and told His disciples to do likewise, and how Peter and Paul and John and James healed great numbers of every type of sickness. The apostles knew, as we know, that not everyone is healed—at least not in the way expected. For Christians, death comes not as something to be dreaded, but as an opening door to perfect healing and everlasting life. As Christians, our task is to do as Jesus commands us, to pray for the healing of the sick, and to pray for the welfare and salvation of others, leaving the results in the hands of God.

The power released through prayer groups is greater than any realize. Good always comes from such prayers, sometimes in terms of miraculous results, sometimes gradually, and very often not noticeable at the time. But always good.

One day I called on a parishioner who was critically ill. Her doctor said he could do no more for her and doubted whether she could live many months. This parishioner was concerned over her granddaughter, who was in trouble, and asked me if we would pray that she might live long enough to see the girl through her difficulty to the right path. I said we would pray both for her prayer request and for her healing. Our prayer group got to work. We prayed, believing God would hear and answer our prayers. Not only did the parishioner live to see her granddaughter out of trouble and restored to the right path, but the woman herself was healed, and is alive today, ten years later.

Sometimes, of course, those for whom we pray that they might be healed die. We all must die, and with death inherit eternal life, and we must keep this larger perspective amid all of our prayers. But our task and duty is to pray affirmatively for healing, trusting completely in the wisdom of our God. God can cure incurable diseases, if it is His will. As the angel said to the Blessed Virgin: "With God, nothing is impossible."

I believe, completely and without reservation, that God hears our every prayer, and that He answers us always. Sometimes the answer is obvious to all. Other times, only a few can discern it, and sometimes no one seems aware of it, but we know within us that the blessing has come. It is important to maintain an affirmative mind, strong in faith, and receptive in heart and soul. I think that sometimes the very negativity of thought and attitude on the part of friends and members of the family members hinders the recovery of sick persons. When we pray, we must pray believing in the presence and power and goodness of God.

There are several questions people often ask regarding intercessory prayers.

In answering prayer, does God act contrary to laws of nature? The laws of nature are made by God. We know only a very few of them and these only in a fragmentary way. God acts according to His wisdom, power, and goodness, all of which far transcend our concepts and the few partial laws we may know.

Do our prayers actually influence God? If God is all-powerful, and knows all things, does He not act without our prayers? The Christian faith holds that our prayers do influence God. In some realms, wherein God has given us a measure of freedom, He does not act until we pray. In other realms, of course, He acts without our prayers.

God tells us in the Bible to pray and makes it evident that He waits for our response to Him. John Wesley says in reference to the realms wherein we are given freedom that "God does nothing but in answer to prayer . . . . Every new victory that a soul gains is the effect of a new prayer." Theologian Karl Barth says that "God does not act in the same way whether we pray or not. Prayer exerts an influence upon God's action . . ."

We are all linked together at certain levels, and, as a social community, share in some measure each other's joys and woes. If we do not care enough for each other and for our common good to pray then we suffer the consequences, individually and collectively. When we care enough to pray, a blessing comes to us and to others in a measure not otherwise possible. Our very intercession plays a part in the redemption of the world. It is what our Sovereign God expects of us.

Are the prayers of some persons more effective than those of others? The biblical answer is in the affirmative. As Saint James writes, "The prayer of faith shall save the sick." The man of faith, the man who is righteous and who prays with all his heart and soul, *believing*—that man's prayer is powerful. To mumble words, not half-believing what you say, obviously is not very effective.

It is the prayer that grows out of real faith in Christ that is truly effective. It is this, coming with all one's heart and soul, that can be the greatest single factor, and often the only factor, in the healing of the sick, in the making of the good life, and in the building of a good world, even a world of peace.

Should we pray for the departed, and do they pray for us? Our God is the God of this world and all worlds, of this level and all levels of life. We should pray for one another here and for those who have departed this life, that the latter may find joy and fulfillment in the eternal world.

The church includes the "church militant" and the "church triumphant," and to pray for each other in the church is to participate in the communion of saints. Even as Saint John tells us in the book of Revelation, the saints in glory pray for us. The more we grow in the spiritual life, the more wondrously real is the experience of knowing that there are those dear and holy ones across the line who are praying for us.

God grant that we might more and more enter into the great spiritual blessedness of praying for one another. In our own intercession, let us remember all who are sick in body or mind, or in conscience or soul. Let us pray for the broken, for the penitent. Let us pray for a new spirit of peace in the hearts of men. Let us pray for the spiritual renewal of all people.

May we pray for one another with faith, with fervor, and out of sincere and compassionate and truthful hearts. And the grace of Our Lord Jesus Christ will be with us all, both now and always.

PRAYER THERAPY

William R. Parker

Such personality characteristics as inferiority feelings, fear, guilt, and hate are impediments to a harmonious relationship between our inner self and our perception of the outer world. Dr. William R. Parker examines these characteristics and shows how prayer and meditation can restore this spiritual harmony.

Dr. Parker is a noted author, a psychologist, and former professor of psychology at the University of Redlands, California. He is a lecturer and is a recognized authority in the area of prayer-therapy. His famous book *Prayer Can Change Your Life* is the basis for the prayer-therapy program. After working with patients who have psychosomatic problems, Dr. Parker is now in private practice in Newport Beach, California.

How can we use prayer and meditation for healing, for peace of mind and to identify with the Creative Force that is the source of all life? Let us approach it from the following four points of departure: (1) Make Prayer a Dialogue, (2) Make Prayer Positive, (3) Make Prayer a Practice in Honesty, and (4) Make Prayer a Regular Activity.

Make Prayer a Dialogue

The human personality is a dual personality that consists of an infantile portion and an adult portion. This is because maturity takes place in the cortex. When the infantile portion (the thalamus) is over-exhibited, we sometimes say to ourselves: "Why don't I grow up?" This may be an empty monologue—an ineffective prayer.

Effective prayer needs to be a dialogue—a talking and listening. It seems to me that the basic reason most prayers are a monologue is that we have been taught, and the majority believe, that God is somewhere in outer space, that we talk to God "out there." Further, we have been taught that God is a person—an anthropomorphic god. The opposite is true; God is not isolated from man. God is in the midst of creation, of creativeness. God is Creativeness. God is Spirit. God is Love. Therefore, if we pray *to* God we imply separation, but if we pray *with* God, this implies integration, oneness, wholeness, unity.

Effective prayer is dependent upon our premises—our ground for understanding. Some of our premises are fearful, some are simply mouthing old concepts we have been taught or heard. Many have a premise that God is a judge, that one is punished from outside. Countless millions make the premise that they are helpless children in the face of an all-powerful God, and under the guise of making themselves humble, they attempt to make themselves small and, invariably, supplicate, plead, beg, and beseech in their prayers. They begin to feel helpless and have little command over their lives. If, now, they would make prayer a dialogue their life and being could begin to change. By talking and identifying with the creative force within, they could begin to sense that they were made in this image and change their self-image to one based on self-acceptance. Self-acceptance is the single most important characteristic of our development. When we begin to appreciate that we are a part of the creative power of the universe, we begin to know that nothing is impossible.

Through dialogue we can be lifted into a state of feeling—a state of love, joy, and peace. Then we are able to listen to the great promptings from within—from God.

By surrendering our inner selves, we stop regarding influence, power, and causation as arising from outside ourselves. We begin to realize that, essentially, the power for good or evil comes from within. Our *new* inner thought will not, actually, change the world, but it will change the world *for us*. It will not change for us if we only think other thoughts—we must do other deeds; we must change our behavior. ("Go and sin no more" (John 8:11).

What can we do? We can stop blaming other people and situations for our mistakes and adopt a new, dynamic attitude toward life. We can stop regretting past mistakes and select a worthy goal to move toward. We can see that we reap as we sow and that we can sow and reap anew. By becoming more aware of the detrimental aspects within us, we can escape reaping inferiority, fear, guilt and hate. They are detrimental to our personal well-being and our way of life. It is a law: the universe will give back action for action. It is clear, then, that we sow from within. We can listen and sow more wisely. We can make prayer a dialogue.

Make Prayer Positive

Positive prayer is not just wishful thinking or being unrealistic and naive. Positive prayer becomes meditation at the point it becomes receptive. As it moves into meditation our prayer becomes an affirmation. Notice how receptive the following affirmation becomes: "So, in thought and deed, we gather up all mankind and hold them in the light, so there might be a benediction on every soul sincerely seeking to do justly, to love mercy, and to walk humbly with his God. We visualize ourselves becoming citizens of the universe."

Great prayer is not begging but affirming. We invariably act, feel, and perform in accordance with what we imagine to be true about ourselves and our environment. It is truly done unto us as we believe. If we do not enjoy suffering, we can change the course of our lives. We do not make things happen; we allow them to happen. Effective prayer, then, is a process, a development.

With the development of the computer, which is an extension of man's brain, we know more about programming ourselves. Our subconscious is the computer part of our brain. What we do in our lives has been programmed into our subconscious. Some of this programming is negative or detrimental. However, we can *reprogram* ourselves at any time.

The memories stored in our subconscious are essentially visual and aural impulses—that is, sight and hearing. These two senses make the greatest imprint. Through new and positive affirmations as well as creative and healing visualizations in our prayer life, the whole subconscious can be altered for the better. Let me give a short example of a meditation that uses the positive concept with the visualization that is necessary for change, renewal, and healing:

"We now become still. In the quietness, we sense that there is one force, one spirit, one presence, one power, and this is of God. It surrounds us and permeates our being. This force is Spirit—this power is all good. We now identify with it and release it in our being.

"We sense a feeling of freshness—of newness—and know that this is the first day of the rest of our lives. We celebrate life and continually restore our health, our harmony and peace in forgiveness and love. As we live in this presence, our hearts are restored and we feel at peace. We now select someone we love and we hold them in the light—the healing light—the light of love. We visualize this white light surrounding them and filling them. It permeates their whole being. We know they are rejuvenated, renewed, refreshed, and set free. We see them happy, well, radiant of spirit, vital, and energetic.

"We simply say, 'Thank you, Father, Creative Spirit, for all our gifts. We, too, have retreated to the mountaintop of meditation, alone, and discovered we are not alone. And so it is. Amen.'"

Positive prayer is not an escape from life. There is a vast difference between *escape* and *losing oneself.* We lose ourselves in the good, the true, and the beautiful. We give energy to our strengths, not to our weaknesses. Erich Fromm has stated that: "Love is based on an attitude of affirmation and respect, and if this attitude does not exist toward oneself, who is after all only another human being and another neighbor, it does not exist at all."

Through positive prayer and meditation, the negative and fearful personalities can be "born again." Those who lack good mental health can, through creative meditation, be transformed by the renewing of their minds. They can grow up again emotionally.

Make Prayer a Practice in Honesty

We need to look at our fear areas so we can discover that there is nothing to fear. We need to go to the trouble spot and not attempt to hide from it, and as we explore our being honestly, we can be set free to choose anew—to become anew. God is not isolated from man. We isolate ourselves by our fear, guilt, and hate. As we harbor these, we feel them; we feel the way a problem looks.

The truth will make us free. We begin to go wrong at the point where we deny, pretend, or lie to ourselves. Prayer works only to the extent that each is honest with himself and, hence, honest with God.

We have a great capacity to hide from ourselves. Let me illustrate this with a true story: Recently I talked with a woman who was a minister's wife. She had suffered from an ulcerated colon for over ten years. She had, through the years, lost weight and had eventually been forced to give up her teaching career. She was mostly bedridden, and her physician offered her little hope of living. She was living on soup alone. Monthly, her condition worsened. She read a book of mine entitled *Prayer Can Change Your Life*. In this book, she had the opportunity of taking a very simple test that measured two things—hostility and honesty. To her surprise, she discovered that she was extremely hostile. Being a minister's wife, she had maintained that she loved everybody. She had said this for so long that she believed it. Now, suddenly, she was faced with the fact that she harbored deep feelings of resentment. It was impossible to rationalize this away—she had taken the test; she had answered the statements. Apparently, she had suffered long enough. Suffering sometimes brings us to honesty. She turned to the only method she knew—that of prayer.

Somehow, now, in this moment of truth, in this moment of revelation, she began to pray to the creative force within herself. She began to enumerate her hatreds, her resentments and verbalized them with feeling. She had every intention of standing in revelation to God and to herself. She poured out everything that she had stored up within herself for years. She then asked for forgiveness and accepted it at once. When she finished with her prayer, she knew that she was healed; she knew she was whole. It wasn't just a wish, a desire; it was a knowing. In this honest dialogue, she had been recreated.

You might say: "But that wasn't positive prayer!" In a way, it was, because of its deep honesty. But she didn't stay on the feeling level with the feelings of resentment. She accepted forgiveness, was deeply thankful and, thereafter, was wholly positive. She used healing affirmations and visualizations that kept her moving in a creative direction. Prayer seems to work only to the extent that each is honest with himself and God. Unless we are honest in prayer, we may merely reinforce the escape mechanisms that keep us from wholeness.

Make Prayer a Regular Activity

Learning how to pray and meditate effectively is a skill, and skills are not mastered by a "hit or miss" method. Prayer needs to be a regular activity, a regulative part of our lives. And, as in all therapeutics, there is a follow-through—a gradual unfolding.

Regular praying is a redirection of creativity. It enables us to recognize our creative potential. However, regular praying may not be enough. Many of our modern illnesses arise from our disturbed mental states. Most of the functional disorders—such as duodenal ulcers, ulcerated colons, asthma, stuttering, rheumatoid arthritis, heart trouble, and so forth—originate from fear, guilt, and misguided love (hate). Lack of love or misguided love is surely the most important of the three. The goal of all therapy is to awaken or help the person to *express a greater capacity to love and be loved.*

We should pray the last thing at night before we retire, letting our minds be filled with positive, loving thoughts—affirming and giving thanks. Pray, also, the first thing in the morning, setting a happy, positive attitude for the day. Throughout the day, utter positive affirmations, for example: "God, I thank thee."

Realize there is unlimited power in the words *I am.* Use your *I am*s upward for health, wisdom, success, and wholeness: "*I am* life," "*I am* whole," "*I am* confident," "God is, and *I am.*" With positive, creative emphasis, we come to love. Through love we are united with others, with all of life. We feel an identity *with* God, and, yet we preserve our own individuality.

Possibly the greatest thing about prayer is that it treats the whole person. This is in keeping with the modern thrust of synthesis rather than analysis. With synthesis comes a greater integration, a greater capacity to love. With love comes the feeling that we are one with *all*, yet we remain ourselves. With this feeling of oneness, we are lifted into the supra-conscious, which is our spiritual center. It is at this level that we receive inspiration and illumination.

One of our great tasks in life is to discover the rest of our selves—to find our place in the thread that weaves through all life. Prayer and meditation are our royal road to this discovery—to wholeness. On this road, we are always leading on to new discovery. Philip Wheelwright in his book *The Burning Fountain* says: "Man lives always on the verge, always on the borderland of a something more . . . . Indeed, the intimating of a something more, a beyond the horizon, belongs to the very nature of consciousness . . . . To be conscious is not just to be, it is to mean, to intend, to point beyond oneself, to testify that some kind of beyond exists, and to be even on the verge of entering into it."

Finally, prayer links us to the unseen. Prayer can make us whole, so that our electromagnetic being vibrates harmoniously. We can reprogram through prayer, so that we identify with creation, with God, with ourselves and others. Prayer lifts us into a new realm, above the mundane, into the spiritual. It moves us beyond doing so we emerge into being.

Through great prayer and meditation, we can realize and accept our divineness and project it out to our world. By this act, we are lifted up and inspire others whose lives we touch. We go from inferiority to self-acceptance, from fear to faith, from guilt to grace, and from hate to love. Harmony lives in our system.

Effective prayer leads to love. Proper love of ourselves, others, and the whole world. At this level, we embrace all mankind. Our world is no bigger than what our heart can embrace; our soul no greater than our capacity and willingness to love. This is the final goal of prayer and meditation—to love. Love outlasts everything.

APERCU OF PRAYER

Ena Twigg

A very beautiful "aperçu"—insight on prayer—came to us from
Hilary Bray on the Other Side, through Mrs. Ena Twigg.

And I said, "Show me what I have to learn."
And my teacher said, "Let me show you people praying."
And it was as though I was looking down on many, many people who
were praying. And he said, "That one is a mother praying for her child.
But she is not praying that God will restore him to health if it is God's
will. She is telling God to make him well. And God is perfect law, so if it
is not in the scheme, the child cannot recover. That prayer does not reach
very far. Although it is intense, and it is pure, it is conditional."
Then I saw a man dressed in a sack, and he was praying, and he said,
"God, I am an unworthy part of you. But if I can be used, use me."
And the man in the sack had a great light come down, and it caught
his prayer—and my teacher said, "That prayer has been accepted."
And then we saw a mass of people in uniform, and they were devising
weapons of destruction; and they were praying that their weapons would be
used successfully—and darkness came over. And my teacher said, "Those
prayers have not been accepted, only by the dark forces. They have no
validity and don't reach out."

And we went round and round, and we were looking at an old lady praying for her husband who was dying, and she was saying. "He belongs to You, God, and although I love him dearly, I give him to You."

That prayer reached out. And again a great blaze of light came down. I was weeping—and my teacher said to me, "Have you learned anything?"

And I said, "Oh, how much I have learned by looking at this thing, much more than I ever learned from my own prayers."

DIMENSIONS OF DEFENSIVE PRAYER

T. N. Tiemeyer

In this selection, Dr. T. N. Tiemeyer discusses how simple and sincere prayer can be used to counter the effect of discarnate evil forces.

Reverend Tiemeyer has a BA in Social Sciences from Elmhurst College, and a BD Divinity Degree from Eden Theological Seminary. He has studied at the University of Cincinnati, Chicago Theological Seminary, Yale University, and the University of Heidelberg. He is a founder and five-year chairman of the South Florida Chapter of Laubach Literacy Movement and a member of the board of directors of the Survival Research Foundation. He is presently the pastor of the Christ Congregation Church in Miami, Florida.

If you accept survival of the human personality, whether by faith or fact, you have probably asked some of these questions: What happens to the unenlightened or the atheist? What about the morally ignorant or spiritually degenerate? Do they ever try to return to influence those still living on this plane?

It is illogical to assume that death is a magic wand that transforms ordinary, worldly minded people into perfected divine beings. Passing through the "valley of the shadow" merely means leaving behind the physical vehicle. To each is offered the opportunity to transfer earth consciousness to the infinite and eternal awareness. But suppose the entity rejects this privilege?

People come in many varieties. Some are ignorant, some evil, some overly sensual, and some corroded with hatred. Since these are mental attitudes, they survive death and continue to dominate discarnate beings. Unable or unwilling to accept survival of mind or reality of spirit, they cannot move on to higher levels. Remaining as close to the material plane as possible, they may seek vicarious fulfillment, revenge, or sadistic satisfactions through those still on the earth plane.

Thus we have a logical basis for belief in spirit possession. In biblical days this was assumed to be fact. In the early scientific era such hypotheses were discarded as medieval superstition. Today, the possibility is again being seriously considered. Not only is it imperative that such afflictions be explored, but the preventions and cures must also be perfected. In this area, prayer has proven itself to be the most powerful defense and the most potent corrective.

"Deliver us from evil" prayed the Man of Nazareth. His interpreter, Paul of Tarsus, amplifies the significance of this petition in these words:

"We are not contending against flesh and blood, but against principalities, against powers, against the world rulers of this present darkness, against spiritual hosts of wickedness in the heavenly places. Therefore take the whole armor of God, that you may be able to withstand the evil . . . and pray at all times in the Spirit with all prayers and supplications. To that end keep alert with all perseverance, making supplication for all the saints" (Eph. 6:10–18).

When Jesus spoke of the fate of the wicked, let it be realized that the imagery of Gehenna (translated as "hell of fire") was not the only one used. Often He spoke of a fate subsequent to this life as being "cast into the outer darkness where there shall be weeping and wailing and gnashing of teeth." How accurately this describes the bewildered souls, released from the flesh, who are not prepared to grasp the significance of a spiritual journey upward! John Bunyan in *Pilgrim's Progress* dramatizes these confused discarnate people, praying for them and in His own defense.

Albrecht Dürer painted them vividly on his canvases as denizens of hell and offers the protective power in his "Praying Hands."

When Jesus cured the madman of Gadarea He addressed himself to an alien spirit that He identified by name (Mark 5:1–14). His "prayer in the spirit" took the form of a command that expelled the foreign entity. At another time He chided His disciples for their inability to set a possessed person free and revealed this secret formula: "This kind can never be driven out by anything but true prayer and fasting" (Matt. 17:21).

Split personality problems have received much attention from psychologists. Many historical incidents have been carefully researched and documented but few conclusions have been reached. There was the familiar Beauchamp case as recorded by Professor Morton Prince of Tufts College. A true and better-known story was that which appeared in the movies under the title *The Three Faces of Eve*. This received more and later attention when a fourth personality made itself evident in the same woman. The strange case of Lurency Vennum of Watseka, Illinois, attracted national interest when for fourteen weeks she assumed the identity of Mary Roff, an entirely different personality who had died some months earlier.

Hugh Lynn Cayce in the magazine *Venture Inward* states, "All mental derangement need not and should not be connected with interference or possession by discarnate entities. It might be well, however, to consider the idea that the psychotic person is one who is aware of activities of the unconscious mind not recognizable to the average person." Cayce carefully avoids fully committing himself on this subject. Yet his more illustrious father, Edgar Cayce, offers one of the best examples of an individual who, while in trance, seemed to be taken over by a completely different intelligence. There are also many qualified authorities on mental paranormalities who believe that most cases reported as evidence of reincarnation can be better explained by temporary spirit possession.

Sigmund Freud's teacher Dr. Pierre Janet recorded this experience in *Body, Mind and Spirit:* "The patient uttered words which seemed to be not his own but those of a possessing spirit and flung about his limbs in obedience to the commands of the demon. I could not cure the sufferer until I parleyed with the obsessing agent and, after a long argument, succeeded in compelling him to obey my orders."

Here is a definite use of a type of prayer to bring mental healing. Invoking the aid of invisible entities and sending commands to the discarnate beings is, by broad definition, a form of prayer. In *Body, Mind and Spirit* Dr. Elwood Worcester of Boston recorded an even more complex healing when He dealt with a woman who was possessed with the spirit of a deceased drug addict. With the assistance of a woman sensitive, the doctor pleaded with the possessed woman's deceased family doctor to lend aid. He, in turn, undertook to expel the spirit and the woman was free.

Two of my own experiences with possible spirit possession occurred in women gifted with the power of automatic writing. In the Indiana case, the young woman in her early twenties had been so closely attached to her father that she spurned a normal social life and friends of her own age. When he died suddenly, she was unable to make an adequate adjustment. One day while writing a letter, a force took over her hand and identified himself as her father, bringing greetings, love, and kind wishes. Each day she looked forward to these messages, which were warm and paternal. One day, however, the tone and penmanship changed. The messages became accusing, then sarcastic, and ultimately obscene. She was powerless to stop the writing. Her family put her into the hands of a psychiatrist.

The second case found me much better prepared to deal with such a situation. The woman this time was more mature and affiliated with my church. She found the messages entertaining until, one day, there was a distinct change in tone. The unknown author warned her to stay away from church, to take instructions only from him in the future, and to ignore the sermons of her pastor. After some months of apprehension, she came to me with the whole story. In the quiet of my study we offered a prayer, surrounding her with angelic forces, and requested that no entity make itself manifest that was not in harmony with the Christ mind.

After a bit of indecisiveness, a distinct message was written through her to this effect: "We have removed the evil force which had been trying to dominate you. You were right in using the precautions you did. Never again attempt automatic writing without protecting yourself with prayer. Better still, give it up unless you feel a very strong compulsion."

Susy Smith, prominent author of numerous volumes relating to mental powers and psychic abilities, for more than ten years was under the influence of an intelligence that expressed itself through her automatic typing. First identifying himself as James, he later claimed to be the late psychologist William James; then through her fingers he not only wrote an entire book but also rewrote and revised it no fewer than four times. A good deal of this manuscript is included in her volumes *Confessions of a Psychic* and *Evidence of Survival*. Not included in the published works is a chapter on spirit possession. Excerpts from that chapter follow:

> If you live for yourself alone, considering your pleasures more important than anything else, you will probably die with nothing better on your mind. You will then be an earth-bound spirit. Such an unenlightened individual hangs closely around the earth for many years. If this entity is an alcoholic, he will remain close to a hard drinker, inciting him to further drink so that he can enjoy the experience vicariously. If he took heroin on earth, he still thinks of himself as a user and will live with addicts, urging them on so he can possess or obsess them when they are under drug influence.
>
> Negative thoughts from the earthbound can intrude themselves upon one who is worried or unhappy and make him twice as miserable. Many entities of a more malicious character know they are dead but do not know what to do about it. They continue to hang around the earth, reveling in the kind of life they used to enjoy. Sex is one of their favorite subjects as you can well imagine. The best way to keep such as these from you is to be the clean living, positive thinking type who does not interest them in the least.
>
> If you are weak-willed and negative in your personality, they may pressure you to indulge excessively in your weaknesses, commit crimes, or even drive you to suicide. Realize that you can protect yourself. Insist orally that you will not allow anyone to influence you who does not come from God in love and peace. Affirm this often, and believe it.

The stark reality of the evil spirit menace has been experienced by Ingrid Sherman, who for two years assisted Tony Agpaoa in performing psychic surgery in the Philippines. "There is a strange magnetism in those islands," she states, "which is conducive to greater activity of sinister psychic elements. I have frequently been under attack by black forces, and once I was dragged around my room at night by an invisible entity. At another time I was visited by what sounded like a 300-pound monster bounding across the living room, coming into my bedroom, and hovering over my bed, breathing heavily."

When asked how she protected herself, she replied, "In this last incident I screamed for Saint Theresa. I then saw a vision of her statue and heard her voice assuring me that everything would be all right." She has used various other modes of protection including a projected white light that she forms into a sword and uses to fight the intruders. Most frequently, however, her means of defense has been a simple, informal prayer. "My saving grace," she states, "was in the confidence I had built up over the years while going along the road of believing in God's forces. Cultivate the awareness that God is there and that your spirit guides are backing you. Then just call on God in prayer and you will receive all the help you need."

The efficacy of prayer in expelling troublesome spirits has long been recognized by the Christian church, which has provided standard prayers for this purpose. Jewish rituals also provide the rabbi with such prayers to expel the "dibbuch" or evil spirit. Various forms of exorcism have had ecclesiastical approval although no one standard ceremony seems to be adequate for all occasions.

Benevolent assistance has been invoked in various but effective ways through the annals of history. Elisha in the Old Testament found it possible to call upon such a powerful host of defenders that his servant, when given clairvoyance, described the protectors as an army of fiery chariots (2 Kings 6:15, 16). The prayers of Shadrach, Meshach, and Abednego brought them a fourth person to protect them in the fiery furnace (Dan. 4:25). The prayer disciplines of Jesus created such a powerful insulation against evil that when His enemies sought to cast Him from the hilltop, they found they could not hold on to Him (Luke 4:29, 30). When the temple soldiers came to arrest Him, they were unable to lay hands upon Him until he, figuratively speaking, turned off the power (John 18:4–6).

Strange assortments of techniques have been employed by those seeking protection from "the forces of darkness." These include singing of hymns, calling aloud sacred words with expectations of magic results, uttering mystical vowel sounds, making the sign of the cross, encasing one's self symbolically within a wall of spirit fire, etc. People have put their faith in a variety of equipment to make themselves "invulnerable," such as rosaries, pentagrams, special gems, holy water, protective light rays, musical vibrations, crucifixes, wolfbane, incense, ointments, dogwood, and mandrake root. None of these by themselves has ever been proven as effective as simple and sincere prayer.

If one admits the possibility of earthbound spirits trying to possess or obsess the carnate individual, one must realize that it cannot happen if that person is fully in control of His consciousness and will. However, there are many people whose wills are weak and whose minds are open to penetration. These include the alcoholic, the drug addict, the sexually promiscuous, the compulsive gambler, the enslaved cigarette smoker, and those who are unable to control excessive eating habits. Any weakness in willpower leaves an opening into which the discarnate evil forces may enter to express themselves or take temporary control.

The danger of leaving the door open is not only for those who have addictions and bad habits. There are many times in the life of the average self-controlled individual when his mind is open to assault. In sickness or extreme fatigue, the self is vulnerable. Under anesthetic in surgery or even in a dentist's chair, evil forces are believed to have entered. The most common time of danger is in sleep. No wonder we are told that the fifteen minutes before sleep is called the day's most critical quarter-hour. Who knows what degenerative elements may attempt to slip into your mind while your consciousness is out of the control room? All the more reason why prayer is so essential before sleeping!

One can now understand the value of teaching children simple bedtime prayers. A highly effective one is that which Hansel and Gretel sing in Humperdinck's opera, with these words: "When at night I go to sleep, fourteen angels watch do keep," etc. I know adults who invoke the four guardian angels—Raphael, Michael, Gabriel, and Uriel—to watch over them from the four directions. Each individual is challenged to devise his own prayer protection so that his sleep will be guarded, untroubled, and safe from invasion by infernal entities.

Lew Smith, a converted Jew, has devised a unique way that to his satisfaction reveals the number of undesirable entities in any person at a given time. Once ascertained, he uses a simple prayer to expel the negative influence. I write from firsthand experience when I state that this is even effective when given over the phone. Skeptic though I was, I cannot deny that I felt a definite tingling starting in the central pelvic portions and moving in both directions to head and feet, followed by a feeling of exhilaration. I make no effort to explain, only to record this unusual reaction to a prayer designed to cleanse one from the influence of harmful or unhealthy spirit forces.

For those who want to try it or who feel the need of such spiritual therapy, here is this prayer, both time-tested and personally attested to:

"Dear God, cleanse, clear, fill, and encapsulate me in the white Christ light of healing and protection. Remove all negative energies and entities from me and send them to their proper plane. Then close my aura against their return and in their place put the highest and most powerful vibrations. Thank you, Father."

PRAYER: HOW AND WHY IN THE LIGHT OF BUDDHISM

Princess Poon Pismai Diskul

Princess Poon Pismai Diskul examines, within the context of Buddhism, the question of how and why one prays. Her exploration of the techniques of and reasons for prayer shows how, with sincerity, sacrifice, and selflessness, one can stay on the Right Path.

The Princess first became widely known for her early work on Buddhism, *Sasanaguna* ("The Value of Religion"). Now in her seventies, she has long been a leading participant in Buddhist activities. Her devotion to the cause of world peace and her painstaking efforts as president of the World Fellowship of Buddhists are acknowledged by all who know her. The Princess received the Royal Medal of the Most Illustrious Order of Chula Chom Klao from the king of Thailand for her humanitarian service in the cause of Buddhism, and she was the first woman president of the Buddhist Association of Thailand.

The role of prayer in Buddhism is both simple and complicated, both easy and difficult to understand, depending partly on the angle of approach and partly on the person who approaches it.

To the question of "how to pray and why," we must first ask, "What is prayer meant in Buddhism?"

To put it in a nutshell, prayer in Buddhism means the desire repeatedly expressed to remind oneself of one's spiritual goal so that one will not waver in the presence of adverse forces of temptations and threats and so that the wish expressed may be achieved through one's own development and maturity as a result of one's own efforts.

To elaborate, Buddhism has as its essential doctrine the "law of karma" determining that, in the Buddha's own words, "Self is the refuge of self," "Be your own refuge," "You must make your own efforts," "Purity and blemish are individual affairs," and several others.

Obviously to some the above quotations may seem to be discouraging and depressing, for it appears that everybody has to struggle alone unaided, relying solely on self-help and being unable to expect assistance from anybody in any way at any time. Should this be absolutely true, even the Buddha would have no place at all and Buddhism would not benefit mankind in any way whatsoever.

Scripturally speaking, the place of the Buddha can be seen in his own words: "I am the pointer of the Way."

Now "pointer of the Way" has several shades or depths of meaning, depending upon the levels of development or maturity of the person who "treads the Way thus pointed."

You may picture the Buddha as a person who stands by the wayside, pointing to the travelers at some remote point far away and telling them to go on, not to sidestep from the main Path—and you will not be wrong, although such a picture is far from perfect and may cause a serious misunderstanding to many.

To get a better idea of this, just study the life of the Buddha. You can see how the Buddha and, of course, his noble disciples, underwent constant and complex troubles through their indefatigable efforts to "point the Way" to those who had not known the right way and also to those who knew the right way but preferred to sidestep from or to stop on the way. To cite only a few examples: the training and conversion of the Five Ascetics; of the 1,000 fire-hermits; of Nanda, his half-brother; of Bhikkhu Tissa, whose whole body was covered with running sores (the Buddha helped clean those sores himself); and the Finger-Necklace Robber; will give us a better picture of how arduous and exacting was the task of "pointing the Way."

Except in the case of some disciples (such as Bahiya and Sankicca Samanera) who won through to attainment rapidly and with ease, in most cases to "point the Way" was *never* to stand passively by the wayside, pointing to an obscure place on the horizon. Even in the case of the seemingly easy attainment the task was "more than what meets the eye." It was not merely talking or cramming the facts into the listeners' heads but it necessitated the Buddha's prior attainment in order to know what level of attainment the listener had come up to at the moment. This required the power of clairvoyance and telepathy before the Teacher could "point the Way" further again so the listener could see a little further ahead. This process could go on steadily to the end, *provided that the person in question matured enough spiritually to be led on to the end.*

If the person was unable to go on, the Buddha would stop for the time being, to go on again soon. The best example of this may be seen in the case of the Buddha's first sermon. At the end of this sermon, the Buddha recognized that the Venerable Kon Danna had realized a great part of his teaching and had crossed the Rubicon of worldlings, but he stopped there and continued his sermon on the days that followed. These examples serve to show how "pointing the Way" is by no means as easy a task as the words imply. In absolute terms, it is a two-way affair, depending upon the Karma of each individual (that is, how mature he or she is), upon how far or how fast he or she can be informed of the various signposts on the way, and partly upon the ability of the person who undertakes to "point the Way."

Bhikkhus in various lands are supposed to say their prayers every day when they chant in the morning and/or in the evening. In Thailand there are, for instance, the passages that say, "This devoted reverence having been paid to the Triple Gem, through whatever merit gained thereof, let not misfortune come to pass," and "To the Buddha I surrender this body-and-mind . . . by the power of uttering this truthfulness may I prosper in the doctrine of the Buddha." These and others serve as verbal reminders of the prior resolutions and also as expressions of the inner goal. Buddhists understand that they are required also to act accordingly:

sincerely, sacrificially, and selflessly. Above all, we Buddhists know we can be helped in proportion to our own self-help (that is, through our own karma). The more we try to help ourselves, the more we can be helped by our own karma, which enables us to draw on help from the sources where help can be drawn. This, therefore, is the Buddhist technique of *how to pray.*

In regard to the question *why to pray,* let us consider first some incidents happening to all of us in our everyday life. When we are ill, for example, we need the doctor's help in the form of advice and medicine, for as laymen we are unable to help ourselves. But then we are required to follow the doctor's advice and take the medicine ourselves. None can do this for us. Again, in education we need our teachers' help in doing our exercises and homework, but we must help ourselves in time of examination. None can help us in such times. In these cases *we are helped in order that we may be able to help ourselves.*

Now we come to the answer *why.* Buddhists "pray" (remind themselves verbally or mentally) to the Triple Gem because they want to strengthen their willpower after they have studied his teaching and known intellectually what is right and what is wrong. They know that to "pray" in the spirit mentioned above is self-strengthening and self-encouraging so that, when occasion arises, they can fight the battle of their lives alone, being at that moment strengthened and encouraged by their previously accumulated karma in the form of sincerity, sacrifice, and selflessness. The more they are sincere, sacrificial, and selfless, the better they can fight against temptations and threats and the sooner their wishes will be granted and their prayers "answered."

Thus in Buddhism a person's karma, or spiritual maturity, is the sum of all possibilities. We can have or be anything if we care and dare to pay the price—a price not of gold and silver but of the steady and progressive accumulation of good karma through walking the Right Path pointed out to us again and again with every step of our progress on that path. To do so we must remember and survey our purposes as often as possible, and repeated "prayer" with the attitude mentioned above is a key to success.

However, frankly speaking, I am of the opinion that the spirit of prayer that characterizes Buddhism can be found to underlie all religious doctrines, the difference being the degree of emphasis and obviousness and also the way of expression. For whereas Buddhism speaks out definitely and unequivocally, in other doctrines the spirit of prayer is sometimes obscured by legends and poetic or figurative expressions and at other times is left understood and needs to be read between the lines, so to speak. There might be various reasons, due to circumstances and the background of listeners at a particular time, and the masters of various religious doctrines are not to blame for this.

To sum up, it is clear that in a relative world we cannot always depend on others' help; nor can we completely boast our self-help. Having been helped by our Master's injunctions, be he the Buddha, Christ, or Mohammed, we must make our own efforts so that we can be better helped and so that we can attain a condition where we shall no longer depend on anybody's help.

And the best way to keep us on the Right Path is to observe, warn, and remind ourselves so that we shall not forget or be led astray on the Way. Repeated prayer, whether mental or verbal, *with the attitude of mind and the mode of practice earlier mentioned*, is the technique for this purpose. This is the answer to *how to pray* in the light of Buddhism.

Now, everybody has a weak point. Repeated prayer, in the sense and method above mentioned, can help build up for him an immunizing power against attacks and setbacks. In "prayer" a Buddhist builds up a karma, or cause, that will produce a vipaka, or effect, he wishes for. It is a self-strengthening and self-encouraging process. It is, in other words, a case of *"deserve* before you *desire."*

PRAYER FOR PEACE
AND HAPPINESS

Ahmad Kuftaro, grand mufti of Syria

Sheikh Ahmad Kuftaro urges that we return to faith and
worship to bring about the brotherhood of man that will unite
nations and bring peace to humanity.

His Excellency the Grand Mufti of Syria received his PhD
in the field of Islamic preaching. He is a world lecturer on
Islam, comparative religions, Muslim-Christian cooperation,
and cooperation among heavenly religions. He is also head of
AL-ANSAR (Social, Cultural and Religious Society in Syria),
head of the Supreme Council of Fatwa, grand mufti of Syria,
permanent member of the World Islamic Organizations and
Conferences, and member of the People Council.

Science says our earth was a burning gas that cooled and froze and became
a planet carrying living things after the inoculated seed turned into a perfect
human being. It also says that our galaxy, together with millions of others,
consists of tremendous worlds, some of which are probably inhabited.
The human mind is unable to count them nor know their dimensions
nor boundaries nor what they do contain. Myriad laws govern them and
keep them in their courses. It is astonishing to look at the minute cells of
the brain, liver, blood, or others and see how they perform their function

with great efficiency and according to laws away from which they cannot divert. There we witness creation and discipline. But when we cast an overall look at the unity of the universe and its laws, from its galaxies to its cells and atoms with their perfect harmony and creative consistency and which have no fault or disorder, surely we will admit that this universe has a great Maker who is all-knowing, merciful, and wise. He granted man his existence and life. He supported him with powers and means by which he attained his aspirations and achieved his goals.

When man contemplates his existence on his planet, which is smaller than the smallest atom of sand in the biggest desert when compared with the galaxies and the infinite worlds, how small he will find himself and how much his poor being is in need of a helpful, great Creator! He is in need of this Creator's kindness, especially when he is in the midst of distress wherein his means of rescue and deliverance have run short. I think under these circumstances man has to look for a means by which he can accomplish a true communion with the great Creator who is the source of power and boundless compassion and by which He can entreat His care and beg for His mercy. This true communion can grant him a well of divine wisdom and true inspiration that can guide him on the right path and give him spiritual happiness and success in all ways of life.

God is aware of the defects of man and his countless needs, so He had granted him what he lacked before he asked for what he wanted. God had opened the gate of response before man asked Him. He says in the Koran: "Pray unto me and I will hear your prayer" (XL, 60).

The most wonderful bounty He ever gave us is the system of prayer that is a school whose instructors are the prophets and their disciples. They have taught us how to utilize this great means with proper efficiency. They have instructed us at the school of prayer with true angelic education whose graduates are adorned with perfect humanity and the most virtuous conduct.

By means of prayer we can prescribe remedy for our spiritual weaknesses and nourishment for our souls. It can give us the power to conquer the spirit of evil and sin that destroys man's happiness in his inner soul, his society, and his world. This spiritual power enabled the prophets and their followers to accomplish full success in achieving their aspirations and ridding themselves of their crises. Prayer was the fortress in which they took refuge in extremities. They could, by prayer, bring up the virtuous, perfect, and happy man.

If I were to mention in this short work what blessings and fruit I and my friends and my faithful disciples have received through prayer, it would take pages and pages. With God's various kinds of help, impossible wishes have been granted and difficulties have been surmounted. Fear and trouble have been changed into tranquility and security, disease into sound health, perplexity and hesitation in making great decisions into infallible inspiration and successful thought.

How to Pray

When the worshipper says his prayers, he has to be clean both in body and apparel with the scent of perfume spreading from him. He has to stand before God in regret for his sins and bad deeds, with a determination to get rid of them, even change them into virtues and good deeds. He has to decide from all his heart to be straightforward and follow the path of good and avoid the path of evil. He has to turn with all his intellect and senses to his Lord the Creator, fearing His greatness and imploring Him to pardon his sins and vices with full confidence of His bounty and mercy and confidence that his prayers will surely be accepted. Thus, obstacles and barriers between the worshipper and God vanish, and man's spiritual communion with his Lord is achieved. His happiness with its rapture diminishes all sensual pleasures and makes it easy for him to bear all shocks and misfortunes. God says in the Koran: "O ye who believe! Seek help in steadfastness and prayer. Lo! Allah is with the steadfast" (II, 153).

Saying prayer under the guidance of efficient instructors is the vitamins and lively nourishment to the spirit of man. This sacred communion infuses the spirit of the worshipper with the attributes of God: with mercy, love, sympathy, kindness, and generosity for the good of man. All moral virtues toward the near and the far and toward all creatures become His. Prophet Mohammed says: "All creatures are God's dependents: the most favored by God is He who is most helpful to them." These virtues do not only accomplish peace for man in this world but also cooperation and brotherhood, bliss and tranquility, happiness, rest of conscience, and satisfaction. Moreover, in the soul of the worshipper some divine traits will appear, as in a drop of ocean water there exist all its properties. These traits are reflected in His heart as a reflection appears in the clear mirror. Thus, man's power is derived from God's power and his wisdom from His wisdom, and his forbearance from His forbearance. The forces of nature are at his command thanks to this lively, true prayer. I do not exaggerate if I say that due to this communion between man and his Lord and with the effects and blessings of prayer, Abraham, Moses, Jesus Christ, and Mohammed, peace be upon them, could heal the ill and could foresee the unseen and foretell the future. With this prayer their wishes were granted and they could perform miracles. The spiritual powers of the worshipper develop so much that his sixth sense becomes alive, enabling him to hear and see what the ordinary eye and ear are unable to see and hear. God's angels and spirit will teach and guide him by means of divine inspiration along the path of good and righteousness in all his bodily and spiritual affairs in the same manner as the prophets and the faithful believers before them had been taught.

If the man of today is far away from faith and worship, it is not because his human nature is corrupted nor because he is no longer apt to accept them. It is because faith and worship have lost much of their beauty and vitality, which used to attract all kinds of men in the past. The mere chanting of the holy books and the mere contentment with the bodily movements in prayer will yield no fruit of virtue in the human character. To say prayers with a sinful spirit will not enable the worshipper to accomplish his spiritual and materialistic objectives and aspirations.

This dead worship will not revive the spirit nor achieve any communion with the spirit of God. This communion will surely call for God's help and care for the worshipper and God's response to his wishes. Worship will not attain its goals nor give its fruit if it is not on the level God enjoins and the manner prophets and messengers taught the believers. If we examine the system of true worship preached by prophets and messengers, we realize why man in the past cherished it whereas the present-day man has neglected it. Christ says: "In your prayer do not be careful of verbosity, for God looks only into the heart. Many pray but their hearts are full of evil, so they are not serious in what they say." He also says: "God does not accept the prayer of a man with a filthy heart: all sea water does not purgate whoever cherishes sins in his heart." He also says: "Whoever prays thoughtlessly mocks his Lord."

Prophet Mohammed says: "Who persistently knocks at the gate will certainly get it open." The Koran says: "I answer the prayer of the suppliant when he crieth unto Me. So let them hear My call and let them trust in Me, in order that they may be led aright" (II, 186).

Mohammed relates the following as said by God: "Not all who say their prayers are good worshippers. I accept the prayers of those who are humble to My greatness and refrain from forbidden sensual desires, and do not persist in their disobedience to Me. They feed the hungry, clothe the needy, have pity on the injured, and give refuge to strangers; they do all that for My sake. I swear by My glory and majesty, the light of their faces is brighter than the light of the sun. I vow to make their ignorance learning and their gloom brilliance. Whenever they ask Me, I readily fulfill their wishes and provide what they beg Me for. My angels are their safeguards and they are always in My Providence. They are like Paradise whose fruit never decays nor changes."

And when we read Matthew—"And all things, whatsoever ye shall ask in prayer, believing, ye shall receive" —it is not strange to see the Koran give witness to Matthew of this truth. It says: "Pray unto me and I will hear your prayer" (XL, 60).

In the gospel according to Barnabas it shows this aim more clearly: "If a man says his prayer properly, he shall surely get what he begs for." Then the Koran comes at last, to emphasize this truth which all divine religions have agreed upon. It says: "Prosperous is he who purifies himself, and remembers the name of his Lord and prays! Nay! but ye prefer the life of this world, while the hereafter is better and more lasting. Verily, this was in the book of yore,—the books of Abraham and Moses."

By virtue of his knowledge and endeavors, man managed to discover many sorts of germs that used to kill millions of human creatures, and consequently he was able to invent drugs and vaccines which have annihilated most of these germs that used to cause misery to mankind.

It is high time present-day man realized war and its devastating effects and catastrophes: orphans, widows, and deformed or distorted warriors on a large scale. Hasn't man understood yet that wars are the result of the microbes of greed and avarice, of selfishness and deceit rooted in merciless hearts and brutal souls? We scarcely perceive any human emotions or moral virtues in the bodily frame of man at present.

All those vices resulted from lack of genuine worship and loss of the spirit and essence of religion or faith. Have the contemporary researchers taken into consideration the necessity of ridding humanity of these fatal microbes that threaten to destroy civilization to the same extent as putting an end to the germs of the body? Will there be endeavors to resort to the drug-stores of prophets and apostles after brushing them of fanaticism and dogmatism and supplying them with true thought and mental freedom? Perhaps we shall restore thereby the efficiency of the drugs that Abraham, Moses, Jesus, and Mohammed made use of to cure humanity of its epidemic, spiritual diseases.

Is there any possibility, as a first step, for creating a Christian-Islamic cooperation for renovating genuine faith and vivid worship in order to attain love, fraternity, and sympathy? Jesus Christ said, "Love your relations as yourself." Mohammed said, "None of you is a true believer unless he loves for his brethren what he loves for himself." It is impossible to achieve this before improving the neglected worship system that is nowadays inadequate for lack of capable trainers. It is essential, too, to renovate faith in human souls that suffer from lack of love, fraternity, cooperation, and human sympathy. Human souls are inflicted with dearth of moral virtues such as truth, faithfulness, and honesty. We have exchanged the blossoms of our souls for the thorns of atheism and the vices of tyranny and imperialism. Everyone knows that the Big Powers spend countless sums of money on the production of military equipment such as transcontinental rockets and all sorts of bombs and space ships. Moreover, scientific institutes and industrial corporations spend huge amounts of wealth on experimentation and research work for the sake of improving man's implements. Have the people in charge ever thought of reinstituting lost humanity and its dignified virtuous morals by means of faith and worship based on learning and the mind?

It is possible to hold a permanent conference to effect cooperation among the heavenly religions—primarily between Islam and Christianity since there is much resemblance between them, especially when one knows that about one-third of the Koran defends and praises Christ, Moses, their holy books, and of all the prophets in the Bible.

I address all believers and free people throughout the world who are concerned about peace and humanity and urge them to study this proposal of mine for which I have been striving for the last 25 years all over the world. I daresay we may, by this experiment (which is able to bring about mercy, peace, and humanitarianism, and which I dearly cherish), go back to the faith or belief that was applied by Abraham, Moses, Jesus, and Mohammed. Let's resort to true worship, which is the greatest link between God and us, with our hands full of His bounties and gifts, and as Saint Matthew said: "And all things, whatsoever ye shall ask in prayer, believing, ye shall receive."

CAN MODERN MAN PRAY?

Rabbi Robert I. Kahn

Modern man has trouble with prayer. The new scientific outlook makes it difficult to believe in the way did our fathers of yesterday. Rabbi Kahn explores the subject and responds with a new outlook on an old practice.

Dr. Robert I. Kahn, rabbi of Congregation Emanu El of Houston, Texas, was ordained in 1935 by the Hebrew Union College-Jewish Institute of Religion. Presently the president of the Central Conference of American Rabbis, he was for six years the chairman of its liturgy committee. He has been visiting lecturer on homiletics at his alma mater, on Jewish mysticism at the Jung Center, and on Judaism at St. Thomas University. He writes a weekly column in the *Houston Chronicle* "Lessons for Life." His more recent books include *Ten Commandments for Today* and *The Letter and the Spirit*. Rabbi Kahn has been given honorary awards by the Boy Scouts of America, the Freedoms Foundation, the Four Chaplains Chapel, and the Scottish Rite.

Prayer is the natural outreach of the human spirit toward the spirit of the universe, as innate as our response to music, as natural as our eye for beauty, as much a part of us as our longing for love.

Nevertheless, as natural as it may be, many of us moderns have trouble praying. Although unable to rid ourselves of the longing, we have lost our faith in its value. I shall never forget the hospital patient who literally clung to my hand and wept, "Rabbi, I want to pray, but I can't. I no longer believe in prayer."

How many of us echo that cry, and how we envy those who are capable of faith-filled worship. There was a woman in my community who had weathered storm after storm with so serene an expression, and so deep a gift of prayer, that everyone used to say, "I wish I had faith like that. I wish I could pray like that."

We have a problem. The hunger for communion is still there, but for many the food has been spoiled. The contemporary thought patterns of our world have shaken our belief in the efficacy of prayer, and the liturgy of our fathers has lost its meaning for us. Both their ideas and their language seem out of date.

Our Jewish prayer book was born in a far different world than ours. The Biblical psalms, the Talmudic *berachot* (blessings), and the medieval *piyyutim* (prayer-poems) were all written in a different context of thought. God was regarded not only as the Creator of the world, but He was also its daily overseer. He was not only First Cause but intermediate and immediate cause of all events. The rains fell by His will, the drought followed His command. Hurricanes and calm weather, sickness and health, defeat and victory all were dependent on Him. In such a world, worship was man's avenue of appeal, adoration was a way to God, thanksgiving was due Him, and petitions were freely addressed to the Almighty. Our prayer book is built on this faith in the value and efficacy of prayer.

In our day, God is regarded as far removed from the daily workings of the world. The universe is no longer a stage upon which He raises and lowers curtains or produces sound effects. In our contemporary worldview, the universe is a machine, wonderfully and fearfully made, and (most agree) the work of a Creative Intelligence, but still a machine, *all* of whose workings can be explored by scientific means and described by so-called laws of nature. Its linked and interlinked chains of chemical and physical cause and effect are quite impersonal. To imagine that prayer can effectuate any change in the workings of this machine would be to indulge in wishful thinking. "For what would we thank God?" the scientific mind asks. "The law of gravity? And for what petition Him? The third principle of thermodynamics?"

More than this, the Creator of this world, once regarded as a near and familiar figure whose central concern was this earth and the inhabitants thereof, who spoke in thunder to Moses and in a still small voice to Elijah, is now revealed to be the Deity of a world so vast that the mind boggles at its infinities. The Earth, in Bible days the center of the universe, is now seen as a tiny planet circling a piddling star which is fifteen thousand light years from the center of its Milky Way galaxy, which in turn is but one of many galaxies, all of them two million and more light years away. "When I behold the heavens, O Lord, what is man?" How can a God who has flung out the stars across the infinite space years attend the prayer of a puny human being who lies weeping on a lonely sickbed?

But our spirits are still hungry, and so there are many who have revised their conception of prayer. No longer able to believe it to be a dialogue between man and God, they take it to be a soliloquy between man and his "better self." No longer convinced of its *objective* efficacy, they praise its *subjective* usefulness as an outlet for the heart's longings.

Let us suppose for a moment that this were so, that prayer were nothing but a cry shouted into a silent void. Would this negate its value or its power? Not entirely. Even subjective prayer can be, has been, enormously effective, changing the objective world by its change of subjective persons in that world. The focusing of attention, which worship can achieve, and the explosive energies which meditation can mobilize, introduce new links into the chain of cause and effect. The chemical and the physical do respond to the spiritual.

Even if one assumes that what Moses experienced at the burning bush was only a mirage, still, what happened later in Egypt was a fact, and the memory of it a powerful force in history. And even if the Maccabees were only talking to themselves, they talked themselves into preserving Judaism. Yes, even if worship were only a subjective experience, prayer would be powerful in restoring personal health, powerful in achieving social reform, powerful in the rewriting of history.

But it is my conviction that prayer is more than a subjective experience, more than a soliloquy. Even as a sunflower on a cloudy day turns toward a sun that is hidden, so the human spirit reaches out to a spirit that is there. And this conviction does not require a leap of faith nor a closing of the eyes to all the accumulation of scientific research and saying, "Nevertheless, I believe!" On the contrary, science itself, in recent groping experiments and hesitant hypotheses on the growing edge of research in psychology, in medicine, in biology, stands on the threshold of the rediscovery of the spiritual aspects of the universe.

Space does not permit the detailing of all the evidence. Let me simply refer you to men and to books and their conclusions.

Carl Jung: "Anyone who has the least knowledge of the parapsychological materials which already exists and has been thoroughly verified, will know that so-called telepathic phenomena are undeniable facts."

Psychosomatic medicine has introduced a new viewpoint in the medical profession. Medical researchers who once conceived of the body as a chemico-physical machine have come to realize that there are nonmechanical factors at work. Where once the minister was regarded by some doctors as an intruder in the sickroom, the hospital chaplain is now a member of the healing team. "Heal us, O Lord, and we shall be healed."

Dr. Edmund Sinnott, professor of botany at Yale University, has put a lifetime of study and research into the physical and chemical processes of plant growth. In his book *The Biology of the Spirit,* he describes a series of biological findings that reveal purposeful goal-seeking "spiritual" qualities in the natural processes: "This self-regulating, pattern-seeking quality of all life may be *described* in chemical terms, but it cannot be explained nor understood except in spiritual terms."

Paleontologist Pierre Teilhard de Chardin in his book *The Phenomenon of Man* unfolds a thesis that is based upon the law of conservation of energy. By this law, everything now in existence was always there. Evolution is the progressive unfolding of qualities that were all previously present, but in so "thin" a form, so to speak, as not to be evident. Before man, there was no self-conscious spiritual groping, yet that quality of man was embryonic in the universe. In sum, that same spiritual quality which was present in the chaos of whirling nebulae, and is found by Sinnott in the groping purposefulness of plant life, comes to flower in the soul of man.

I would also recommend the reading of Loren Eiseley's *The Unexpected Universe.* This naturalist, student, and biographer of Charles Darwin lifts the heart and feeds the spirit. For real inspiration, read the chapter "The Star Thrower."

So it is with the sociologist Peter L. Berger in his book *A Rumor of Angels*, which is subtitled "Modern Society and the Rediscovery of the Supernatural." He turns for "rumors of angels" not to philosophy, nor to science, but to the structure of man's heart, his love of order, his capacity for play, his faith in the future. It is a stimulating book and will open windows in your soul.

All of these contemporary witnesses testify that we are formed by the same forces, chemical, physical, and spiritual, which hold the stars in their orbit, thrust up the mountains, scoop out the seas, bring the rose to bloom, teach the hawk to fly, the horse to neigh. "If I climb up unto the heavens, behold thou art there, and if I go to the ends of the earth, behold thou art there."

Prayer is not the lonely cry of a "tailless monkey-playing ape to his dreams," nor a shout into an empty void answered only by its own echo. Prayer is the spirit within us reaching out to the Spirit of the universe; and prayer is that Spirit responding to us. Even as the sun, 92 million miles away, spinning through space with the planets in its train, still (as Galileo pointed out) ripens a bunch of grapes as though that were all it had to do, so does the God of the infinite light years lean down close to the suffering to hear their cry.

And thus we realize that although the prayers of our fathers may seem naive, they penetrated intuitively to the core of truth—that prayer is dialogue between the spirit of man and the Spirit of God.

Yet, as natural as the hunger for dialogue with God may be, it must still be learned. Just as the eye must be trained to appreciate beauty, and the ear, great music, so the soul must be taught to pray.

How shall we learn to pray?

Luckily, we do not have to start from scratch; we can begin by learning how our fathers prayed.

To understand our Jewish liturgy takes study (and this is true I believe of all traditional forms of worship). Our liturgy resembles classical poetry. Anyone who has taken a course in literature knows that without a knowledge of Greek mythology, it is difficult to make sense of much English poetry. But with that knowledge, those poems not only become clear to the mind, but glow with beauty as well. The study of traditional prayer will make the seemingly arbitrary symbols and oddly worded blessings stand out like the colors in a medieval painting that has been cleansed and restored.

Another aspect of our prayer book that we need to understand is the fact that it speaks from and to so many different hearts. People are not alike religiously any more than they are physically. Some like their faith all systematic and intellectual; others like their faith all mystic and emotional. The prayer book was written by men of equally wide differences. The *Adon Olam* expresses the intellectual precision of a Maimonides, the *L'cho Dodi*, the poetic mysticism of kabbalism. The prayer book speaks to every heart. There are prayers for the quiet of the study, for militant social action, for the sick at heart, for the radiant of faith.

Would you learn to pray? Begin with the book of prayer.

And then continue by making your prayer a *keva*, a fixed habit, in your private devotions, your family rituals and your public worship. Customarily we separate these and weigh their comparative importance. Personally, I cannot see much distinction between them nor any possibility of getting along without all of them. A private prayer is like an aria sung in the shower, the family ritual is like singing the same selection together around the piano in the living room, public worship is like attending a concert. All enrich, all supplement. In private devotions there is a depth of insight that cannot be measured; in family devotions a quality of warmth beyond description; and among the "multitude keeping holy day," a limitless strengthening and broadening of faith. And all of these must be regular, our private exercises in a daily time and place, our family devotions at the table, daily, and on Sabbaths and holy days, our public worship weekly. We pump our Exercycles religiously, keep our golf dates ceremoniously, and buy season tickets to the symphony so we won't miss a one. Let us learn to pray by regular prayer.

But the key to prayer, as the psalmists knew, is the mood of prayer.

Leo Baeck was quoted recently by one of his students as saying that "a person achieves real *Kavanah* [inspired devotion] in rare moments." So our faith supplies us a prayer book that helps us reach "at least a certain height." The prayer book can reach high levels of inspiration, and high levels of inspiration can lift the prayer book above routine.

I would suggest another way to lift the level of the prayer book's impact. The creating and sustaining of a deep mood can best be achieved by recall, a recall of those moments in your life when time stood still, when you felt at one with the universe. It may have been a sunset, or your first glimpse of a snow-capped mountain, or looking at your sleeping baby. There have been moments in all our lives, whether we called them prayerful or not, when awe and wonder rose in our hearts like the tide on the shore, and at such moments we knew, without words, the meaning of life.

Would you make your routine prayers meaningful? Close your eyes and remember moments of grandeur and glory.

And if there have not yet been such moments, and if your every effort at communion seems dry and sterile, all I can say is keep trying.

Perhaps a personal experience will help clarify what I mean.

In high school, my senior English teacher taught us that Shakespeare was the greatest of dramatists and *Hamlet* the greatest of dramas. I accepted her judgment but did not appreciate the play at all. The soliloquy was over my head, the madness of Ophelia seemed without motive, the graveyard puns made no impression.

Then, at the University of Cincinnati, where I majored in English, a professor made the same claim. This time I tried to find out why he felt *Hamlet* the greatest of plays. But I could not understand the play, its characters, or its greatness. And, sophomore-like, I decided the whole thing was a plot; no one had the courage to say the king was really naked.

Twenty years later, I read that Laurence Olivier would play Hamlet, and so I went to see the movie. Nothing! And this time I was angry. The whole world couldn't be all wrong. So on coming home that very night, I took out my Shakespeare and read *Hamlet* until two in the morning. No contact. It was still beyond my ability to see what moved everyone else.

Ten more years later, a performance of *Hamlet* was advertised by a Houston theater-in-the-round. You would think that by this time I would have known better, but I went. And I do not know what happened that night, nor why, but suddenly *Hamlet* came alive. I realized why Ophelia had gone mad, I doubled up in laughter at the gravediggers' puns, I recognized what the soliloquy was about. Now I knew why *Hamlet* was called the greatest of dramas. It had taken years, but I knew, I knew.

And so it will be if our souls reach out in prayer again and again to the soul of the universe. Jeremiah said it best: "If with all your hearts you truly seek Me, you shall find Me."

BIBLIOGRAPHY:

Berger, Peter L. *A Rumor of Angels*. Garden City, NY: Doubleday & Co.,
     Inc., 1969. de Charden, Pierre Teilhard. *The Phenomenon of Man*.
     New York: Harper & Row, 1959.
Eiseley, Loren. *The Unexpected Universe*. New York: Harcourt, Brace &
     World, Inc., 1969.
Sinnott, Edmund W. *The Biology of the Spirit*. New York: The Viking
     Press, 1955.

APPENDICES

I
WISDOM OF THE AGES

The selections below represent the ancient and modern wisdom of mystics, theologians, educators, scientists, and men who had a glimpse of the Infinite Light.

KNOW THYSELF

People should think less about what they ought to do and more about what they ought to be. If only their being were good, their works would shine forth brightly.

—Meister Johannes Eckhart, 1260–1328,
German scholar, mystic

One must be able to strip oneself of all self-deception, to see oneself naked to one's own eyes before one can come to terms with the elements of oneself and know who one really is.

—Frances G. Wickes, 1875–1967,
American psychotherapist

In other living creatures ignorance of self is nature; in man it is vice.

—Boethius, ca. 480–524,
Roman philosopher

Cleanse your own heart, cast out from your mind pain, fear, envy, ill will, avarice, cowardice, passion uncontrolled. These things you cannot cast out unless you look to God alone; on Him alone set your thoughts, and consecrate yourself to His commands. If you wish for anything else, with groaning and sorrow you will follow what is stronger than you, ever seeking peace outside you, and never able to be at peace; for you seek it where it is not, and refuse to seek it where it is.

—Epictetus, AD 60–120,
Greek philosopher

Contemplation is a perception of God or of divine things; simple, free, penetrating, certain, proceeding from love and tending to Love.

—Louis Lallemant, 1587–1635

The difference between a good and a bad man does not lie in this, that the one wills that which is good and the other does not, but solely in this, that the one concurs with the living inspiring spirit of God within him, and the other resists it, and can be chargeable with evil only because he resists it.

—William Law, 1686–1761,
English clergyman, mystic

A man has many skins in himself, covering the depth of His heart. Man knows so many things; he does not know himself. Why, thirty or forty skins or hides, just like on an ox's or a bear's, so thick and hard, cover the soul. Go into your own ground and learn to know yourself there.

—Meister Johannes Eckhart

If the doors of perception were cleansed, everything would appear to man as it is, infinite.

For man has closed himself up, till he sees all things thro' narrow chinks in his cavern.

—William Blake, 1757–1827,
English poet, artist, mystic

By false desires and false thoughts man has built up for himself a false universe: as a mollusc, by the deliberate and persistent absorption of lime and rejection of all else, can build up for itself a hard shell which shuts it from the external world, and only represents in a distorted and unrecognizable form the ocean from which it was obtained. This hard and wholly unnutritious shell, this one-sided secretion of the surface-consciousness, makes as it were a little cave of illusion for each separate soul.

—Evelyn Underhill, 1875–1944,
English writer, mystic

Every thoughtful person who has ever considered the matter realizes that the doctors are right when they tell us that resentment, hate, grudge, ill will, jealousy, vindictiveness, are attitudes which produce ill-health. Have a fit of anger and experience for yourself that sinking feeling in the pit of your stomach, that sense of stomach sickness. Chemical reactions in the body are set up by emotional outbursts that result in feelings of ill-health. Should these be continued either violently or in a simmering state over a period of time, the general condition of the body will deteriorate.

—Norman Vincent Peale, 1898–1993,
American preacher

It is foolish to seek for God outside of oneself. This will result either in idolatry or in skepticism.

—Toyohiko Kagawa, 1888–1960,
Japanese social reformer and evangelist

All the great works and wonders that God has ever wrought . . . or even God Himself with all His goodness, can never make me blessed, but only insofar as they exist and are done and loved, known, tasted, and felt within me.

—*Theologia Germanica*, 1497

GOD

I am the holy Spirit of inspiration within thee, I am thy power to fulfill it.

—Anonymous

God is the natural appellation, for us Christians at least, for the supreme reality, so I will call this higher part of the universe by the name of God. We and God have business with each other; and in opening ourselves to His influence our deepest destiny is fulfilled. The universe, at those parts of it which our personal being constitutes, takes a turn genuinely for the worse or for the better in proportion as each one of us fulfills or evades God's demands.

—William James, 1842–1910,
American philosopher

LOVE

Love is infallible; it has no errors, for all errors are the want of love.

—William Law, 1686–1761,
English clergyman, mystic

Never wait for fitter time or place to talk to Him. To wait till thou go to church or to thy closet is to make Him wait. He will listen as thou walkest.

—George Macdonald, 1824–1905,
Scottish novelist and poet

God forces no one, for love cannot compel, and God's service, therefore, is a thing of perfect freedom.

—Hans Denk, 1495–1527,
German mystic

To love God with all our hearts and all our souls and all our minds means that every cleavage in human existence is overcome.

—Reinhold Niebuhr, 1892–1971,
American theologian, educator, author

You are a distinct portion of the essence of God; and contain part of Him in yourself. Why, then, are you ignorant of your noble birth? Why do you not consider whence you came? Why do you not remember, when you are eating, who you are who eat; and whom you feed? Do you not know that it is the Divine you feed? The Divine you exercise? You carry a God about with you, poor wretch, and know nothing of it.

—Epictetus, AD 60–120,
Greek philosopher

PRAY

If the heart wanders or is distracted, bring it back to the point quite gently and replace it tenderly in its Master's presence. And even if you did nothing during the whole of your hour but bring your heart back and place it again in Our Lord's presence, though it went away every time you brought it back, your hour would be very well employed.

—Saint Francis de Sales, 1567–1622,
French Archbishop of Geneva

Our safety does not lie in the present perfection of our knowledge of the will of God, but in our sincerity in obeying the light we have, and in seeking for more.

—Edward Worsdell, 1853–1908,
English teacher

God is bound to act, to pour Himself into thee as soon as He shall find thee ready.

—Meister Johannes Eckhart

God wants only one thing in the whole world, the thing which it needs . . . that thing is to find the innermost part of the noble spirit of man clean and ready for Him to accomplish the divine purpose therein. He has all power in heaven and earth, but the power to do His work in man against man's will, He has not got.

—Johann Tauler, ca. 1304–1361,
German friar-preacher

But open your eyes and the world is full of God.

—Jacob Boehme, 1575–1624,
German mystic

The right relation between prayer and conduct is not that conduct is supremely important and prayer may help it, but that prayer is supremely important and conduct tests it.

—William Temple, 1881–1944, archbishop of Canterbury

Immediately you awake set your first thought on God. Keep your mind on Him for a few seconds. Do not think of Him subjectively, as to your relation to Him, your failures, your sins, or your needs, but rather objectively. Let your whole self become conscious of Him. Think of Him as shining beauty, radiant joy, creative power, all-pervading love, perfect understanding, purity, and serenity. This need only take a moment or two once the habit has been formed, but it is of inestimable importance. It sets the tone for the whole day . . . .

One's waking mood tends to correspond to the state of mind in which one falls asleep. If, therefore, as a result of a disturbed night or simply because of lack of practice, this first thought of God should evade you, look out of the window for something obviously made by Him, trees, flowers, the sky, or a wind-shaped cloud, even a gray one, and ponder on the perfection of His handicraft . . . .

Never get into bed with a burdened or a heavy mind; whether it be a vague oppression or a definite fear, shame or remorse, anger or hate, get rid of the evil thing before you lie down to sleep. Night is a holy time, a time of renewing and refreshment. He giveth to His beloved while they sleep; our unconscious mind is active during our slumber. Settle down restfully to let your mind get clear and your spirit unclogged.

—Muriel Lester, 1885–1968,
English author, social worker

Your enjoyment of the world is never right till every morning you awake in Heaven; see yourself in your Father's palace; and look upon the skies, the earth and the air as celestial joys; having such a reverent esteem of all, as if you were among the Angels. The bride of a monarch, in her husband's chamber, hath no such causes of delight as you.

—Thomas Traherne, ca. 1637–1674,
English poet, religious writer

A frequent intercession with God, earnestly beseeching Him to forgive the sins of all mankind, to bless them with His providence, enlighten them with His Spirit, and bring them to everlasting happiness, is the divinest exercise that the heart of man can be engaged in.

—William Law

Our prayer for others ought never to be: "God! give them the light Thou hast given to me!" but: "Give them all the light and truth they need for their highest development!"

—Mahatma Gandhi, 1869–1948,
Indian statesman, national leader

The seed of God is in us. Given an intelligent and hard-working farmer, it will thrive and grow up to God, whose seed it is; and accordingly its fruits will be God-nature. Pear seeds grow into pear trees, nut seeds into nut trees, and God seed into God.

—Meister Johannes Eckhart

II
MYSTICS AT PRAYER

In this section we have carefully selected prayers of mystics, sages, saints, and those whom the Light of our Creator inspired.

To derive continual benefit in your spiritual development we recommend you refer to these prayers daily.

Grant that no word may fall from me against my will unfit for the present need.

—Pericles, Athenian statesman, 495–429 BC

With bended knees, with hand outstretched, I pray to You, my LORD, O INVISIBLE BENEVOLENT SPIRIT!
Vouchsafe to me in this hour of joy,
All righteousness of action, all wisdom of the good mind,
That I may thereby bring joy to the Soul of Creation.

—Zoroaster, founder of ancient Persian religion Zoroastrianism, sixth century BC

Grant me to be beautiful within, and all I have of outward things to be at peace with those within.

—Socrates, Athenian philosopher, 469–399 BC

O GOD, the FATHER, ORIGIN of DIVINITY, GOOD beyond all that is good, FAIR beyond all that is fair, in WHOM is calmness, peace and concord; bring us all back into an unity of love, which may bear some likeness to Your sublime nature.

—Jacobite liturgy, AD third century

Our Father in heaven, hallowed be your name, your kingdom come, your will be done on earth as it is in heaven.
Give us today our daily bread, and forgive us the wrong we have done as we forgive those who wrong us.

Subject us not to the trial but deliver us from the evil one.

—Jesus Christ, the Savior

Thanks be to YOU, O GOD, for everything.

—Saint Chrysostom, Greek Father of the Church,
born in Syria, 347–409

Steer THOU the vessel of our life towards THYSELF, THOU tranquil Haven of all storm-tossed souls. Show us the course wherein we should go.

—Saint Basil the Great, 330–379

May the Strength of GOD pilot us. May the Power of GOD preserve us. May the Wisdom of GOD instruct us. May the Way of GOD direct us.

—Saint Patrick, Christian saint, Apostle of Ireland, ca. 389–461

O GOD of Unchangeable Power, let the whole world feel and see that things which were cast down are being raised up, that those which had grown old are being made new and that all things are returning to perfection.

—Gelasian Sacramentary, Saint Gelasius,
AD fifth century

Grant us, O LORD, not to mind earthly things, but to love things heavenly; and even now while we are placed among things that are passing away, to cleave to those that shall abide.

—Leonine Sacramentary, Citta Leonina,
part of ancient Rome, AD fifth century

O LORD, grant us to love THEE; grant that we may love those that love THEE; grant that we may do the deeds that win THY love. Make the love of THEE to be dearer than ourselves, our families, than wealth, and even than cool water.

—Muhammad ibn 'Abdullah,
the founder of the religion of Islam, 570–632

Come LORD and work. Arouse us and incite. Kindle us, sweep us onwards. Be fragrant as flowers, sweet as honey. Teach us to love and to run.

—Saint Augustine, Bishop of Hippo, 354–430

LORD, teach me to know YOU, and to know myself.

—Saint Augustine

Take THOU possession of us. We give our whole selves to THEE, make known to us what THOU requirest of us, and we will accomplish it.

—Saint Augustine

O ETERNAL LIGHT, shine into our hearts. O ETERNAL GOODNESS, deliver us from evil. O ETERNAL POWER, be THOU our support. ETERNAL WISDOM, scatter the darkness of our ignorance. ETERNAL PITY, have mercy upon us.

—Alcuin, archbishop, English theologian, 735–804

I love THEE because I love; I love that I may love.

—Saint Bernard, French ecclesiastic, 1091–1153

If YOU, LORD, are so good to those who seek, what shall YOUR goodness be to those who find?

—Saint Bernard

Grant me fervently to desire, wisely to search out, and perfectly to fulfill all that is well-pleasing unto THEE.

—Saint Thomas Aquinas, philosopher, theologian, doctor of the Church, ca. 1225–1274

Praise be to THEE, O HIDDEN ONE and MANIFESTED ONE. Praise be to THY Glory, to THY Might, to THY Power, and to THY Great Skill.

O ALLAH, to THEE all greatness belongs. O THOU who possessest the Power and Beauty and Perfection. THOU are the Spirit of All.

Praise to THEE, O SOVEREIGN of all Monarchs; to THEE, O MASTER of all affairs; to THEE, O CONTROLLER of all things; to THEE, RULER of all BEINGS.

THOU art free from death, free from birth and free from all limitations. O THOU ETERNAL ONE, THOU art free from all conditions, pure from all things. O ALLAH, THOU art the GOD of Souls on earth; THOU art the LORD of Hosts in the Heavens.

—Sufi invocation, developed in Persia

O LORD, I gasp in my desire for THEE, yet can I not consume THEE. The more I eat—the fiercer is my hunger; the more I drink—the greater is my thirst. I follow after that which flieth from me, and as I follow, my desire groweth greater.

—Jan van Ruysbroeck,
1293–1381

Grant me, O LORD, heavenly wisdom, that I may learn above all things to seek and to find THEE; above all things to relish and to love THEE; and to think of all other things as being what indeed they are, at the disposal of THY wisdom.

—Thomas à Kempis, Christian mystic, 1380–1471

LORD, we pray not for tranquility, nor that our tribulations may cease; we pray for THY Spirit and THY love that THOU grant us strength and grace to overcome adversity.

—Girolamo Savonarola, Christian martyr, 1452–1498

Defend me, O GOD, from myself.

—Sir Thomas Browne, English philosopher, 1605–1682

O give me grace to see YOUR face and be a constant mirror of ETERNITY.

—Thomas Traherne 1636–1674

LORD, I give YOU all.

—Blaise Pascal, French philosopher and mathematician,
1623–1662

LORD, I know not what I ought to ask of THEE; THOU only knowest what I need; THOU lovest me better than I know how to love myself. O FATHER, give to THY child that which he himself knows not how to ask.

—François de Salignac Fénelon,
archbishop of Cambrai, author, 1651–1715

ALMIGHTY GOD, grant me THY grace to be faithful in action, and not anxious about success. My only concern is to do THY will, and to lose myself in THEE when engaged in duty. It is for THEE to give my weak efforts such fruits as THOU seest fit, none, if such be THY pleasure.

—François de Salignac Fénelon 1651–1715

O Loving-Kindness so old and still so new, I have been too late in loving THEE.

O Lord, enlarge the chambers of my heart that I may find room for THY love.

Sustain me by THY Power, lest the fire of THY love consume me.

—Brother Lawrence, Christian mystic, 1614–1691

Draw near to my heart and inflame it. Touch my uncircumcised lips with a burning coal from THINE altar, that I may not speak of THINE ardent love in a cold or feeble manner.

—Gerhard Tersteegen, poet and ascetic, 1697–1769

O ADMIRABLE WISDOM, that circlest all eternity, receivest into THYSELF all immensity, and drawest to THYSELF all infinity; from the inexhaustible fountain of THY light, shed some ray into my soul that I may more and more love whatever tends to THY glory and honour.

—Blaise Palma, seventeenth century mystic

O GOD, in THEE alone can our wearied souls have full satisfaction and rest, and in THY love is the highest joy. LORD, if we have THEE, we have enough.

—Melchior Ritter, seventeenth century mystic

O LORD, let us not live to be useless.

—John Wesley, founder of Methodism, 1703–1791

Pour upon us THY Spirit of meekness and love. Annihilate selfhood in us. Be THOU all our life.

—William Blake

I am born to serve THEE, to be THINE, to be THY instrument. Let me be THY blind instrument. I ask not to see, ask not to know; I ask simply to be used.

—John Henry Newman, English cardinal and author, 1801–1890

Grant us grace from rest from all sinful deeds and thoughts, to surrender ourselves wholly unto THEE, and keep our souls still before THEE like a still lake, so that the beams of THY grace may be mirrored therein, and may kindle in our hearts the glow of faith and love and prayer.

—Collect from the eighteenth century

If THOU speakest not, I will fill my heart with THY silence and endure it. I will keep still and wait like the night with starry vigil and its head bent low with patience. The morning will surely come, the darkness will vanish, and THY voice pour down in golden streams, breaking through the sky.

—Rabindranath Tagore, Bengali poet and mystic, 1861–1941

Dear GOD and FATHER of us all, forgive our faith in cruel lies; forgive the blindness that denies; forgive THY creature when he takes, for the all-perfect Love THOU art, some grim creation of His heart.

—John Greenleaf Whittier, American poet, 1807–1892

They who never ask anything but simply love, THOU in their heart abidest for ever, for this is THY very home.

—Hindu prayer

Out of the unreal, lead me to the Real.
Out of the darkness, lead me into the Light.
Out of death, lead me to Deathlessness.

—Hindu prayer

Grant, GOD, protection
And in protection, strength
And in strength, understanding
And in understanding, knowledge
And in knowledge, the knowledge of the just,
And in the knowledge of the just, the love of it,
And in the love of it, the love of all existences.
And in the love of all existences, the love of GOD,
GOD and all GOODNESS.

—Gorsedd (Welsh bard) prayer

O GOD, I thank THEE for all the joy I have had in life.

—Earl Brihtnoth of the Northmen,
?– 991

O GOD, THINE is the kingdom, the power and the Glory, for ever
and ever. Amen.

—Sister E. T. Cawdry, African mystic

For health, prosperity and happiness
To THEE I pray,
But most of all a smile to greet
The newborn day.

—Beatrice Colony, author

Let not our sins be a cloud between THEE and us.

—John Colet, Dean of St. Paul's, London, mystic,
1467–1519

THY glory alone, O GOD, be the end of all that we say;
Let it shine in every deed, let it kindle the prayers that I pray;
Let it burn in my innermost soul till the shadow of self pass away,
And the light of THY glory, O GOD, be unveiled in the dawning of day.

—F. W. Scott, English writer

Behold THY creature; do with me what THOU wilt. I have nothing, my GOD, that holds me back. I am THINE alone.

—Scupoli, mystic

Tomorrow
I am content to leave with him
Who gives today
For today the sun smiles
And the earth responds,
And a twinkling, singing sea
Forms lacy patterns on the sand.
O, GOD,
I am grateful
For this day!

—E. C. Wilson, American writer and philosopher

GOD be merciful to me, a fool.

—Edward Rowland Sill, American poet and author,
1841–1887

May it be Thy will, O God, that we return to Thee in perfect penitence, so that we may not be ashamed to meet our fathers in the life to come.

—Talmud

SELECTED BIBLIOGRAPHY

The listing below represents a basic core of books published in English on prayer and fasting. Especially recommended books on prayer are marked with an asterisk.

Books on Prayer:

*   Allen, Charles L., *All Things Are Possible Through Prayer*, 1958

*   Armstrong, H. Parr, *Living in the Currents of God*, 1962

Austin, Mary, *Can Prayer Be Answered?* 1934

Baillie, John, *A Diary of Private Prayer*, 1950

Baker, F. Augustine, *Holy Wisdom, or Directions for the Prayer of Contemplation*, n.d.

Banks, J. B., *The Master and the Disciple—Devotional Reading*, 1954

Barry, J. G. H., *On Prayer to the Dead*, 1922

Bauman, Edward W., *Intercessory Prayer*, 1958

Belden, Alfred, *The Practice of Prayer*, n.d.

Boggis, R. J. E., *Praying for the Dead*, 1913

Bro, H. H., *Dreams in the Life of Prayer, The Approach of Edgar Cayce*, 1970

Bro, M., *More Than We Are*, 1965

Campbell, James H., *The Place of Prayer in the Christian Religion*

Carrel, Alexis, *Prayer*, 1949

Casteel, John H., *Renewal in Retreats*, 1959

Clark, Glenn, *I Will Lift Up Mine Eyes*, n.d.

Clarke, James Freeman, *The Christian Doctrine of Prayer*

Dallas, Helen Alex, ed., *Communion and Fellowship (Aids to the Bereaved)*, 1921

Day, Albert E., *An Autobiography of Prayer*, 1952

Fillmore, Charles and Cora, *Teach Us to Pray*, 1941

* Fillmore, L., *The Prayer Way to Find Health, Wealth, and Happiness*, 1964

Fluck, D., *Better Health Through Prayer*, n.d.

Forsythe and Greenwell, *The Power of Prayer*

Fosdick, Harry Emerson, *The Meaning of Prayer*, 1915

Freer, Harold, *God Meets Us Where We Are*, 1967

Freer and Hall, *Two or Three Together: A Manual for Prayer Groups*, 1954

* French, R.M., *The Way of a Pilgrim*, 1960

Frost, B., *The Art of Mental Prayer*, 1931

Gordon, S. D., *Quiet Talks on Prayer*, 1967

Grou, J. N., *How to Pray*, 1955

Hanky, P., *Signposts on the Christian Way*, 1962

Harkness, G., *Prayer and the Common Life*, 1948

Heard, Gerald, *Preface to Prayer*, 1944

Herman, E., *Creative Prayer*, n.d.

Herrman, Wilhelm, *Communion With God*

Ikin, A. Graham, *Life, Faith and Prayer*, 1954

Jones, Rufus, M., *The Double Search*

Kelly, T. R., *Testament of Devotion*, 1941

Lake, Alexander, *Your Prayers Are Always Answered*, 1956

* Laubach, F. C., *Prayer, The Mightiest Force in the World*, 1946

Leen, Edward, *Progress Through Mental Prayer*, 1935

* Loehr, Franklin, *The Power of Prayer on Plants*, 1959

* Mack, Gwynne, *Talking With God: The Healing Power of Prayer*, 1961

Maclachlan, L., *Common Sense About Prayer*, 1962

——, *How to Pray for Healing*, 1963

——, *Intelligent Prayer*, 1946

——, *The Teaching of Jesus on Prayer*, 1952

——, *Twenty-One Steps to Positive Prayer*, 1965

Magee, John, *Reality and Prayer*, 1957

Magee, Raymond, *Call to Adventure—The Retreat as Religious Experience*, 1967

Mann, Stella, *Change Your Life Through Prayer*, 1955

— —, *How to Live in the Circle of Prayer*, 1959

Matson, Archie, *A Month With the Master*, 1958

McComb, Samuel, *Prayer, What It Is and What It Does*

McFadyen, John Edgar, *The Prayer of the Bible*

Murray, A., *With Christ in the School of Prayer*, 1885

Neville, *Prayer, The Art of Believing*, 1943

* Parker, and St. Johns, *Prayer Can Change Your Life*, 1957

Poulain, A., *The Graces of Interior Prayer*, N.D.

Rawson, F. L., *The Nature of True Prayer*, 1930

— —, *Right Thinking, the Basis of True Prayer*, 1919

Russell, A. J., *God Calling*, 1948

Sherman, Harold, *How to Use the Power of Prayer*, 1958

* Shoemaker, H., *The Secret of Effective Prayer*

* Steere, Douglas, *Dimensions of Prayer*, 1962

— —, *Prayer and Worship*, 1938

Strong, Anna Louise, *The Psychology of Prayer*

Swetenham, L., *Conquering Prayer*

Trumbull, H. Clay, *Prayer, Its Nature and Scope*

Weatherhead, L. D., *A Private House of Prayer*, 1958

Winslow, Jack C., *When I Awake*, 1938

Wuellner, F., *Prayer and the Living Christ*

Books on Fasting:

Bragg, Paul C., *The Miracle of Fasting*, 1972

Brown, Harold R., *The Fast Way to Health and Vigor*, 1961

Carrel, Alexis, *Man, the Unknown*, 1932

Carrington, Hereward, *Fasting for Health and Long Life*, 1953

Carrington, *Vitality, Fasting and Nutrition* 1908

Ehret, Arnold, *Rational Fasting*

Hazzard, Linda B., *Scientific Fasting*, 1963

Langfield, Herbert S., "On the Psychophysiology of a Prolonged Fast"; *Psychological Monographs*, Volume XVI, No. 5; Harvard University: July 1914

MacFadden, Bernarr A., *Fasting for Health*, 1934

Prince, Derek, *Restoration Through Fasting*

Shelton, Herbert M., *Fasting Can Save Your Life*, 1964
Sinclair, Upton, *The Fasting Cure*
Wallis, Arthur, *A Spiritual and Practical Guide to Fasting*, 1972

Yogi Amrit Desai
Dr. Frank C. Laubach
Sister Cecile Sandra
Princess Poon Pismai Diskul
Dr. Emmet Fox
The Grand Mufti of Syria
Rabbi Robert I. Kahn
The Archbishop of Canterbury

These people, and many more—
—as rich and varied as the world
itself—speak out in testimony to
the working of faith and prayer
through God, and love . . . of
man, of God, of God for man.

BIBLIOGRAPHY

Abbott, Walter M., and Chapman, Geoffrey, eds. *The Documents of Vatican II*, with notes by Protestant and Orthodox authorities, 1966.

Acklom, George Moreby. "The Man and the Book." In Maurice R. Bucke, *Cosmic Consciousness: A Study in the Evolution of the Human Mind*. New York: E. P. Dutton & Co., 1901 and 1975.

Adler, M. J., editor-in-chief. *The Great Ideas: A Syntopicon of Great Books of the Western World*. Chicago: Encyclopaedia Britannica, Inc, 1971.

Affifi, Abu'l-'Ala. *The Mystical Philosophy of Muhyid'Din Ibnul-'Arabi*. Cambridge, 1936.

Afterman, Allen. *Kabbalah and Consciousness*. Riverdale, NY: Sheep Meadow Press, 1992.

Amaldi, E. "The Unity of Physics." *Physics Today*, September 1973.

Ambjorn, J. and Wolfram, S. "Properties of the Vacuum. 1. Mechanical and Thermodynamic." *Ann. Phys. 147* (1983): 1–32.

— —. "Properties of the Vacuum. 2. Electrodynamic." *Ann. Phys. 147* (1983): 33–56. Andrews, Allan A. *The Teachings Essential for Rebirth: A Study of Genshin's Ojoyoshu*. Tokyo: Sophia University Press, 1973.

Anesaki, Masaharu. *Nichiren, the Buddhist Prophet*. Cambridge, MA: Harvard University Press, 1916.

Ansari, Muhammad Abdul-Haq. *Sufism and Shari'ah: A Study of Shaykh Ahmad Sirhindi's Effort to Reform Sufism*. Leicester, England: The Islamic Foundation, 1986.

Aquinas, Thomas. *On Being and Essence*. Translated by Armand Maurer. Toronto: The Pontifical Institute of Medieval Studies, 1949.

—— ——. "Summa Theologica." Vol. 19, *The Great Books of the Western World.* Chicago: Encyclopaedia Britannica, Inc., 1971.

Aristotle. *Topics*, Vol. 8, bk. 4, ch. 1, *The Great Books of the Western World.* Chicago: Encyclopaedia Britannica, Inc. 1971.

Armstrong, Karen. *A History of God.* New York: Ballantine Books, 1993.

Ashvagosha. *The Awakening of Faith.* Translated by D. T. Suzuki. Chicago: Open Court, 1900.

Assagioli, Roberto. *La Vie dello Spirito.* Rome: G. Filipponio, 1974.

Athenagoras. "A Plea for the Christians." Translated by Rev. B. P. Pratten. Vol. 2, *Fathers of the Second Century.* Peabody, MA: Hendrickson Publishers, 1999.

Atiyah, Michael. "Topology of the Vacuum." *The Philosophy of Vacuum.* Oxford: Oxford University Press, 1991.

Attar, Fariduddin. *Muslim Saints and Mystics.* Translated by A. J. Arberry. London: Routledge and Kegan Paul, 1966.

Augustine. "The City of God." Vol. 18, *Great Books of the Western World.* Chicago: Encyclopaedia Britannica, Inc., 1952.

—— ——. *On the Gospel of St. John.* Grand Rapids: Wm B. Eerdmans Publishing Co., 1987.

Aurobindo, Sri. *The Light Divine.* New York: The Sri Aurobindo Library, Inc., 1949.

—— ——. *Essays on the Gita.* Pondicherry: Sri Aurobindo Ashram Press, 1950.

—— ——. *The Ideal of Human Unity.* New York: E. P. Dutton & Co., 1950.

—— ——. *The Mind Light.* New York: E. P. Dutton & Co., 1953.

—— ——. *The Life Divine.* Pondicherry: Sri Aurobindo Ashram Press, 1960.

—— ——. *Birth Centenary Library.* 30 vols. Pondicherry, India: Sri Aurobindo Ashram Press, 1972.

—— ——. *The Future Evolution of Man.* Wheaton, IL: The Theosophical Publishing House, 1974.

Baba, Meher. *God to Man and Man to God.* Edited by C. B. Purdom. Myrtle Beach, SC: Sheriar Press, 1975.

—— ——. *Sparks from Meher Baba.* Myrtle Beach, SC: Sheriar Press, 1962.

Baba, Satya Sai. *Teachings of Sri Satya Sai Baba.* Edited by Roy Eugene Davis. Lakemont, GA: CSA Press, 1974.

Bailey, Alice A. *The Consciousness of the Atom.* New York: Lucis Publishing Company, 1922.

____. *The Soul and Its Mechanism.* London: Lucis Trust, 1971.

____. *From Intellect to Intuition.* London: Lucis Trust, 1971.

Bandera, Cesareo. *The Sacred Game: The Role of the Sacred in the Genesis of Modern Literary Fiction.* Penn. State Studies in Romance Literatures.

Barnstone, Willis, ed. "The Gospel of Thomas." *The Other Bible.* San Francisco: HarperCollins Publishers, 1984.

Barrett, C. K. *From First Adam to Last, A Study in Pauline Theology.* New York: Scribner, 1962.

Basler, Roy P., and others. *The Collected Works of Abraham Lincoln. 8 vols.* New Brunswick: Rutgers University Press, 1953.

Bedrij, Orest, ed. *Yes, It's Love: Your Life Can Be A Miracle.* New York: Pyramid Publications, 1974.

____. *One.* San Francisco: Strawberry Hill Press, 1977.

____. *You.* Warwick, NY: Amity House, 1988.

____. "Grand Unification of the Science of Physics through the Cosmolog." *Abstracts: Amer. Assoc. for the Adv. of Sci.* Annual Meeting, 1990.

____. "Fundamental Constants in Quantum Electrodynamics." *Dopovidi: Proceedings of the National Academy of Sciences of Ukraine,* no. 3 (March 1993).

____. "Scale Invariance, Unifying Principle, Order and Sequence of Physical Quantities and Fundamental Constants." *Dopovidi: Proc. of the Nat. Acad. of Sci. of Ukr., no. 4 (*April 1993).

____. "Connection of p with the Fine Structure Constant." *Dopovidi: Proc. Of the Nat. Acad. of Sci. of Ukr., no. 10 (*1994).

____. "Revelation and Verification of Ultimate Reality and Meaning through Direct Experience and the Laws of Physics." *Ultimate Reality and Meaning 23 (2000).*

____. *La Preuve Scientifique de L'Existence de Dieu.* Montreal: Courteau Louise Ed., 2000.

____. "New Relationships and Measurements for Gravity Physics." Vol. 43, pt. 2, *Proc. of the Fourth Inter. Conf. Symmetry in Nonlinear*

Mathematical Physics, Proc. of Nat. Acad. of Sci. of Ukr. Institute of Mathematics, 2002.

Bedrij, O., and Fushchych, W. I. "On the Electromagnetic Structure of Elementary Particles' Masses," in Russian. *Doklady, Ukr. SSR Academy of Sciences,* no. 2 (February 1991).

———. "Fundamental Constants of Nucleon-Meson Dynamics." *Dopovidi: Proc. of the Nat. Acad. of Sci. of Ukr, no. 5 (1993).*

———. "Planck's Constant Is Not Constant in Different Quantum Phenomena." *Dopovidi: Proc. of the Nat. Acad. of Sci. of Ukr, no. 12 (1995).*

Bell, J. S. "On the Einstein-Podolsky-Rosen Paradox." *Physics* 1 (1964): 195.

———. "On the Problem of Hidden Variables in Quantum Mechanic." *Reviews of Modern Physics* 38 (1966): 447.

———. *Speakable and Unspeakable in Quantum Mechanics.* Cambridge: Cambridge University Press, 1987.

———. *Collected Papers in Quantum Mechanics.* Cambridge: Cambridge University Press, 1987.

Benardete, José. *Infinity.* Oxford: Clarendon Press, 1964.

Benjamin, Barbara. *Face to Face.* Yonkers, NY: Nepperham Press, 2009.

Besant, Annie. *The Self and Its Sheaths.* Adyar, Madras, India: The Theosophical Publishing House (TPH), 1948.

———*An Autobiography.* TPH: Adyar, Chennai, 1984.

———*Esoteric Christianity.* Preface. Adyar, Chennai: TPH, 1989.

———*Thought Power.* Wheaton, IL: TPH, 1988.

Bhagavad-Gita, The in Sanskrit. Many English translations are available, among them that of Swami Prabhavananda and Christopher Isherwood, a Mentor Paperback, 1954; that of Ann Stanford, New York: Herder & Herder, 1971; that of P. Lal, Calcutta: Writers Workshop, 1965; and that of Swami Nikhilanada, New York: Ramakrishna-Vivekananda Center, 1952. Also a complete edition with original Sanskrit text by His Divine Grace A. C. Bhaktivedanta Swami Prabhupada. Bhatnagar, R. S. *Dimensions of Classical Sufi Thought.* Delhi: Motilal Banarsidass, 1984.

Bible, Holy: From the Ancient Eastern Text. George M. Lamsa's Translation from the Aramaic of the Peshitta. Philadelphia: A.J.Holman Co., a division of B. Lippincott Co., 1933.

Bible, The Holy: New International Version. Grand Rapids, MI: Zondervan Bible Publishers, 1978.

Bible, The Holy. New Revised Standard Version. London: Collins Publishers, 1989.

Bible, The New American. Translated from the Original Languages with Critical Use of All the Ancient Sources. Washington, DC: Confraternity of Christine Doctrine, 1970.

Blake, William. *The Complete Writings of William Blake*. Edited by Geoffrey Keynes. Oxford: Oxford University Press, 1969.

Blavatsky, H. P. *The Theosophical Glossary*. Los Angeles: The Theosophy Co., 1930.

__ __. *Collected Writings*. 15 vols. Wheaton, IL; Adyar, Chennai, India: Theosophical Publishing House, 1966–91.

__ __. *The Secret Doctrine*. Adyar, Madras, India: Theosophical Publishing, 1987.

Boehme, Jacob. *The Incarnation of Jesus Christ*. Translated by J. R. Earle. London: Constable, 1934.

Bohm, David. *Quantum Theory*. New York: Prentice-Hall, 1951.

__ __. *The Special Theory of Relativity*. New York: W. A. Benjamin, 1965.

__ __. *Wholeness and the Implicate Order*. Boston: Routledge & Kegan Paul Ltd., 1980. Reprint. London: Associated Book Publishers Ltd.; Ark Paperbacks Ltd., 1983.

Bohm, D., and Hiley, B. *The Undivided Universe: An Ontological Interpretation of Quantum Theory*. London: Routledge, 1993.

Bohr, N. *Atomic Theory and the Description of Nature*. Cambridge: Cambridge University Press, 1934.

__ __. *Essays 1958–1962 on Atomic Physics and Human Knowledge*. New York: Wiley-Interscience, 1963.

Bokser, Rabbi Ben Zion, ed. and trans. *The Essential Writings of Abraham Isaac Kook*. Warwick, NY: Amity House, 1988.

Bolzano, Bernard. *Paradoxes of the Infinite*. New Haven, CT.: Yale University Press, 1950.

Boole, George. *An Investigation of the Laws of Thought on Which Are Founded the Mathematical Theories of Logic and Probabilities*, 1854.

Bromley, D. A., ed. "The Unity of Physics." *Physics in Perspective*. Washington, DC: National Academy of Sciences, 1972.

Bruno, Giordano. *On the Infinite Universe and Worlds.* Translated by Dorothy Singer. New York: Greenwood Press, 1968.

Brunton, Paul. *The Hidden Teaching Beyond Yoga.* New York: Samuel Weiser, 1972.

Bruteau, Beatrice. *Worthy Is the World: The Hindu Philosophy of Sri Aurobindo.* Rutherford, NJ: Fairleigh Dickinson University Press, 1971.

_____. *Evolution Toward Divinity: Teilhard de Chardin and the Hindu Traditions.* Wheaton, IL.: The Theosophical Publishing House, 1974.

Bub, Jeffrey. *Interpreting the Quantum World.* Cambridge: Cambridge University Press, 1997.

Buber, Martin, *Hasidism.* New York: Philosophical Library, 1997.

Bucke, Maurice R. *Cosmic Consciousness: A Study into Evolution of the Human Mind.* New York: E. P. Dutton & Co., 1901 and 1975.

Burghardt, Walter J. *The Image of God in Man according to Cyril of Alexandria.* Washington, DC: Catholic University of America, 1957.

Buswell, Robert E. Jr., trans. and ed. *The Korean Approach to Zen: The Collected Works of Chinul.* Honolulu: University of Hawaii Press, 1983.

_____. *The Zen Monastic Experience.* Princeton, NJ: Princeton University Press, 1992.

Cantor, Georg. *Contributions to the Founding of the Theory of Transfinite Numbers.* Translated by Philip E. B. Jourdain. La Salle, IL: Open Court, 1952.

Capra, Fritjof. *The Tao of Physics.* 3rd ed. Boston: Shambhala Publications, Inc., 1991.

_____. *The Turning Point.* New York: Simon & Schuster, 1982.

Capra, Fritjof and Steindl-Rast, David with Matus, Thomas. *Belonging to the Universe: Explorations on the Frontiers of Science and Spirituality.* San Francisco: HarperCollins Publishers, 1991.

Carey, Ken. *Vision.* Kansas City, MO: Uni Sun, 1985.

_____. *Starseed: The Third Millennium.* San Francisco: HarperCollins Publishers, 1991.

Carpenter, Edward. *The Drama of Love and Death*. London: George Allen & Unwin Ltd.

Carter, Robert E. *The Nothingness beyond God: An Introduction to the Philosophy of Nishida Kitaro*. New York: Paragon House, 1989.

Catherine of Genoa. *Vita Mirabile e Dottnna Celeste de Santa Catherina de Genova*. Insieme Col Trattato del Purgatorio e col Dialogo Della Santa, 1743.

Catherine of Siena,. *The Divine Dialogue of Saint Catherine of Siena*. Translated by Alger Thorold. 2nd ed. London, 1926.

Chaden, Charlene Leslie-. *A Compendium of the Teachings of Sathya Sai Baba*. Prasanthi Nilayam: Sai Towers Publishing, 1997.

Champawat, Narayan. "Rabindranath Tagore." In *Great Thinkers of the Eastern World. Edited by Ian P. McGreal*. New York: HarperCollins Publishers, 1995.

Chan, Wing-Tsit, ed. and trans. *The Platform Scripture*. New York: St. John's University Press, 1963. An unabridged translation of the Tun-huang (Dunhuang) manuscript, found in a cave in Dunhuang, northwest China, in 1900.

— —. trans. and comp. *A Source Book in Chinese Philosophy*. Princeton, NJ: Princeton University Press. 1963. Chapter 28 discusses Chou and gives a variety of selections from his books.

Chang, Garma C. C. *The Buddhist Teaching of Totality: The Philosophy of Hwa Yen Buddhism*. University Park, PA.: Penn State Press, 1971.

Chapple, Christopher Key, and Yogi Ananda Viraj (Eugene P. Kelly Jr.), trans. *The Yoga Sutras of Patanjali: An Analysis of the Sanskrit with Accompanying English Translation*. Delhi: Sri Satguru Publications, 1990.

— —. "Mahavira," In *Great Thinkers of the Eastern World, edited by Ian P. McGreal*. Harper Collins Publishers, 1995.

Chardin, Pierre Teilhard de. *The Appearance of Man*. New York: Harper & Row, 1956.

— —. *The Divine Milieu*. New York: Harper & Row, 1956.

— —. *The Making of a Mind*. New York: Harper & Row, 1956.

— —. *The Phenomenon of Man*, trans. by Bernard Wall. London: Collins, 1959.

— —. *The Future of Man*. New York: Harper & Row, 1959.

__ __. *Building the Earth.* Wilkes-Barre, PA: Dimension Books, 1965.

__ __. *Hymn of the Universe.* New York: Harper & Row, 1965.

__ __. *Activation of Energy.* New York: Harcourt Brace Jovanovich, 1971.

__ __. *Christianity and Evolution.* New York: Harcourt Brace Jovanovich, 1971.

__ __. "The Evolution of Chastity." *Toward the Future.* New York: Harcourt Brace Jovanovich, 1975.

Cheney, Sheldon. *Men Who Have Walked With God.* New York: Alfred A. Knopf, 1945.

Chittick, William C. *The Sufi Path of Knowledge.* Albany: State University of New York Press, 1989.

Chuang Tzu. *The Book of Chuang Tzu,* trans. Martin Palmer with Elizabeth Breuilly. London: Arkana, 1996.

Chuang-Tzu. *Musings of a Chinese Mystic.* London, 1920.

Chung, Bruya. *Zhuangzi Speaks!* Princeton, NJ: Princeton University Press, 1992.

Chu Ta-kao, trans. *Tao-Te Ching.* Boston: Mandala Books, 1982.

Cidade Calelixnese manuscript, found in Oxyrynchus, Egypt. Located in the British Library, Department of Manuscripts, London.

Cleary, Thomas. *The Dhammapada: The Sayings of Buddha.* New York: Bantam Books, 1994.

Clement of Alexandria. "The Stromata, or Miscellanies," *Ante-Nicene Fathers.* Peabody, MA: Hendrickson Publishers, 1999. Vol. 2. , in Eusebius, *Ecclesiastical History* 6.14.7.

Confraternity of Christian Doctrine. The New American Bible. New York: Catholic Book Publishing Co., 1986.

Conze, Edward, ed. and trans. *Buddhist Wisdom Books: The Diamond Sutra and Heart Sutra.* London: George Allen & Unwin, 1958.

__ __. *Buddhist Scriptures.* Harmondsworth: Penguin Books Ltd., 1959.

Corbin, Henri. "Imagination créatrice et prière créatrice dans le soufisme d'Ibn 'Arabi." *Eranos-Jahrbuch* 25 (1956).

__ __. *Creative Imagination in the Sufism of Ibn 'Arabi.* Princeton: Princeton University Press, 1969.

Danielou, Jean, and Herbert Musurrillo, *From Glory to Glory: Texts from Gregory of Nyssa's Mystical Writings.* London, 1961.

Das, Bhagavan, *The Essential Unity of All Religions*. Quest Book Edition. Wheaton: The Theosophical Publishing House, 1973.

Datta, Dhirenda Mohan. *The Philosophy of Mahatma Gandhi*. Madison: The University of Wisconsin Press, 1972.

___ ___. *Six Ways of Knowing*. Calcutta: University of Calcutta, 1972.

Dauben, Joseph W. *Georg Cantor, His Mathematics and Philosophy of the Infinite*. Cambridge: Harvard University Press, 1979.

Davidson, H. "Avicenna's Proof of the Existence of God as a Necessarily Existent Being." In *Islamic Philosophical Theology*. Edited by P. Morewedge. Albany: SUNY Press, 1979.

Descartes, Rene. "Rules for the Direction of the Mind," trans. by Elizabeth S. Haldane and G. R. T. Ross. Vol. 31, *The Great Books of the Western World*. Chicago: Encyclopaedia Britannica, Inc., 1971.

Deussen, Paul. *The Philosophy of the Upanishads*. Edinburgh: T&T Clark, 1906.

Dhammapada. *Dhammapada: Wisdom of the Buddha*, trans. by Harischandra Kaviratna. Pasadena, CA: Theosophical University Press. 1889.

___ ___. *The Dhammapada: With Introductory Essays, Pail Text, English Translation and Notes*. Translated by S. Radakrishnan. London: Oxford University Press, 1966.

Digha Nikaya. *Thus Have I Heard: The Long Discourses of the Buddha*. Translated by Maurice Walshe. London: Wisdom Publications, 1987.

Dirac, P. A. M. *Quantum Mechanics*. 4th ed. Oxford: Clarendon Press, 1958.

___ ___. *Directions in Physics*. New York: John Wiley and Sons, 1978.

Donald, David Herbert. *We Are Lincoln Men: Abraham Lincoln and His Friends*. New York: Simon & Schuster, 2003.

Dossey, Larry, MD. *Space, Time & Medicine*. Boston: New Science Library, Shambhala, 1985.

Dowman, Keith, trans. Sky Dancer: The Secret Life and Songs of the Lady Yeshe Tsogyel. London: Routledge & Kegan Paul, 1984.

Downs, Robert B. *Books That Changed the World*. New York: The New American Library, Inc., 1956.

Dundas, Paul. *The Jainas*. London: Routledge, 1992.

DuNouy, Lecomte. *Human Destiny*. New York: Longmans, Green & Co., 1947.

Dyson, Freeman J. *Infinite in All Directions*. New York: Harper & Row, 1988.

Eckhart, Meister. *Meister Eckhart: A Modern Translation*, trans. Raymond Bernard Blankney. New York: Harper Torchbook, 1941.

—— —. *Works*, trans. by C. B. Evans. London, 1924.

Eddington, Sir Arthur Stanley. *The Mathematical Theory of Relativity*. Cambridge, MA: Cambridge University Press, 1923.

—— —. *The Nature of the Physical World*. New York: Macmillan, 1929.

—— —. *Science and the Unseen World*. New York: Macmillan, 1929.

—— —. *Fundamental Theory*. Cambridge: Cambridge University Press, 1946.

—— —. *Space, Time and Gravitation*. New York: Harper Torchbooks, 1959.

Ehrman, Bart D. *Lost Scriptures: Books that Did Not Make It into the New Testament*. Oxford: Oxford University Press, 2003.

—— —. *Lost Christianities: The Battles for Scripture and the Faiths We Never Knew*. Oxford: Oxford University Press, 2003.

Einstein, Albert. "Prinzipielles rur Allgemeinen Relativitaetstheorie [Principles Concerning the General Theory of Relativity]." *Ann d. Physik* 55 (1918).

—— —. *Über den Äther*. Schweizerische Naturforschende Gesellschaft Verhanflungen, 105 (1924): 85–93. For translation, see S. Saunders and H. R. Brown 1991, below.

—— —. "Religion and Science," *New York, NY Times Magazine*, November 9, 1930. German text published in *The Berliner Tageblatt*, November 11, 1930.

—— —. *Mein Weltbild*. Amstterdam: Querido Verlag, 1934.

—— —. "Education for Independent Thought." New York: *New York Times*, October 5, 1952.

—— —. "Generalization of Gravitation Theory." *The Meaning of Relativity*. Reprint of appendix 2 from 4th ed. Princeton: Princeton University Press, 1953.

—— —. Message conveyed at Leyden, Holland, 1953, for the honor of the 100th anniversary of the birth of Lorentz. Published in *Mein Weltbild*. Zurich: Europa Verlag, 1953.

—— —. *The New York Post*, November 18, 1972.

Einstein, A., B. Podolsky, and N. Rosen. *Phys. Rev.* 45 (1935): 777.

Eliot, T. S. *Four Quarters.* London: Faber and Faber, 1944.

———. *Collected Poems.* London: Faber and Faber, 1963.

Emerson, Ralph Waldo. *The Works of Ralph Waldo Emerson.* Roslyn, NY: Black's Readers Service, 2000.

———. *The Journals and Miscellaneous Notebooks of Ralph Waldo Emerson.* Edited by William H. Gilman, et al. 16 vols. Cambridge: Harvard University Press. 1960–1982.

Erkes, Eduard. *Ho-shang Kung's Commentary on Lao-tse.* Ascona, Switzerland: Artibus Asiae, 1958. d'Espagnat, Bernard. *Conceptual Foundations of Quantum Mechanics. 2nd ed.* Reading, MA: W. A. Benjamin, 1976.

———. "The Quantum Theory and Reality." *Scientific American,* November 1979, 158–181.

———. *Veiled Reality.* Reading, MA: Addison-Wesley, 1995.

Evans-Wentz, W. Y., ed. *Tibet's Great Yogi Milarepa.* London: Oxford University Press, 1951.

———. *The Tibetan Book of the Great Liberation.* London: Oxford University Press, 1954.

———. *Tibetan Yoga and Secret Doctrines.* London: Oxford University Press, 1958.

Fehrenbacher, Don, ed. *Abraham Lincoln: Speeches and Writings 1832–58,* and *Abraham Lincoln: Speeches and Writings 1859–65.* Library of America, two-volume set, as well as the one-volume edition. New York: Vintage, 1965.

Feng, English. *Chuang Tsu: The Inner Chapters.* New York: Vintage Books, 1974.

Feuerstein, Georg. *Yoga-Sutra of Patanjali: A New Translation and Commentary.* Feynman, Richard. *QED.* Princeton, NJ: Princeton University Press, 1985.

———. "The Distinction of Past and Future." In *The Character of Physical Law.* Cambridge, MA: The MIT Press, 1965.

———. "The Distinction of Past and Future," in *The World Treasury of Physics, Astronomy, and Mathematics.* Edited by Timothy Ferris. Boston: Little, Brown and Company, 1991.

Feynman, R. and Weinberg, S. *Elementary Particles and the Laws of Physics.* Cambridge: Cambridge University Press, 1999.

Finegan, Jack. *Light from the Ancient Past.* Princeton: Princeton University Press, 1946.

Finkelstein, D. "Theory of Vacuum." *The Philosophy of Vacuum.* Oxford: Oxford University Press, 1991.

Fleming, G. N. *The Vacuum on Null Planes.* Presented to the 1987 Oxford University Symposium on the Vacuum in Quantum Field Theory.

Foard, James Harlan. *Ippen and Popular Buddhism in Kamakura Japan.* PhD diss., Stanford University, 1977. Ann Arbor, Mich.: Xerox University Microfilms.

Fox, Emmet. *The Sermon on the Mount: A General Introduction to Scientific Christianity in the Form of a Spiritual Key to Matthew V, VI, and VII.* New York: Harper & Row, 1938.

Fremantle, Anne. *Woman's Way to God.* New York: St. Martin's Press, 1977.

Friedman, M., ed. *Martin Buber's Life and Work: The Early Years 1878–1923.* New York: E. P. Dutton, 1981.

Fung, Yu-lan, trans. *Chuang Tzu, A New Selected Translation with an Exposition of the Philosophy of Kuo Hsing.* Shanghai: Commercial Press, 1933.

— —. *A History of Chinese Philosophy.* Translated by Derk Bodde. 2 vols. Princeton: Princeton University Press, 1953.

— —. *A Taoist Classic: Chuang Tzu.* Beijing: Foreign Language Press, 1989.

Gabor, Dennis. *Inventing the Future.* Harmondsworth, England: Penguin, 1964.

Galloway, Allan D. *The Cosmic Christ.* New York: Harper Brothers, 1951.

Gandhi, Mohandas K. *The Way to God.* (The original title of this work is *Pathway to God*). Berkeley, CA: Berkeley Hills Books, 1999.

Gell-Mann, Murray, and Ne'eman, Yuval. *The Eightfold Way.* New York: W. A. Benjamin, Inc., 1964.

Gill, Pritam Singh. *The Doctrine of Guru Nanak.* Jullundher: New Book Company, 1969.

Gilson, Etienne. *The Mystical Doctrine of Saint Bernard.* London: 1940.

Girard, Rene. *Deceit, Desire & the Novel*. Baltimore: The John Hopkins University Press, 1961.

— —. *Things Hidden Since the Foundation of the World*. Stanford, CA: Stanford University Press, 1978.

Glasberg, R. "Internal and External Perspectives on Immediate and Ultimate Reality: Toward the Unity of Knowledge." *Ultimate Reality and Meaning* 22 (1999): 2–142.

Gödel Kurt. *The Consistency of the Continuum Hypothesis*. Princeton, NJ: Princeton University Press, 1940.

— —. *Collected Works*. Vols. I (II) Feferman, Solomon, et al., eds. New York: Oxford University Press, 1986 (1990).

— —. *On Formally Undecidable Propositions of Prtincipia Mathematica and Related Systems*. Translated by B. Meltzer. New York: Dover, 1992.

Goddard, Dwight, ed. *A Buddhist Bible*. Boston: Beacon Press, 1994.

Goldstein, S. March. "Quantum Theory without Observers—Part One." *Physics Today*. College Park, MD: American Institute of Physics, 1998.

Gollancz, Victor. *Man and God*. Boston: Houghton Mifflin Company, 1951.

Good News for Modern Man. New York: American Bible Society, 1970.

Gopal, Sarvelli. *Radhakrishnan, A Biography*. London: Unwin Hyman Ltd., 1989.

Gospel According to Thomas, The. Coptic text established and translated by A. Guillaumont, et al. San Francisco: Harper & Row, 1959.

Gospel of Thomas, The. York, England: The Ebor Press, 1987.

Gospel of Thomas Comes of Age, The. Harrisburg, PA: Trinity Press International, 1998.

Goswami, Amit. *The Self-Aware Universe*. New York: Tarcher, 1993.

Chuang-tzu: The Inner Chapters. London: George Allen & Unwin, 1981.

Great Treasures of Ancient Teachings. 627 vols. Berkeley, CA: Dharma Publishing, 1983–93.

Greenberger, Dadiel M., and Zeilinger, eds. Vol. 755, *Fundamental Problems in Quantum Theory: A Conference Held in Honor of Professor John A. Wheeler*. New York: The New York Academy of Sciences, 1995.

Greene, Brian. *The Fabric of the Cosmos: Space, Time, and the Texture of Reality.* New York: Vintage Books, 2004.

Gregory of Nyssa, *The Life of Moses.* Translated by Abraham J. Malherbe and Everett Ferguson. New York: Paulist Press, 1978.

Griffiths, Bede. *Return to the Center.* London: Collins Fontana, 1978.

———. *River of Compassion.* Warwick, NY: Amity House, 1987.

Guthrie, Kenneth Sylvan, comp. and trans. *The Pythagorean Sourcebook and Library.* Grand Rapids, MI: Phanes Press, 1987.

Hafiz. *The Gift.* Translated by Daniel Ladinsky. New York: Arkana, Penguin Group, 1999.

Haich, Elizabeth. *Sexual Energy and Yoga.* London: George Allen & Unwin Ltd. Hakeda, Yoshito, trans. *Kukai: Major Works.* New York: Columbia University Press, 1972.

Hammarskjöld, Dag. *Markings.* Translated from Swedish by Leif Sjöberg and W. H. Auden. New York: Ballantine Books, 1993.

Hardy, G. H. *Orders of Infinity, the 'Infinitärcalcul' of Paul DuBois Reymond.* Cambridge, England: Cambridge University Press, 1910.

Harman, W. Willis. "Business as a Component of the Global Economy." *Noetic Sciences Review*, November 1971.

Harman, Willis, and Hormann, John. *Creative Work: The Constructive Role of Business in a Transforming Society.* Indianapolis, IN: Knowledge Systems, 1990.

Harman, Willis and Rheingold, Howard. *Higher Creativity: Liberating the Unconscious for Breakthrough Insights.* Los Angeles: Jeremy P. Tarcher, Inc., 1984.

Harold, Preston, and Babcock, Winifred. *Cosmic Humanism and World Unity.* New York: Dodd, Mead, 1971.

Haughey, John C. *The Conspiracy of God.* Garden City, NY: Image Books, 1976.

Hawking, Stephen. Singularities in the Universe, *Physical Review Letters* 17.

———. *A Brief History of Time.* New York: Bantam Books, 1988.

Hawking, S. W. and Ellis, G. F. R. *The Large Scale Structure of Space-Time.* Cambridge, England: Cambridge University Press, 1973.

Hawkins, Donald J., ed. *Famous Statements, Speeches and Stories of Abraham Lincoln.* Scarsdale, NY: Heathcote Publications, 1981.

Heath, Sir Thomas L., trans., "The Thirteen Books of Euclid's Elements." *The Great Books of the Western World*. Vol. 11. Chicago: Encyclopaedia Britannica, Inc., 1952.

Heidegger, M. *The Basic Problems of Phenomenology*. Ttranslated by Albert Hofstadter. Indianapolis: Indiana University Press, 1998.

Heisenberg, Werner. *The Physical Principles of the Quantum Theory*. New York: Dover Publications, Inc., 1930.

— —. *The Physicist's Conception of Nature*. New York: Harcourt and Brace, 1955.

— —. *Physics and Philosophy: The Revolution in Modern Science*. New York: Harper & Row, 1958.

— —. *Across the Frontiers*. New York: Harper & Row, 1974.

Herbert, Nick. *Quantum Reality: Beyond the New Physics*. New York: Doubleday, 1985.

Heschel, Abraham Joshua Heschel. *The Prophets*. New York: HarperCollins, 1969.

— —. *I Asked for Wonder: A Spiritual Anthology*. Edited by Samuel H. Dresner. New York: Crossroad, 2000.

Hiley, Basil. "Vacuum or Holomovement." *The Philosophy of Vacuum*. Oxford: Oxford University Press, 1991.

Hirtenstein, S., ed. *Journal of the Muhyiddin Ibn 'Arabi Association*. Oxford: 1981.

Hodson, Geoffrey. *The Hidden Wisdom in the Holy Bible*. (An examination of the idea that the contents of the Bible are partly allegorical.) 3 vols. Wheaton, IL: The Theosophical Publishing House, 1955.

— —.Lecture Notes from *The School of Wisdom*. Vol. 2. Adyar, Madras, India: The Theosophical Publishing House, 1955.

— —. *The Brotherhood of Angels and Men*. Wheaton, IL.: The Theosophical Publishing House, 1983.

Horvath, T. "A Study of Man's Horizon-Creation: A Perspective for Cultural Anthropology." *The Concept and Dynamic of Culture*. Edited by B. Bernardi. The Hague: Mouton Publishers, 1976.

— —. "Methods and Systematic Reflections: The Structure of Scientific Discovery and Man's Ultimate Reality and Meaning." *Ultimate Reality and Meaning* 3 (1980):2–161.

— —. "John Neumann's Idea of Ultimate Reality and Meaning." *Ultimate Reality and Meaning* 20 (1997):134–7.

Huffines, LaUna. *Bridge of Light: Tools of Light for Spiritual Transformation.* New York: H. J. Kramer Inc., Pub., 1993.

___. *Healing Yourself with Light: How to Connect with the Angelic Healers.* New York: H. J. Kramer Inc., Pub., 1995.

Hughes, David. *The Star of Bethlehem Mystery. An Astronomer's Confirmation.* New York: Walter & Co., and London: Dent & Sons, 1979.

Hume, Robert Ernest, trans. *The Thirteen Principal Upanishads,* from Sanskrit, with an outline of the philosophy of the Upanishads. London: Oxford University Press, 1971.

Humes, James C. *The Wit and Wisdom of Abraham Lincoln.* New York: Gramercy Books, 1999.

Huxley, Aldous. *The Perennial Philosophy.* New York: Meridian Books, 1968.

Huxley, Julian, *Aldous Huxley 1894–1963; A Memorial Tribute.* London: Chato and Windus; New York: Harper & Row.

Hyujong. *Choson sidae p'yon. Han'guk Pulgyo chonso [Comprehensive Collection of Korean Buddhism].* Vol. 7. Seoul: Tongguk Taehakkyo Ch'ulp'anbu, 1990, in classical Chinese.

___. *The Seven Days of the Heart.* Translated by Pablo Beneito and Stephen Hirtenstein. Oxford: Anqua Publishing, 2000.

Ibn 'Arabi. "Bezels of Wisdom." *Classics of Western Spirituality,* trans. by Ralph Austin. New York: Paulist Press, 1980.

Inada, Kenneth. *Nagarjuna: A Translation of his Mula-madhyamaka-karika with an Introductory Essay.* Tokyo: Hokuseido Press, 1970.

Irenaeus. *Adversus Haereses. The Ante-Nicene Fathers.* Vol. 1, bk. 2., ch. 28, 4. Edited by A. Roberts and J. Donaldson. Grand Rapids, MI: Eerdmans, 1958.

Jaeger, W. *Two Rediscovered Works of Ancient Christian Literature: Gregory of Nyssa and Macarius.* Leiden, 1954.

Jahn, R. G., and Dunne, B. J. *Margins of Reality: Role of Consciousness in the Physical World.* San Diego: Harcourt, Brace, Jovanovish, 1988.

Jaini, Padmanabh S. *The Jaina Path of Purification.* Berkeley, CA: University of California Press, 1979.

Jammer, Max. *The Conceptual Development of Quantum Mechanics.* New York: McGraw-Hill, 1966.

___. *The Philosophy of Quantum Mechanics.* New York: John Wiley, 1974.

— —. *Concepts of Space: The History of Theories of Space in Physics.* New York: Dover Publications, 1993.

James, Joseph. *The Way to Mysticism.* London: Jonathan Cape, 1950.

James, William. *The Varieties of Religious Experience.* London: Longmans Green, 1919.

— —. *William James: The Essential Writings.* Edited by Bruce W. Wilshire. Albany: State University of New York, 1984.

— —. *A Pluralistic Universe.* Lincoln: University of Nebraska, 1996.

— —. *William James: The Essential Writings.* Edited by Bruce W. Wilshire. Albany: State University of New York, 1984.

Jami, Maulana Abdurrahman. *Lawā'ih.* Tehran, 1342 sh./1963.

— —. *Diwan-I kamil,* ed. Hashim Riza. Tehran, 1962.

Jeans, Sir James. *The Mysterious Universe.* Cambridge: Cambridge University Press, 1931.

John of the Cross. *Dark Night of the Soul.* New York: Doubleday, 1959.

— —. *The Collected Works of St. John of the Cross.* Translated by Kieran Kavanaugh and Otilio Rodriguez. Washington, DC: Institute of Carmelite Studies, 1973.

— —. *Flame of Love, Spiritual Canticle.* Classics of Western Spirituality. New York: Paulist Press, 1984.

John Paul II. Encyclical Letter of John Paul II to The Catholic Bishops of the World on the Relationship Between Faith and Reason. Rome: L'Osservatore Romano, 1998.

Kalupahana, David J. *Nagarjuna: The Philosophy of the Middle Way.* Albany, NY: SUNY Press, 1986.

Kanamori, Akihiro. *The Higher Infinite.* Berlin: Springer-Verlag, 1997.

Kawai, Hayao. *The Buddhist Priest Myoe: A Life of Dreams.* Translated by Mark Unno. Venice, CA: Lapis Press, 1992.

Keating, Thomas. *Open Mind, Open Heart.* Warwick, NY: Amity House, 1986.

Keel, Hee Sung. *Chinul: The Founder of the Korean Son [Zen] Tradition.* PhD diss., Harvard University, 1977.

Kempis, Thomas à. *Imitation of Christ.* New York: Doubleday, 1955.

Kerner, Fred, ed. *A Treasury of Lincoln Quotations.* New York: Doubleday & Co., 1965.

Kerrigan, A. *St. Cyril of Alexandria: Interpreter of the Old Testament.* Rome, 1952.

Keynes, Geoffrey, ed. *The Writings of William Blake.* 3 vols. London, 1925.

Kieffer, Gene, ed. *Kundalini for the New Age: Selected Writings by Gopi Krishna.* New York: Bantam Books, 1988.

King, Martin Luther Jr. *Stride Toward Freedom.* New York: Harper & Row, 1958.

Kitaro, Nishida. *Intelligibility and the Philosophy of Nothingness.* Translated by R. Schinzinger. Tokyo: Muruzen, 1958; also reprint, Westport, CT.: Greenwood Press, 1973.

Kiyota, Minoru. *Shingon Buddhism: Theory and Practice.* Los Angeles: Buddhist Books International, 1978.

__ __. *Last Writings: Nothingness and the Religious Worldview.* =Translated by D. A. Dilworth. Honolulu: University of Hawaii Press, 1987.

Klotz, Neil Douglas. *The Hidden Gospel.* Wheaton, IL: Quest Books, 1999.

Kochumuttom, Thomas. *A Buddhist Doctrine of Experience: A New Translation and Interpretation of the Works of Vasubandhu the Yogacarin.* Delhi: Motilal Banarsidass, 1982.

Kodlubovsky, E. and Palmer, G.E.H. *Early Fathers from the Philokalia.* London: Faber and Faber Limited, 1954.

Koestler, Arthur. *The Act of Creation.* New York: Dell, 1964.

Krishna, Gopi. *Kundalini: The Evolutionary Energy in Man.* Berkeley, CA, 1970.

__ __. *The Biological Basis of Religion and Genius.* New York: Harper & Row, 1972.

__ __. *Higher Consciousness: The Evolutionary Thrust of Kundalini.* New York: The Julian Press, 1974.

__ __. *The Awakening of Kundalini.* New York: Dutton, 1975.

La Fleur, William R., ed. *Dogen Studies.* Honolulu: University of Hawaii Press, 1985.

Landry, Tom, with Greg Lewis. *Tom Landry: An Autobiography.* New York: Harper Collins, 1990.

Lao Tzu. *Tao Te Ching.* Translated by D. C. Lau. Baltimore: Penguin Books, 1963.

——. *The Tao Teh King: Sayings of Lao Tzu.* Translated with Commentary by C. Spurgeon Medhurst. Wheaton, IL: The Theosophical Publishing House, 1972.

——. *Lao Tsu: Tao Te Ching.* Translated by Gia-Fu Feng and Jane English. New York: Vintage, 1972.

——. *Lao-Tzu: Te-Tao Ching: A New Translation Based on the Recently Discovered Ma-wang-tui Texts.* Translated by Robert G. Henricks. New York: Ballantine, 1989.

Lavine, Shaughan. *Understanding the Infinite.* Cambridge, MA: Harvard University Press, 1994.

Lawson, John. *The Biblical Theology of Saint Irenaeus.* London: Epworth Press, 1948.

Leadbeater, C. *The Chakras.* Wheaton, IL: The Theosophical Publishing House, 1969.

——. *The Hidden Side of Things.* Wheaton, IL: Theosophical Publishing House, 1974.

——. *The Science of the Sacraments.* Adyar, India: Theosophical Publishing House, 1974

——. *The Christian Gnosis,* Ojai, CA: St. Alban's Pres, 1983.

Lebreton, J. *History of the Dogma of the Trinity from its Origins to the Council of Nicaea.* London: Burns, Oates, and Washbourne, 1939.

Lee, Peter H., ed. *The Silence of Love: Twentieth Century Korean Poetry.* Honolulu: The University Press of Hawaii, 1980.

——. ed. *Sourcebook of Korean Civilization.* New York: Columbia University Press, 1993.

Legge, James, trans. and ed. *The Life and Work of Mencius.* Oxford: Clarendon Press, 1895.

Lewis, Gilbert N. *The Anatomy of Science.* New Haven: Yale University Press, 1926.

Liu, Ming-wood. *The Teaching of Fa-Tsang: An Examination of Buddhist Metaphysics.* Ann Arbor, MI: University Microfilms International, 1979.

Logan, Alastair H. B. *Gnostic Truth and Christian Heresy: A Study in the History of Gnosticism.* Edinburgh, Scotland: Hendrickson Publishers, 1996.

Lombardi, Vince, with Heinz, W. C. *Run to Daylight*. Englewood Cliffs, NJ: Prentice Hall, 1963.

Lopez, Donald S., and Steven C. Rockefeller, eds. *Christ and the Bodhisattva*. Albany, NY: State University of New York Press, 1987.

Lorimer, David, ed. *The Spirit of Science: From Experiment to Experience*. New York: Continuum, 1999.

Lovejoy, Arthur. *The Great Chain of Being*. Cambridge, MA: Harvard University Press, 1953.

MacGregor, G. H. C. *St. John's Gospel*. London: Hodder & Stoughton, 1936.

Mackay, Alan L. *A Dictionary of Scientific Quotations*. Bristol and Philadelphia: Institute of Physics Publishing, 1992.

Mahamudra. *Mahamudra: The Quintessence of Mind and Meditation*. Translated and annotated by Lobsang P. Lhalungpa. Boston: Shambhala Publications, Inc., 1986.

Maimonides, Moses. *The Guide for the Perplexed*. Translated by M. Friedlander. New York: Dover Publications, 1956.

Manaka, Fujiko. *Jichin Kasho oyobi shugyokushu no kenkyu* [*Master Jien and the Collection of Gleaned Jewels*]. Kawasaki, Japan: Mitsuru Bunko, 1974.

Mandino, Og. *The Greatest Salesman in the World*. New York: Frederick Fell Publishers, 1973.

Margenau, Henry. *The Nature of Physical Reality*. New York: McGraw-Hill, 1950.

Margenau, Watson, and Montgomery. *Physics Principles and Applications*. New York: McGraw-Hill Book Company, 1953.

Mason, S.F. *A History of the Sciences*. London: Routledge, 1953.

Matt, Daniel C. *Zohar: The Book of Enlightenment*. Mahwah, NJ: Paulist Press, 1983.

_____. *The Essential Kabbalah*. San Francisco: Harper San Francisco, 1996.

Maurice, Nicoll. *The New Man*. Baltimore: Penguin Books, 1972.

Mayotte, Ricky Alan. *The Complete Jesus*. South Royalton, VT: Steerforth Press, 1997.

McGreal, Ian P., ed. *Great Thinkers of the Eastern World*. HarperCollins Publishers, 1995.

Mearns, David, ed. *Lincoln Papers*. 2 vols. New York: Doubleday & Co., 1948.

Mechtchild of Magdeburg. *Das Flieszende Licht der Gottheit von Mechtchild von Magdeburg [The Flowing Light of the Godhead]*. Berlin, 1909.

Mei, Yi-Pao. *The Ethical and Political Works of Motse*. Westport, CT: Hyperion Press, 1973.

Mersch, Emile. *The Whole Christ*. Milwaukee: Bruce & Bruce, 1938.

Merton, Thomas. *New Seeds of Contemplation*. New York: New Directions Books, 1961.

———. *The Asian Journal of Thomas Merton*. Edited by Naomi Burton, Brother Patrick Hart, and James Laughlin. New York: New Directions Press, 1973.

———. *The Way of Chuang Tzu*. New York: Norton Co., 1975.

———. *The Intimate Merton*. Edited by Patrick Hart and Jonathan Montaldo. New York: HarperCollins Publishers, 1999.

Milarepa, Jetsun. *One Hundred Thousand Songs of Milarepa*. Translated and annotated by Garma C. C. Chang. 2 vols. Boulder: Shambala, 1977.

Miller, William Lee. *Lincoln's Virtues: An Ethical Biography*. New York: Alfred A. Knopf, 2002.

Miller, W. R. *Nonviolence: A Christian Interpretation*. New York: Schocken, 1966.

Misner, C. W., Thorne, K. S., and Wheeler, J. A. *Gravitation*. San Francisco: Freeman, 1973.

Mitchell, Donald. *Spirituality and Emptiness: The Dynamics of Spiritual Life in Buddhism and Christianity*. New York,: Paulist Press, 1991.

Mitchel, Stephen. *The Enlightened Mind*. New York: Harper Perennial, 1993.

Montague, G. *Growth in Christ*. Kirkwood, MO: Maryhurst Press, 1961.

Moore, Gregory H. *Zermelo's Axiom of Choice: Its Origins, Developments, and Influence*. New York: Springer-Verlag, 1982.

Morgan, Tom, ed. *A Simple Monk*. Novato, CA: New World Library, 2001.

Morris, James. *Introduction to Wisdom of the Throne*. Translation of Mulla Sadra's *al-Hikmat al-'arshiyyah*. Princeton, NJ: Princeton University Press, 1981.

Muktananda, S. P. *Guru*. New York: Harper & Row, Publishers. 1971.

__ __. *Kundalini: The Secret of Life*. South Fallsburg, NY: SYDA Foundation, 1979.

__ __. *Play of Consciousness*. New York: Harper & Row, 1980.

Muller, Robert. *New Genesis: Shaping a Global Spirituality*. Garden City, NY: Image Books, 1984.

__ __. *What War Taught Me about Peace*. New York: Doubleday, 1985.

__ __. *A Planet of Hope*. Warwick, NY: Amity House, 1985.

Murray, Bruce C. *Navigating the Future*. New York: Harper & Row, Publishers, 1975.

Namgyal, Takpo Tashi. *Mahamudra: The Quintessence of Mind and Meditation*. Translated and annotated by Lobsang P. Lhalungpa. Boston: Shambhala Publications, Inc., 1986.

Nanopoulos, D. V. "Tales of the Gut Age." *Grand Unified Theories and Related Topics*. Edited by M. Konuma and T. Maskawa. Proceedings of the 4th Kyoto Summer Institute 5–63. 1981.

Nasr, Seyyed Hossein. *Three Muslim Sages*. New York: Carvan Books, 1969.

__ __. *Sadr al-Din Shirazi and His Transcendental Theosophy*. Tehran: Iranian Academy of Philosophy, 1978.

Nazi Conspiracy and Aggression, Official Records of the International Military Tribunal at Nuremberg. 8 vols. New York: United Nations, 1946.

Needleman, Jacob. *Lost Christianity*. New York: Bantam Books, 1980.

Neumann, J. von. *The Mathematical Foundations of Quantum Mechanics*. Translated by R. T. Beyer. Princeton, NJ: Princeton University Press, 1955.

__ __. *Collected Works*. Edited by A. H. Taub. Oxford: Pergamon, 1961.

Neumann, J. von, and Morgenstern, Oskar. *The Theory of Games and Economic Behavior*. Princeton, NJ: Princeton University Press, 1959.

__ __. *Theory of Self-Reproducing Automata*. Urbana, Ill.: University of Illinois Press, 1966.

New American Bible, The. Translated from the Original Languages with Critical Use of All the Ancient Sources. Washington, DC: Confraternity of Christine Doctrine, 1970.

Newton, I. "Mathematical Principles of Natural Philosophy." Vol. 34. *Great Books of the Western World.* Chicago: Encyclopaedia Britannica, Inc., 1971.

Nicolaevsky, Boris, ed. *The Crimes of the Stalin Era.* New York: The New Leader, 1962.

Nicoll, Maurice. *The New Man.* Baltimore: Penguin Books, 1972.

Nikaya, Digha. *Thus Have I Heard: The Long Discourses of the Buddha.* Translated by Maurice Walshe. London: Wisdom Publications, 1987.

Nikilananda, Swami. *The Upanishads.* 4 vols. New York: Harper & Brothers, 1959.

Nishitani, Keiji. *Religion and Nothingness.* Translated by Jan van Bragt. Berkeley: University of California Press, 1982.

Novak, Philip. *The World's Wisdom: Sacred Texts of the World's Religions.* New York: HarperCollins Publishers, 1994.

Novikov, I. D. *The River of Time.* Cambridge: Cambridge University Press, 1998.

Nyingma Edition of the Tibetan Buddhist Canon. 120 vols. Berkeley, CA: Dharma Publishing, 1981.

O'Leary, Brian. *Miracle in the Void.* Kihei, Hawaii: Kamapua'a Press, 1996.

Ooms, Herman. *Tokugawa Ideology: Early Constructs, 1570–1680.* Princeton, NJ: Princeton University Press, 1985.

Origen. *Origenes Werke.* 8 vols. Leipzig, 1899–1925.

Osborne, E. F. *The Philosophy of Clement of Alexandria.* Cambridge: Cambridge University Press, 1957.

Osbourne, Arthur. *Ramana Maharshi and the Path of Self-Knowledge.* New York: Samuel Weiser, 1973.

Pagels, Elaine. *The Gnostic Gospels.* New York: Random House, 1980.

Pagels, Heinz. *The Cosmic Code.* London: Penguin Books, 1994.

Pak, Chong-hong. "Wonhyo's Philosophical Thought." *Assimilation of Buddhism in Korea: Religious Maturity and Innovation in the Silla*

Dynasty. Edited by Lewis R. Lancaster and C. S. Yu. Berkeley, CA: Asian Humanities Press, 1991.

Pantanjali. *How to Know God: The Yoga Aphorisms of Pantanjali.* Translated by Swami Pascal, Blaise. *Pensees and Other Writings.* Translated by Honor Levi. Oxford: Oxford University Press, 1995.

Paul VI, Pope. *Ecclesiam Suam.* New York: Paulist Press, 1965.

Pauling, Linus. *The Nature of the Chemical Bond.* New York: Cornell University Press, 1960.

Peebles, P. J. E. *Principles of Physical Cosmology.* Princeton, NJ: Princeton University Press, 1993.

Peierls, R. E. *The Laws of Nature.* George Allen, 1955.

Pelikan, Jaroslav. *The Idea of the University: A Reexamination.* New Haven, CT: Yale University Press, 1992.

Penrose, Roger. "Gravitational Collapse and Space-Time Singularities." *Physical Review Letters.* 1965.

_ _. *Cosmology.* London: BBC Publications, 1974.

_ _. "Singularities in Cosmology," *Confrontation of Cosmological Theories with Observational Data.* Edited by Longair, M. S. Boston: D. Reidel.

_ _. "Singularities and Time-asymmetry." *General Relativity: An Einstein Centenary Survey.* Edited by Stephen Hawking and W. Israel. Cambridge: Cambridge University Press, 1979.

_ _. *Shadows of the Mind.* Oxford: Oxford University Press, 1994.

_ _. *The Large, the Small and the Human Mind.* Cambridge: Cambridge University Press, 1997.

Petley, B. *The Fundamental Physical Constants and the Frontier of Measurement,* Bristol, England: Adam Hilger Ltd., 1985.

Phillips, Donald T. *Run to Win: Vince Lombardi on Coaching and Leadership.* New York: St. Martin's Press, 2001.

Planck, Max. *Where Is Science Going?* New York: Norton, 1932.

Plato. "Dialogues of Plato: Parmenides." *Great Books of the Western World.* Chicago: Encyclopaedia Britannica, Inc., 1971.

_ _. "Timaeus." Vol. 7, *Great Books of the Western World.* Chicago: Encyclopaedia Britannica, Inc., 1952.

Plotinus. *"The Six Enneads."* Vol. 17, *Great Books of the Western World.* Chicago: Encyclopaedia Britannica, Inc., 1952.

—— ——. *Works*. Translated by A. H. Armstrong. London: Heinemann, 1996–1984.

Poincare, H. *La Valeur de la Science*. Paris: Flammarion. 1904.

—— ——. *Revue de métaphysique et de morale* 20 (1912): 486.

Popper, Karl Raimund. *The Logic of Scientific Discovery*. London: Hutchison, 1959.

—— ——. *Conjectures and Refutations: The Growth of Scientific Knowledge*. New York: Basic Books, 1963.

—— ——. *Objective Knowledge: An Evolutionary Approach*. Oxford: Clarendon Press, 1972.

Prabhupada, A. C., and Bhaktivedanta Swami. *Bhagavad-Gita as It Is*. Los Angeles: Macmillan Publishing, 1973.

—— ——. *Sri Isopanisad*. Los Angeles: The Bhaktivedanta Book Trust, 1995.

Preston, Harold. *Cosmic Humanism and World Unity*. New York: Dodd, Mead, 1971.

Prigogine, I. *From Being to Becoming*. San Francisco: Freeman, 1980.

Quine, W. V. O. *Set Theory and Its Logic*. Cambridge, MA: Harvard University Press, 1963.

Qushayri, al-. *Principles of Sufism*. Translated by B. R. Von Schlegel. Berkeley, CA: Mizan Press, 1990.

Radhakrishnan, Sarvepalli. *The Bhagavadgita*. London: Allen and Unwin, 1948.

—— ——. *The Principal Upsanishads*. New York: Harper & Brothers, 1953.

Radhakrishnan, Sarvepalli, and Moore, Charles. *A Sourcebook in Indian Philosophy*. Princeton, NJ: Princeton University Press, 1957.

Radin, D. I. *The Conscious Universe*. San Francisco: Harper Edge, 1997.

Rahula, Walpola. *What the Buddha Taught*. New York: Grove Press, 1974.

Rama, Swami. *The Book of Wisdom*. Kanpur, India: Himalayan International Institute of Yoga, Science & Philosophy, 1972.

Ramakrishna. *Ramakrishna: Prophet of New India*. Translated by Swami Nikhilananda. New York: Harper & Brothers, n.d.

Randall, J. C. *Mr. Lincoln* 4 vols. New York: Dodd Mead, 1945.

Rayfield, Donald. *Stalin and His Hangmen*. New York: Random House, 2004.

Reichenbach, Hans. *Experience and Prediction.* Chicago: University of Chicago Press, 1938.

——. *Philosophic Foundations of Quantum Mechanics.* Berkeley: University of California Press, 1946.

——. *The Direction of Time.* Berkeley: University of California Press, 1956.

Reischauer, A. K. "Genshin's Ojo Yoshu: Collected Essays on Birth into Paradise." *Transactions of the Asiatic Society of Japan 7, 2nd ser. (1930)*: 16–97.

Reiser, Oliver. *Cosmic Humanism.* London: Schenkman, 1966.

Rele, Vasant. *The Mysterious Kundalini.* India: D. B. Taraporevala Sons & Company. Renan, Ernest. *The Life of Jesus.* Translated by C. E. Wilbur. New York: Everyman's Library, E. P. Dutton, 1987.

Ribera, Francisco de, *Vida de S. Teresa de Jesus.* Barcelona: Nuova ed., 1908.

Richards, I. A. *Mencius on the Mind.* London: Kegan Paul, Trench, Trubner & Company, 1932.

Richardson, Robert D. Jr. *Emerson.* Berkeley: University of California Press, 1995.

Rinpoche, K. *Gently Whispered: Oral Teachings.* Compiled, edited, and annotated by E. Selandia. Tarrytown, NY: Station Hill Press, Inc.

Roberts, Alexander, DD, and James Donaldson, LLD, eds. "The writings of the Fathers down to CE 325." *Ante-Nicene Fathers.* Vols. 1–10. Peabody, Mass: Hendrickson Publishers, 1999.

Robinson, James M., gen. ed., *The Nag Hammadi Library in English.* San Francisco: Harper & Row, 1988.

——. "The Gospel according to Thomas." *The Nag Hammadi Library in English.* San Francisco: Harper & Row, 1988.

Roche de Coppens, Peter. *Spiritual Man in the Modern World.* Washington: University Press of America, 1976.

——. *Spiritual Perspective II: The Spiritual Dimension and Implications of Love, 1984.*

——. *The Nature and Use of Ritual for Spiritual Attainment.* St. Paul, MN: Llewellyn Publications, 1985.

——. *Apocalypse Now.* St. Paul, MN: Llewellyn, 1988.

——. *The Art of Joyful Living.* Rockport, MA: Element, 1992.

_____. *Divine Light and Fire: Experiencing Esoteric Christianity.* Rockport, MA: Element, 1992.

_____. *The Spiritual Family in the 21ˢᵗ Century.* Philadelphia: Xlibris Book Publishers, 2005.

_____. *Religion, Spirituality and Healthcare.* Philadelphia: Xlibris, 2007.

Rodd, Laurel Rasplica. *Nichiren: Selected Writings.* Honolulu: University Press of Hawaii, 1980.

Rotman, Brian. *Signifying Nothing.* Stanford, CA: Stanford University Press, 1987.

Rucker, Rudy. *Infinity and the Mind.* New York: Bantam Books, 1983.

Rumi, Jalal al-Din. *The Discourses of Rumi*, Translated by A. J. Arberry. London: Murray, 1961.

_____. *Teachings of Rumi the Masnavi*, translated and abridged E. H. Whinfield. New York: E. P. Dutton & Co., 1975.

_____. *Light upon Light.* Translated by Andrew Harvey. Berkeley: North Atlantic Books, 1996.

_____. *The Essential Rumi.* Translated by Coleman Barks with John Moyne, A. J. Arberry, and Reynold Nicholson. New York: Quality Paperback Book Club, 1998.

Rump, Ariane. *Commentary on the Lao Tzu by Wang Pi.* Honolulu: University of Hawaii Press, 1979.

Russell, Bertrand. *Introduction to Mathematical Philosophy.* New York: The MacMillan Company and George Allen & Unwin Ltd., 1919.

_____. *Mysticism and Logic.* Totowa, NJ: Barnes & Noble Books, 1981.

_____. *Human Knowledge, Its Scope and Limits.* New York: Simon and Schuster, 1948.

_____. *The Analysis of Mind.* London: George Allen and Unwin, Ltd., 1956.

_____. *Wisdom of the West.* New York: Doubleday and Company, Inc., 1959

Russell, Bertrand, and Whitehead, Alfred North. *Principia Mathematica.* 2nd ed. 3 vols. London: Cambridge University Press, 1935.

Russell, Peter. *The Global Brain: Speculations on the Evolutionary Leap to Planetary Consciousness.* Los Angeles: J. P. Tarcher, Inc., 1983.

Sahn, S. *The Compass of Zen.* Boston: Shambhala Publications, Inc., 1997.

Sandburg, Carl. *Abraham Lincoln*. 6 vols. New York: Charles Scribner & Sons, 1943.

___ ___. *Abraham Lincoln*. Norwalk, CT: The Easton Press, 1954.

Sanella, Lee, MD. *Kundalini—Psychosis or Transcendence?* San Francisco: Sannela, 1976.

Sanford, John A. *The Kingdom Within*. New York: Harper & Row, 1987.

Santayana, George. *Reason in Common Sense*. New York: Charles Scribner and Sons, 1927.

Sartre, Jean-Paul. *Being and Nothingness*. Translated by Hazel Barnes. New York: Philosophical Library, 1956.

Sastri, S. S., and Raja, C. K., trans. and eds. *The Bhamati of Vacaspati*. Madras, India: The Theosophical Publishing House, 1933.

Satprakashanada, Swami. *Methods of Knowledge*. Calcutta: Advaita Ashrama, 1974.

Saunders, S. and Brown, H. R., eds. *The Philosophy of Vacuum*. Oxford: Oxford University Press, 1991. Philip, ed. "A Select Library of the Christian Church." Vols. 1–28. *Nicene and Post-Nicene Fathers*. Peabody, MA: Hendrickson Publishers, 1999.

___ ___. *History of the Christian Church. 8 vols*. Peabody, MA: Hendrickson Publishers, Inc., 2002.

Schilpp, Paul A, ed. *The Philosophy of Sarvepalli Radhakrishnan*. New York: Tudor Publishing Company, 1952.

Schimmel, Annemarie. *Mystical Dimensions of Islam*. Chapel Hill: The University of North Carolina Press, 1975.

Schrödinger, Erwin. *What Is Life?* Cambridge: The MacMillan Company, 1946.

Schuhmacher, Stephan. *The Encyclopedia of Eastern Philosophy and Religion*. Boston: Shambhala, 1994.

Schure, Edouard. *The Great Initiates*. Translated by Gloria Rasberry. San Francisco: Harper & Row, 1980.

Seife, Charles. *Zero: The Biography of a Dangerous Idea*. New York: The Penguin Group, 2000.

Sells, Michael A. "Foundations of Islamic Mysticism." *Classics of Western Spirituality*. New York: Paulist Press, 1994.

Sharma, B. N. K. *The Brahmasutras and their Principal Commentaries: A Critical Exposition.* 3 vols. Bombay: Bharatiya Vidya Bhavan. Vol. 1, 1971; vol. 2, 1974; vol. 3. 1978.

Sheldrake, R. *A New Science of Life: The Hypothesis of Formative Causation.* London: Blond & Briggs, 1981.

Shipov, Gennady. *A Theory of Physical Vacuum: A New Paradigm.* Moscow: Russian Academy of Natural Sciences, 1998.

Simonetti, Manlio. *Biblical Interpretation in the Early Church: An Historical Introduction to the Patristic Exegesis.* Translated by John A. Hughes. Edinburgh: T&T Clark, 1994.

Singh, Gopal Singh, trans. and ed. *Sri Guru Granth Sahib: An Anthology.* Calcutta: M. P. Birla Foundations, 1989.

Singh, Maharay Charan. *Light on Saint John.* Punjab, India: Radha Soami Satsang Beas, 1985.

Skolimowski, Henry. "Global Philosophy as the Canvas for Human Unity." *The American Theosophist.* May 1983.

Skovorodá, Hryhorij Savych. *Hryhory Skovorodá: Works in Two Volumes.* Translated by M. Kashuba and W. Shewchuk. Cambridge-Kyiv: Ukr. Research Institute of Harvard University, Shevchenko Inst. of Literature, Nat. Academy of Sciences of Ukraine, 1994.

Smith, Margaret. *Rabi'a the Mystic.* Cambridge: Cambridge University Press, 1984.

Snyder, Louis L. *The War, A Concise History, 1939–45.* New York: Julian Messner, Inc., 1960.

Solzhenitsyn, Aleksandr. *The Gulag Archipelago Two.* New York: Harper & Row, 1975.

Sorokin, Pitirim. *The Ways and Power of Love.* Boston: Beacon Press, 1950.

Srinivasa, K. R. *Sri Aurobindo: A Biography and a History.* 2 vols. Pondicherry, India, 1980.

Stein, Edith. *Finite and Eternal Being: An Attempt at an Ascent to the Meaning of Being.* Translated by K. F. Reinhardt. Washington, DC: ICS Publications, 2002.

———. *Edith Stein Gesamtausgabe* (ESGA, The Complete Edition of Works of Edith Stein). Edited by M. Linssen, O. C. D., and H. B. Gerl-Falkovitz. Wien: Herder, 2000.

Stulman, Julius. *Evolving Mankind's Future*. Philadelphia: J. B. Lippincott, 1967.

Sullivan, Lawrence E. *Icanchu's Drum: An Orientation to Meaning in South American Religions*. New York: Macmillan Publishing Company, 1988.

Suzuki, D. T. *An Introduction to Zen Buddhism*. New York: Grove Press, 1964.

__ __. *The Field of Zen*. New York: Harper & Row 1970.

__ __. *Mysticism: Christian and Buddhist*. Westport, CT: Greenwood, 1976.

Svarney, Patricia Barnes. Editorial Director, *Science Desk Reference*. New York: Macmillan, 1995.

Swan, Laura. *The Forgotten Desert Mothers*. New York: Paulist Press, 2001.

Symeon the New Theologian. *Hymns of Divine Love*. Translated by George A. Maloney, SJ. Denville, NJ: Dimension Books, 1968.

Tagore, Rabindranath. *The Religion of Man*. London: Allen & Unwin, 1931.

__ __. *Gitanjali*. New York: Macmillan Publishing Co., Inc. 1973.

Taimni, I. K. *Man, God and the Universe*. Wheaton, IL: The Theosophical Publishing House, 1969.

Talbot, George Robert. *Electronic Thermodynamics*. Los Angeles: Pacific State University Press, 1973.

__ __. *Philosophy and Unified Science*. 2 vols. Madras, India: Ganesh & Company, 1977.

Tarada, Toru, and Yaoko, Mizuno, eds. *Dogen*. 2 vols. Tokyo: Iwanami, 1971.

Tarski, Alfred. *Introduction to Logic*. London: Oxford University Press, Inc., 1941

Tatia, Nathmal. *Studies in Jaina Philosophy*. Banares, India: Jaina Cultural Research Society, 1951.

Tauler, Johan. *Theologica Germanica*. Translated by Winkworth. London, 1937.

Taylor, Edwin F., and Wheeler, John A. *Space Time Physics*. San Francisco: W.H. Freeman and Co., 1966.

Taylor, L. H. *The New Creation*. New York: Pageant Press, 1958.

Tehrani, Kazem. *Mystical Symbolism in Four Treatises of Suhrawardi*. PhD diss., Columbia University, 1974.

Teller, P. "Relativity, Wholeness, and Quantum Mechanics." *British Journal for the Philosophy of Science 37* (1986): 71–81.

Templeton, John Marks. *The Humble Approach: Scientists Discover God*. New York: Continuum, 1995.

Teres, Gustav, SJ. *The Bible and Astronomy: The Magi and the Star in the Gospel.* Budapest: Springer Orvosi Kiado Kft., 2000.

Teresa, Mother. *A Simple Path.* Compiled by Lucinda Vardey. New York: Ballantine Books, 1995.

———. *The Joy in Loving.* New York: Viking Penguin, 1997.

Teresa of Avila. *The Interior Castle.* Translated and edited by E. Allison Peers. Garden City, NY: Image Books, 1944.

Thackston, W. M. *Mystical and Visionary Treatise of Suhrawardi.* London: The Octagon Press, 1982.

Theophilus of Antioch. "Thoeophilus to Autolycus." Translated by Marcus Dods, A. M. Vol. 2, *Fathers of the Second Century.* Peabody, Mass: Hendrickson Publishers.

Thibaut, George, trans. "The *Vedanta Sutras* with the Commentary of Ramanuja." In *The Sacred Books of the East.* Vol. 48. Oxford: The Clarendon Press, 1904.

Thomas, D. J. "The Gospel of Thomas." *The Nag Hammandi Library in English.* San Francisco: Harper & Row, Publishers, 1988.

Thomson, E. J. *Rabindranath Tagore: Poet and Dramatist.* London: Oxford University Press, 1948.

Tiller, William A. *Science and Human Transformation: Subtle Energies, Intentionality and Consciousness.* Walnut Creek, CA: Pavior Publishing, 1997.

Tiller, William A., Dibble, Walter E. Jr., and Kohane, Michael J. *Conscious Acts of Creation: The Emergence of a New Physics.* Walnut Creek, CA: Pavior Publishing, 2001.

Tirtha, Swami Mahjaraj Vishnu. *Devatma Shakti*, India. Tishby, Isaiah, and Lachower, Fischel. *The Wisdom of the Zohar.* New York: Oxford University Press, 1989.

Tollinton, R. B. *Clement of Alexandria.* Vols. 1 and 2. London: Williams and Norgate, 1914.

Tolstoy, Leo. *Tolstoy's Writings on Civil Disobedience and Nonviolence.* New York: New American Library, 1968.

Tower, Courtney. "Mother Theresa's Work of Grace." *Reader's Digest.* December 1987.

Toynbee, Arnold, and Ikeda, Daisaku. *Choose Life: A Dialogue.* London: Oxford University Press, 1976.

Tranter, Gerald. *The Mystery Teachings and Christianity.* Wheaton, IL: The Theosophical Publishing House, 1969.

Trump, Ernest. *The Adi Granth, or the Holy Scriptures of the Sikhs.* New Delhi: Munshiram Manoharlal, 1970.

Trungpa, Chögyam. *Orderly Chaos: The Mandala Principle.* Boston: Shambhala, 1991.

Tseu, Augustinus A. *The Moral Philosophy of Mo-tzu.* Taiwan: Fu Jen Catholic University Press, 1965.

Tyler, Royall, trans. *Selected Writings of Suzuki Shosan.* Cornell University East Asia Papers, no. 13. Ithaca, NY: China-Japan Program, Cornell University, 1977.

Udanavarga. *The Dhammapada with the Udanavarga,* ed. by Raghavan Iyer. The Pythagorean Sangha, 1986.

Ueda, Yoshifumi, and Hirota, Dennis. *Shinran: An Introduction to His Thought.* Kyoto: Hongwanji International Center, 1989.

Underhill, Evelyn. *Mysticism: A Study in the Nature and Development of Man's Spiritual Consciousness.* New York: E. P. Dutton & Co., Inc., 1961.

Upanishads, The. *The Thirteen Principal Upanishads.* Translated by Robert Ernest Hume. London: Oxford University Press, 1971.

Utke, A. "The Cosmic Holism Concept: An Interdisciplinary Tool in the Quest for Ultimate Reality and Meaning." *Ultimate Reality and Meaning,* 9 (1986):134–55.

U.S. Congress House Committee on Un-American Activities. *The Crimes of Khrushchev: Hearings.* Washington, DC: Government Printing Office, 1959.

U.S. Congress Senate Committee on Foreign Relations. *The Genocide Convention: Hearings before a Subcommittee,* January 23–February 9, 1950, on Executive Order. Washington, DC: Government Printing Office, 1950.

U.S. Congress Senate Committee on Judiciary. *Soviet Empire: Prison House of Nations and Races.* Washington, DC: Government Printing Office, 1958.

__ __. *Soviet Empire: A Study in Genocide, Discrimination and Abuse of Power.* Washington, DC: Government Printing Office, 1958.

Vatican II, The Documents of, with notes by Protestant and Orthodox authorities. Edited by Walter M. Abbot, and Geoffrey Chapman, 1966.

Verster, F. "Silence, Subjective Absence and the Idea of Ultimate Reality and Meaning in Beethoven's Last Piano Sonata, Op. 111." *Ultimate Reality and Meaning* 22 (1999): 4–23.

Vivekananda. *Living at the Source*. Boston: Shambhala, 1993. da Vinci, Leonardo. *The Notebook*. Translated and edited by E. Macurdy. London, 1954.

Vishnu Tirtha, Swami Maharaj. *Devarma Shakti*. India.

Waldenfels, Hans. *Absolute Nothingness: Foundations for a Buddhist-Christian Dialogue*. Translated by James W. Heisig. New York: Paulist Press, 1980.

Waley, Arthur. *The Way and Its Power: A Study of the Tao Te Ching and Its Place in Chinese Thought*. New York: Evergreen, 1958.

Warder, A. K. *Indian Buddhism*. Delhi: Motilal Banarsidass, 1980.

Watson, Burton. *Chuang Tzu: Basic Writings*. New York: Columbia University Press, 1964.

— —. *Basic Writings of Mo Tzu, Hsun Tzu, and Han Fei Tzu*. New York: Columbia University Press, 1967.

— —. *Complete Writings of Chuang Tzu*. New York: Columbia University Press, 1968.

Watts, Alan. *The Book: On the Taboo against Knowing Who You Are*. New York: Random House, 1972.

Weber, Max. *Protestant Ethic and the Spirit of Capitalism*. New York: Charles Scribner's Sons, 1976.

Weinberg, Steven. *Gravitation and Cosmology: Principles and Applications of the General Theory of Relativity*. New York: John Wiley, 1972.

— —. *The First Three Minutes: A Modern View of the Origin of the Universe*. New York: Basic Books, 1976.

— —. *Dreams of a Final Theory*. New York: Pantheon Books, 1992.

Weingart, R. "Making Everything Out of Nothing." *The Philosophy of Vacuum*. Oxford: Oxford University Press, 1991.

Weizsacker, C. F. von. *The Unity of Nature*. Translated by Francis J. Zucker. New York: Farrar, Strauss, Giroux, 1980.

— —. *The Unity of Physics in Quantum Theory and Beyond*. Edited by Ted Bastin. Cambridge: Cambridge University Press, 1971.

Weyl, Hermann. *Philosophy of Mathematics and Natural Science*. Princeton, NJ: Princeton University Press, 1949.

— —. *Theory of Groups and Quantum Mechanics.* Translated by H. P. Robertson. New York: Dover, 1950.

— —. *Space Time Matter.* Translated by H. L. Brose. New York: Methuen, 1922; repr. Mineola, NY: Dover Publications, Inc., 1950.

— —. *The Continuum: A Critical Examination of the Foundation of Analysis.* New York: Dover Publications, Inc., 1987.

Wheeler, John Archibald. *Frontiers of Time.* Amsterdam: North Holland, 1979.

— —. *At Home in the Universe.* Woodbury, NY: American Institute of Physics, 1994.

Wheeler, J. A., and Zurek, W. H., eds. *Quantum Theory and Measurement.* Princeton, NJ: Princeton University Press, 1983.

White, John, ed. *The Highest State of Consciousness.* New York: Doubleday, 1972.

— —. *Kundalini, Evolution and Enlightenment.* New York: Anchor Books/Doubleday, 1978.

— —. *Theory and Beyond.* Edited by Ted Bastin. Cambridge: Cambridge University Press, 1971.

— —. *What Is Enlightenment.* Los Angeles: Jeremy P. Tarcher, Inc., 1984.

Whitehead, Alfred North. *Process and Reality.* New York: The Macmillan Company, 1929.

— —. *Adventure of Ideas.* New York: Macmillan Company, 1933.

— —. *Essays in Science and Philosophy.* New York: Philosophical Library, 1947.

— —. *An Introduction to Mathematics.* London: Oxford University Press, 1984.

Whitehead, Alfred North, and Bertrand Russell. *Principia Mathematica.* 3 vols. Cambridge: Cambridge University Press. Vol. 1, 1910; vol. 2, 1912; vol. 3, 1913.

Whitman, Walt. *Leaves of Grass.* New York: Quality Paperback Book Club, 1992.

Whitrow, G. J. *What Is Time?* London: Thames and Hudson, 1972.

— —. *The Natural Philosophy of Time.* Oxford: Oxford University Press, 1980. *Time in History.* Oxford: Oxford University Press, 1989.

Wick, David. *The Infamous Boundary: Seven Decades of Controversy in Quantum Physics.* Boston: Birkhäuser, 1995.

Wigner, Eugene P. "The Limits of Science," *Proceedings of the American Philosophical Society* 94 (1950).

Wilbur, Ken. *The Atman Project*. Wheaton, IL: The Theosophical Publishing House, 1980.

———. *Quantum Questions*. London: New Science Library, 1984.

———. *Sex, Ecology and Spirituality*. Boulder, CO: Shambhala, 1995.

Wilhelm, M. *Education: The Healing Art*. Houston, TX: Paideia Press, 1995.

Wilkenhause, A. *Pauline Mysticism*. Freiburg: Herder, 1956.

Williams, R. *Jaina Yoga: A Survey of the Mediaeval Sravkacaras*. London: Oxford University Press, 1963.

Wilson, Peter Lamborn. Fakhruddin Iraqi: Divine Flashes," New York: Paulist Press, 1982.

Wingate. *Tilling the Soul*. Santa Fe, NM: Aurora Press, 1984.

Yampolsky, Philip, ed. and trans. *The Platform Sutra of the Sixth Patriarch: The Text of the Tunhuang Manuscript*. New York: Columbia University Press, 1967.

Yogananda, Paramahansa. *Men's Eternal Quest*. Los Angeles: Self-Realization Fellowship, 1982.

Yusuf 'Ali, 'Abdullah. *The Meaning of the Holy Qur'an*. Beltsville, MD: Amana Publications, 1994.

Zaehner, R. C. *Matter and Spirit: Their Convergence in Eastern Religions, Marx, and Teilhard de Chardin*. New York: Harper & Row, 1963.

———. *The Bhagavad Gita, with Commentary Based on Original Sources*. London: Oxford University Press, 1969.

Zuzuki, Daisetz Teitaro. *Studies in Zen Buddhism*. London, 1927.

———. *Collected Writings on Shin Buddhism*. Kyoto: Shinshu Otaniha, 1973.

INDEX

PERSONAL NOTES

ABOUT THE AUTHOR

Orest Bedrij is the founder and chairman of the Institute for Advanced Study of '**1**'. For the past forty years he has been "unifying" the foundations of the universe, the nature of God, the theory of everything, and the observer—which he finds one and the same in nature and essence—and '**1**' in physical relationships of the laws of physics, which he describes in his various works.

At the age of twenty-nine, Bedrij was IBM's technical director at the NASA Jet Propulsion Laboratory, California Institute of Technology. He was responsible for the development of the Space Flight Operation Facility computer complex that controlled the first soft landing on the moon. Bedrij is also founder of several high-technology companies in computers, semiconductors, finance, and human resource development and the author of books including: *Yes It's Love: Your Life Can Be A Miracle* (1974), *One* (1977), *You* (1988), *Seeing God Face to Face* (2004), *Celebrate Your Divinity: The Nature of God and the Theory of Everything* (2005) and *'1': The Foundation and Mathematization of Physics* (2008). He is married and the father of three children.

LaVergne, TN USA
30 November 2010

206819LV00001B/47/P